# The mobility of labor and capital

# THE MOBILITY OF LABOR
# AND CAPITAL

*A study in international investment
and labor flow*

## SASKIA SASSEN

Professor of Urban Planning
Graduate School of Architecture and Planning,
Columbia University

The right of the
University of Cambridge
to print and sell
all manner of books
was granted by
Henry VIII in 1534.
The University has printed
and published continuously
since 1584.

## CAMBRIDGE UNIVERSITY PRESS
CAMBRIDGE

NEW YORK   PORT CHESTER   MELBOURNE   SYDNEY

Published by the Press Syndicate of the University of Cambridge
The Pitt Building, Trumpington Street, Cambridge, CB2 1RP
40 West 20th Street, New York, NY 10011, USA
10 Stamford Road, Oakleigh, Melbourne 3166, Australia

First published 1988
Reprinted 1989
First paperback edition 1990

**Printed in Great Britain at the University Press, Cambridge**

*British Library cataloguing in publication data*

Sassen, Saskia
The mobility of labor and capital: a study
in international investment and labor flow.
1. Labor mobility   2. Alien labor
I. Title
331.12′791   HD5717

*Library of Congress cataloguing in publication data*

Sassen, Saskia.
The mobility of labor and capital.
Includes index.
1. Alien labor.   2. Capital movements.
3. Investments, Foreign.   I. Title.
HD6300.S37 1987   331.12′791   87-14586

ISBN 0 521 32227 8 hardback
ISBN 0 521 38672 1 paperback

# Contents

v

# Tables

# Acknowledgements

I began research on international investment and migration flows in 1980 while a Fellow of the Inter-American Research Program at New York University, funded by the Tinker Foundation and the Ford Foundation. The focus of this early research was the coexistence in the U.S. during the 1970s of rapid growth in the export of low-wage jobs and a high immigration from low-wage countries. For their support, I am most grateful to the staff of the Center for Latin American and Caribbean Studies, especially its director, Christopher Mitchell, and the administrator, Deborah Truhan. Catherine Benamou's research assistance was outstanding; I could not have done the work without her intelligent and imaginative help. While at the Center, I spent many good hours discussing the subject with Mary Garcia Castro, Fernando Urrea, Sherri Grasmuck, and Patricia Pessar.

In doing the research on U.S. direct investment abroad, I had come across evidence of growing levels of direct foreign investment in the U.S. A fellowship at the Center for United States–Mexico Studies, University of California, San Diego, allowed me to continue this research in 1982–83. It became a study on the use of foreign capital and foreign labor in Southern California. I am most grateful to Wayne Cornelius, the Center's director, and the staff for their support. I also want to thank the Tinker Foundation for funding the fellowship. While at the Center, I had the opportunity to discuss my ideas with a number of people, especially Maria Patricia Fernandez Kelly, Rosalía Solorzano, Leo Chavez and Cassio Luiselli.

The Centro de Estudios de la Frontera Norte de México (CEFNOMEX), in Tijuana, was of invaluable help for research and discussions; I am particularly grateful to Jorge Bustamante and Jorge Carrillo.

During Spring 1983 I did research in Los Angeles. My visiting appointment at the Graduate School of Architecture and Urban Planning of the University of California, Los Angeles, gave me ample opportunity to talk with students and colleagues interested in economic restructuring. I am most grateful to Rebecca Morales, Leo Estrada, Wendy Grover, and John Friedmann. The Research Foundation of the City University of New York provided funding for the research.

The research in New York City during 1984–85 benefited from the first year of a three-year project supported by the Revson Foundation on the employment of Hispanic women in the electronics and garment industries in the New York City Metropolitan area.

My single largest debt is to Soon Kyoung Cho. We shared a relentlessness as researchers and a sense of excitement about the inquiry that kept us working into the early hours of the morning, with the University cleaning staff doing their job all around us and often sharing our findings. Whenever I left New York City and went off tracking data, Soon joined the effort.

Susan Allen-Mills, my editor at Cambridge, and Lynn Hieatt, the subeditor, were immensely helpful and gracious in their support. For their indispensable help at various stages in the preparation of the manuscript, I would like to thank Escheal Segan, Norma Gayne, and Eric Canin.

There are many more people and institutions to thank, many referred to in the text. Three that were particularly helpful, though in very different ways, were the U.S. Department of Commerce, the New York Institute for the Humanities, and Asia Labor Monitor (Hong Kong).

I would also like to thank the following publishers and journals for allowing me to reprint segments of several articles and chapters. The publishers are the Society for the Study of Social Problems, Sage and Academic Press; the journals, *Development and Change*, *International Migration Review*, *Environment and Planning*, *Social Problems*, and *Journal of Ethnic Studies*.

And then there is my son, Hilary, who learnt about migrant workers when he barely walked; by the time he was four years old I could count on him introducing the subject at any event, appropriate or not.

# Introduction

Capital mobility has created new conditions for the mobility of labor. Economic practices and technology have contributed to the formation of a transnational space for the circulation of capital. Policies, many originating in the United States, delimit, regulate and make this space viable. What economic theory as well as governments define as movement between countries is also movement within one single entity encompassing those countries. The central question organizing the inquiry in this book concerns the impact of such a transnational space for the circulation of capital on the formation and directionality of international labor migrations.

This is a new version of an old question. In the late nineteenth century some of the leading political economists debated the impact of free trade on the international movement of labor and capital. Eighteenth-century free trade theory rested on the assumption of international factor immobility; the international circulation of commodities was seen as a process separate from the mobility of capital and labor. These were considered to have mobility only within a country. The transformations brought about by international trade were to be absorbed by the internal mobility of labor and capital across classes and across occupations. The movement of capital and labor from England to its overseas territories was seen as part of the colonization process and, unlike free trade, requiring state regulation. Debating the impact of free trade on the international mobility of labor and capital represented, then, an advance over the discussions of the eighteenth and early nineteenth centuries, which had excluded reference to such a possibility. Today, much of the literature about international labor migrations on the one hand and international trade and investment on the other is characterized by the same absence of mutual references.

In his landmark study on international migration in the Atlantic economy of the 1800s, Brinley Thomas (1973) posits that free trade contributed to the formation of a system that encompassed England, Germany, and the U.S.A., and functioned as a single entity. International movements of labor and capital from England to the U.S. took place inside this system rather than between two countries. Thomas shows theoretically and empirically that free trade did induce international migration of capital and labor, and he formalizes these elements into a central hypothesis: that free trade under conditions of social stratification – that is to say, immobility of labor and capital across social classes – brings about emigration. In Thomas's analysis, the emigration of capital and labor from England went to a country, the United States, where there was no such stratification.

Applied to a different historical period, this same question evinces novel interactions. The concrete forms assumed by the process of internationalization today are different. And so are the leading investment sectors and the spatial organization of investment activity. The gravitational force attributed to free trade in the eighteenth and nineteenth centuries has now shifted to various forms of the international circulation of capital. To the internationalization of trade, so central to the free trade era and the theory, we now must add the internationalization of production sites through foreign investment. The question then becomes what are the specific forms under which the internationalization of production contributes to the formation of labor migrations; also the related question arises of what are the specific forms under which international labor migrations become incorporated into the internationalization of production?

The book addresses these questions by focusing on processes that contain pronounced forms of this internationalization. Three stand out. One, beginning in the middle 1960s, is the development of production for export in several Third World countries through a massive increase of direct foreign investment and international subcontracting by industrialized countries. We are seeing the development of an off-shore production sector for these countries, especially in agriculture and manufacturing but now increasingly also in clerical work. Export Processing Zones are the most formalized instance. A second process is the development of major cities into nodes for the control and management of the global economic system. These cities become production sites for a wide array of specialized services, including financial services, necessary for such management and control and thus produced mostly for export. New York City and

Los Angeles are leading examples. A third process is the recent emergence of the United States as the major recipient of direct foreign investment in the world, after being the main exporter of capital for thirty years. In these three locations we can posit an intersection between the internationalization of production and international labor migrations. The major task of the empirical analysis in this book is to document and explain the concrete forms of this intersection.

The crucial period for analysis is the one beginning in the middle of the 1960s, when there are significant transformations in the magnitude and composition of global foreign investment flows. This is also the period of massive new migrations. The largest of these flows are the migration from Southern Europe and North Africa to Western Europe, from the Caribbean Basin and South-East Asia to the U.S., and from the Middle East and South Asia into the Arab oil-exporting countries. The main focus of this book is on the U.S., a central participant in both the growth of direct foreign investment and the emergence of new international migrations.

The current migration to the U.S. shares a number of general traits with earlier migration phases. But it is also predicated on specific conditions that arise out of the reorganization of the world economy over the last two decades. Emphasizing the latter, as this book does, is not a denial of the weight of the general conditions at work in most migrations. It is, rather, an attempt to identify the particular historical and political context of the current migration phase. It means, for example, viewing the 1965 liberalization of U.S. immigration policy as but one instance of a whole series of policies, from the lifting of import–export restrictions to the implementation of the eurodollar market, that had the effect of internationalizing the country's economy. The overall result was the formation of a transnational space within which the circulation of workers can be regarded as one of several flows, including capital, goods, services, and information.

However, the fact that not all countries became large-scale senders of immigrants points to the need for specifying the manner in which countries are incorporated into this transnational space. A key assumption in much thinking about immigration in the U.S. is that poverty, overpopulation and a stagnant economy are the central causes for emigration. Most countries in the Third World have one or more of these conditions; yet most do not have significant emigration flows. We need to understand whether there are specific kinds of linkages between the U.S. and those countries that do become major senders of immigrants to the U.S. It may well be that particular forms of incorporation into the internationalization of production coalesce with basic conditions such as poverty or unemployment to promote a migration inducing situation.

In what follows I will briefly discuss how these conventional variables fail to explain the current migration phase adequately and whence the need to recognize the migration impact of other conditions.

### THE CLASSICS: OVERPOPULATION, POVERTY, ECONOMIC STAGNATION

Population growth in Third World countries cannot be disregarded, as it signals the possibility of increased emigration. However, there is considerable evidence that not all countries with high population growth have high emigration. A second consideration that needs to be incorporated into the analysis of population growth and migration is the relation between population growth and population density. Some of the countries with high population growth in the Third World do not necessarily have high density, certainly not compared with countries such as France, the Netherlands, or Luxembourg. The assumption that migrants come from countries with very high population growth where there is simply no room left for them requires careful examination. Excessive population density may not necessarily be the main reason for migration. While it would be very useful to have a criterion as simple and quantifiable as population growth to predict what countries will be emigration countries, the migration reality is less tidy and more elusive. The issue of population growth needs to be placed in context precisely because it has received so much attention and because it makes intuitive sense to see it as a key factor promoting emigration.

Once we posit that a country with high population growth may have high, medium, or low population density and may have high, medium, or no emigration, then the relation between these demographic variables and emigration emerges as more complex than is usually assumed or explicitly postulated. It then becomes clear that we need to introduce a number of other factors into the analysis. This need to introduce additional factors is evident and generally accepted in the case of war refugees. Few, if any, would insist that refugee flows are generated by high population growth and density, even though refugees may come from countries with those characteristics and even though these may lead to war. Yet an insistence on demographic explanations is common in the analysis of labor migrations. Further, refugee policies acknowledge indirectly that U.S. military activities abroad make the U.S. accountable, at least to some degree, for the fate of an ally's displaced people. Refugee entitlements carry such an acknowledgement. One might ask whether people displaced because of commercial developments by U.S. corporations abroad, i.e. large-scale export crops, are entitled to certain indemnities for being forced to become emigrants. This kind of formulation is never introduced into the immigration debate.

There is a similar need for a critical examination of the relation between emigration and poverty. Poverty is held to be a basic migration push factor. This raises two questions. First, why are *not* all countries with extensive poverty emigration countries? Secondly, why is it that large-scale emigration in what are today the main sending countries started when it did and not earlier, since many of these countries were poor long before emigration commenced? Haiti was poor long before massive emigration began in the early 1970s. The Dominican Republic had considerable unemployment, under-employment, and poverty long before large-scale emigration began in the middle 1960s.

Finally, it becomes necessary to examine the relation between emigration and economic growth. Again, one key assumption has been that emigration is a consequence of stagnant economic growth. Yet growth rates in employment and domestic product in the main migrant-sending countries were relatively high during the 1970s, certainly compared with those of developed market economies. These high growth rates do not preclude the existence of unemployment insofar as job creation, even if high, may not be able to keep up with labor force growth or with unemployment in sectors of the economy other than those experiencing high growth. But what does need to be emphasized is that these growth rates were considerably higher than rates in other countries which did not have high emigration. That is to say, the long-held assumption that a stagnant economy generates emigration is not necessarily borne out by the facts in the current emigration phase. To cite one of the most blatant examples: South Korea, with one of the highest growth rates in GDP, in general employment, and particularly in manufacturing employment, also was one of the countries with the highest growth rate in migration to the U.S.

The possibility of migration pressures under conditions of poverty unemployment, and overpopulation cannot be denied. Yet it has become evident that by themselves these conditions will not promote large-scale emigration. It is necessary to identify processes that transform these conditions into a migration inducing situation. This distinction may carry significant implications for policy. Given U.S. attempts to regulate immigration, what may be needed is a recognition of such intervening processes. Thinking and policies stemming from this recognition may carry a rather different focus from current U.S. policies aimed at controlling the border or reducing population growth and promoting economic growth in Third World countries. Recognition of intervening processes may move the focus away from conditions in emigration countries and invite an examination of processes that link the U.S. to those countries and may contribute to the initiation of new migration flows to the U.S. And it would invite an examination of labor demand conditions in the U.S. that may contribute to the continuation of such flows. Policies stemming from such a recognition may have to address issues not usually considered relevant to immigration.

A DOMESTIC OR AN INTERNATIONAL ISSUE?

A focus on high population growth, poverty, and economic stagnation easily leads one to view migration as a domestic matter, and the inadequacy of socio-economic conditions and policies in countries of origin as promoting emigration. Immigration, in turn, becomes a domestic matter (or "problem") for the receiving country. For humanitarian or more pragmatic reasons, a receiving country, such as the U.S., commits itself to accept immigrants under certain conditions. The acceptance of immigrants is based ultimately on factors internal to the U.S., including a tradition of immigration. If international factors are brought to bear on immigration policies or decisions concerning immigrants they are typically not viewed as pertaining to migration but rather to other economic or diplomatic ties between the countries involved. Migration simply becomes an obvious, handy, or unavoidable arena within which these other issues can also be played out. A classic example is the use of the migration situation in oil negotiations between Mexico and the U.S.

This book introduces international factors into the analysis of migration, specifically the effects of U.S. foreign policies and activities in migrant sending countries and in the U.S. domestic economy. Once we introduce international factors it becomes evident that U.S. immigration policies and practices address, wittingly or not, both domestic and international issues that have to be dealt with in the domestic arena, i.e., inside the territory of the U.S. In its most extreme version, the current phase of U.S. immigration could be seen as representing, in addition to all the other dimensions it represents, a domestic consequence of U.S. activities abroad. One can point to the active role of U.S. firms in the disruption of "traditional" economies due to large-scale development of commercial agriculture with its associated displacement of small-holders and subsistence growers, or due to massive recruitment of young women into wage labor for export manufacturing. By "traditional" economies I refer to a whole range of activities, from subsistence and semi-waged types of work to industrial activity geared to the local or national market, with no or little foreign investment and typically less mechanized than would be the case in highly developed countries. As I discuss at length in Chapter 4, the disruption of these forms of work need not be an inevitable consequence of the development of agriculture and manufacturing for export. Yet historically that has tended to be the case. Furthermore, this disruption does not necessarily generate emigration. Other objective and ideological linkages need to be established between the sending and receiving countries. It is here that the facts of foreign investment and general cultural westernization acquire weight, as do a liberal immigration policy and a tradition of immigration.

In each of the major countries sending immigrants to the U.S. today, we can find a specific set of conditions which, together with poverty and unemployment, induce outmigration. As these will be discussed at length in Chapter 2 in their general form and in Chapter 4 in the forms specific to the current phase, here I briefly touch upon items that have not received sufficient attention in the debate on immigration to show the importance of introducing international factors into the analysis.

Emigration from the Dominican Republic began in the middle of the 1960s. Subsequent to the election victory of Bosch in the Dominican Republic, the U.S. government sent marines to Santo Domingo. This occupation had, among others, two effects that directly bear on emigration: (1) it created a stream of middle-class political refugees who came to the U.S. and (2) it created objective linkages with the U.S. Both of these eventually evolved into conditions that facilitated further emigration of Dominicans to the U.S. and, very importantly, the emergence of emigration to the U.S. as an option actually perceived by individuals as available to them. Further linkages were consolidated via direct foreign investment in agriculture and manufacturing for export.

In the case of Haiti, insufficient attention has been given to the change in economic development strategy and the types of upheaval these brought about. The transition from the older Duvalier to his son was also a transition from one type of economic regime to another. There was an opening to foreign investment and large-scale development of commercial agriculture and manufacturing for export. The United States was the key partner in this new strategy. The development of commercial agriculture, export processing zones, and manufacturing for export outside the zones, had one thing in common: they required securing a labor supply. We observe, indeed, large-scale displacements of small-holders who become laborers on plantations or in the cities. There is some evidence that the intensification of police violence in the countryside may be in part explained by the need to secure wage-labor in the context of a tradition of subsistence farming and the associated resistance to becoming wage-labourers.

An aspect of Mexican immigration that is not sufficiently emphasized is that a number of studies show the large-scale emergence of illegal Mexican flows to be associated with a *legal* program. The development of the "bracero" program created objective linkages between the U.S. and Mexico and promoted the whole notion of migrating to the U.S. Thus an arrangement made by the U.S. with Mexico had unanticipated consequences. Something instructive regarding the possibility of initiating guest worker programs with various countries is that they may emerge as a mechanism promoting emigration to the U.S. outside the bounds of such programs. This is particularly significant if such treaties were to be signed with a country that has not had a history of migration to the U.S. It could set the stage for the occurrence of new migration flows.

In the case of South-East Asian migration to the U.S., we cannot disregard the fact that after World War II and the Korean War, U.S. strategy sought to build up U.S. business in the region and promote economic development as a means to "stabilize" the region politically. U.S. business and military interests coalesced to create a vast array of linkages with the Asian countries sending immigrants to the U.S. over the last decade. The massive increase of direct foreign investment during that same period reinforces these patterns.

All the above examples accentuate, first, the fact that U.S. business, military, or diplomatic activities were a strong presence in countries that have significant migration to the U.S. It is important to emphasize that not any kind of U.S. presence will have this effect. Secondly, it is important to emphasize that the *combination* of poverty, unemployment, or underemployment *with* the emergence of objective and ideological linkages probably operates as a migration-inducing factor. It then becomes necessary to make distinctions: what kind of U.S. military, political, and economic policies abroad have the potential, in conjunction with unemployment, or underemployment and poverty, to create a migration-inducing situation? In this context, the image of the U.S. as a country of immigrants with opportunities for all, and the 1965 liberalization of immigration policy, become significant. In combination with objective conditions and linkages, the existence of such an open migration policy becomes truly consequential. Without this context of linkages, it is difficult to see how such a policy could have generated massive immigration to the U.S. Thus the 1965 Act should be seen in combination with military and economic policies facilitating a wide range of U.S. activities abroad. This would explain not only the massive increase in immigration, but also why the countries that sent most of the new migrants are not necessarily the ones that should have done so according to the stipulations of the Act. And it would explain why most countries in the world are far from using their quota of immigrant visas to the U.S.

## OUTLINE OF THE BOOK

Displacing the locus of explanation away from poverty or economic stagnation in sending countries and onto the processes that link sending and receiving country introduces a set of variables into the analysis not usually thought of as pertaining to immigration. Such linkages are constituted through processes that are historically specific. In the current period, the internationalization of production

is central in the constitution of such linkages, even when there may be
purely political objectives associated with aspects of that internationalization. A wide array of countries are incorporated as
production sites into a single encompassing system or, more tentatively, a transnational space. The next chapters, particularly 4, 5, and
6, document the concrete forms through which labor migrations
intersect with the more general process of the internationalization of
production as it takes place in key locations.

Chapter 1 is a brief overview of the main lines of conceptual and
empirical analysis in the book. This chapter also describes traits in the
current immigration phase to the U.S. which raise questions about
conventional explanations and suggest the need to introduce additional variables. Chapter 2 presents the general historical and
theoretical background for the analysis. It points to the weight of
economic development in the formation of labor migrations. This
chapter also contains an overview of the main labor migrations in the
post-World War II era; this discussion should serve in placing the new
immigration phase to the U.S. in a broader context. Chapter 3
introduces the empirical information for the particular case study, the
new migrations to the U.S. beginning in 1965 and continuing today.
Chapters 4, 5, and 6 are detailed discussions of major locations of the
internationalization of production. Chapter 4 focuses on the main
locations in the development of manufacturing for export; these are in
South-East Asia (used here to describe East and Southeast Asia) and
the Caribbean Basin (used here to describe the nations on and in the
Caribbean). Central to the analysis is the rapid and massive
mobilization of young women into wage labor, a movement that
would not have happened on this scale and at this speed without the
large influx of direct foreign investment for the development of export
manufacturing. Chapter 5 examines the rapid growth of major cities
into global centers for the regulation and servicing of the global
production system, international financial markets and other components of the world economy. These cities and their metropolitan
areas are also the main destinations of the new migration from the
Caribbean Basin and South-East Asia. The analysis seeks to establish
whether there is any articulation between the two processes. To that
end it examines the economic base, and particularly the job supply, in
these cities to see whether the absorption of immigrant workers is
associated with the expanding growth sectors linked to internationalization, rather than merely with declining economic sectors

in need of cheap labor for survival. Does the economic base, often thought of as post-industrial, resulting from these cities' role in the global economy generate a demand for the kinds of workers that immigrants represent? Chapter 6 focuses on the U.S. as the leading recipient of global direct foreign investment flows and examines the composition of this investment by sectors, location and national origin. The magnitude of direct foreign investment in the U.S. since 1981 and the fact that it represents almost half of global direct foreign investment makes this a new development. The major recipient areas are California and the New York–New Jersey region. The organizing question for the rather preliminary presentation in Chapter 6 is whether these areas are emerging as new investment zones in a global marketplace of production sites; changes in the organization of production alongside a large supply of immigrant workers may make these areas competitive with locations in the Third World.

# Foreign investment: a neglected variable

There is considerable evidence both on international labor migrations and on the internationalization of production. But they are
mostly two separate bodies of scholarship. Analytically these two
processes have been constructed into unrelated categories. As socio-
economic givens, there are certain locations where one can identify
the presence of both. Our question then becomes whether there is an
articulation between these two processes and, if so, how we can
capture this analytically. Furthermore, the notion of the internationalization of production needs to be elaborated in order to
incorporate more of its central components. Theoretical and empirical studies of this process have focused largely on one particular
component: the massive shift of jobs to Third World countries
through direct foreign investment, resulting in the development of an
off-shore manufacturing sector.

The question about the articulation of these two processes stems
from both a broader theoretical argument on the nature of the world
economy and from the concrete details of the new migrations to the
U.S. Similarly, the need to elaborate the notion of the internationalization of production stems from that broader theoretical
argument as well as from the concrete details of the U.S. economy
over the last twenty years. In this chapter I briefly review the main
conceptual and empirical lines of analysis that bring these various
concerns together.

The new Asian and Caribbean Basin immigration to the U.S.
reveals patterns that escape prevailing explanations of why migrations occur. Two of these patterns are of interest here. One concerns
the timing, magnitude and origins of the new immigration. Why did
the new immigration take place at a time of high unemployment in
the U.S., including major job losses in sectors traditionally employing
immigrants, and of high growth rates in the major immigrant sending
countries? There are two separate issues worth considering here, to

wit, the *initiation* of a new migration flow and its *continuation* at ever higher levels. Understanding why a migration began entails an examination of conditions promoting outmigration in countries of origin and the formation of objective and subjective linkages with receiving countries that make such migration feasible. Understanding why a migration flow continues and sustains high levels invites an examination of demand conditions in the receiving country. This brings up the second pattern, the continuing concentration of the new immigration in several major cities which are global centers for highly specialized service and headquarters activities, an economic base we do not usually associate with immigrant labor. The questions raised by these patterns in the new immigration become particularly acute when we consider that the major immigrant-sending countries are among the leading recipients of the jobs lost in the U.S. and of U.S. direct foreign investment in labor-intensive manufacturing and service activities. If anything, this combination of conditions should have been a deterrent to the emergence of new migrations or at least a disincentive to their continuation at growing levels. Why is it that the rapidly industrializing countries of South-East Asia, typically seen as the success stories of the Third World, are the leading senders of the new immigrants? I will briefly examine each of these patterns.

Immigrant entry levels since the late 1960s are among the highest in U.S. immigration history. Legally admitted immigrants numbered 265,000 in 1960. By 1970 such entries reached half a million, a level sustained since then with a gradual tendency to increase over the years. The overall estimate now is that the combination of all different types of entry had reached about 1 million a year by 1980 (see INS, 1978; 1985; Teitelbaum, 1985). The highest numbers of immigrants from 1970 to 1980 came from Mexico, the Philippines, and South Korea, followed by China (Taiwan and People's Republic), India, the Dominican Republic, Jamaica, Colombia, and several Caribbean Basin countries. New entries and natural growth resulted in the pronounced expansion of the Asian and Hispanic populations in the U.S. From 1970 to 1980, the Asian population increased by 100 percent and the Hispanic by 62 percent (U.S. Bureau of the Census, 1981). These growth rates were surpassed by some nationalities, notably the 412 percent increase of South Koreans.

The new Caribbean Basin and South-East Asian immigration, by far the largest share in the current immigration, is heavily concentrated in cities with high job losses in older industries, and job growth in high-technology industries and specialized services. Asians have gone largely to Los Angeles, San Francisco, and New York City; these have the three largest concentrations of Asians. West Indians and the new Hispanics (excluding Mexicans and Cubans) have gone largely to New York City. What conditions in the economies of these cities have facilitated the absorption of such massive immigrant flows and induced their continuation at ever higher levels? The fact that these are traditional destinations and contain large immigrant communities goes a way towards answering the question. And so does the fact that declining sectors of the economy need cheap labor for survival. But the magnitude and new origins of the immigrant influx, its continuation at ever higher levels and the extent of job losses in sectors historically employing immigrants point to the need for additional explanations.

The increase in immigration took place at a time of rather high economic growth in most countries of origin. For example, annual GNP growth in the decade of the seventies hovered around 5 to 9 percent for most of these countries. Growth rates in manufacturing employment were even higher. Massive increases in direct foreign investment, mostly from the U.S. but also from Japan and Europe, contributed to these growth rates.

While U.S. direct foreign investment generally accelerated from 1965 to 1980 and continues to go to Europe and Canada, it quintupled in the less developed countries. This is a noteworthy trend, since much of it goes to a few select countries in the Caribbean Basin and South-East Asia. The average annual growth rate of U.S. direct foreign investment from 1950 to 1966 was 11.7 percent for developed countries and 6.2 percent for developing countries; from 1966 to 1973 these rates were, respectively, 10.7 percent and 9.7 percent, and, from 1973 to 1980, 11.8 percent and 14.2 percent (these figures exclude the petroleum industry). There has also been a massive increase of Western European direct foreign investment during the 1970s, mostly in these same countries. Given the particular conceptualization of the migration impact of such investment posited in this book, and briefly described later in this chapter, this increase of European and Japanese investment in countries sending migrants to the U.S. is also significant. The average annual growth rates of direct foreign investment in developing countries by all major industrial countries were 7 percent from 1960 to 1968; 9.2 percent from 1968 to 1973, and 19.4 percent from 1973 to 1978.

Furthermore, a growing share of direct foreign investment in developing countries over the last two decades has gone into production for export, mostly to the U.S. As I will discuss later, export manufacturing and export-agriculture tend to be highly labor-intensive kinds of production which have mobilized new segments of the population into waged-labor and into regional migrations. The main migrant-sending countries to the U.S. over the last fifteen years all have received large export-oriented foreign investment. This would seem to go against a central proposition in the development literature, to wit, since foreign investment creates jobs it should act as a deterrent to emigration; this deterrent should be particularly strong in countries with high levels of export-oriented investment because of its labor-intensive nature.

Using Export Processing Zones (EPZs) as an indicator of export-oriented direct foreign investment, a distinct pattern emerges. These zones, all built in the last fifteen years, tend to be concentrated in a few countries, most of which represent the areas of origin of the overwhelming share of new immigrants. In Latin America, and the Caribbean, the three countries with the largest number of zones are Mexico, Colombia and the Dominican Republic. In 1975 they accounted for sixteen of the twenty-two zones. These are also countries with large export-agriculture sectors. And they account for a very large share of all Hispanic immigrants. We find a similar situation in South-East Asia. The question then is whether there is any connection between large increases in foreign investment and large-scale emigration.

While the change in U.S. immigration legislation can explain a good part of the increase in entries to the U.S. after 1965, it is insufficient to explain the magnitude of the increase and the disproportionate weight of certain countries of origin. Indeed, the family reunion emphasis in the 1965 legislation was expected to bring in largely Europeans because the main immigrant stock in the U.S. was European. It was not expected that Asian and Caribbean Basin nationalities would dominate the flow and would do so in such high numbers. This lack of correspondence between the expectations associated with the legislation changes and the ensuing reality has led one historian to call the 1965 Immigration and Naturalization Act the "unintended reform" (Reimers, 1983).

Though not necessarily addressed directly to these questions, the migration literature does contain partial explanations as to why migration would occur under the conditions described above. Elements of answers can be found in explanations that emphasize a combination of strong push factors such as high unemployment in the sending country; resources for mobility, i.e., it is not the poorest who migrate; and *perceived* opportunity in the country of destination (Reubens, 1981). Secondly, explanations that emphasize the importance of an already existing immigrant community as a pull factor and as a structure that facilitates access to employment and housing for newly arrived immigrants (Chaney, 1976; Wilson and Portes, 1980; Sassen-Koob, 1979). Thirdly, explanations that emphasize the internal differentiation of the labor market in industrialized countries to explain the co-existence of growing unemployment and relative labor scarcity in declining and/or backward industries in need of cheap labor for survival (Piore, 1979; Bailey and Freedman, 1981). Fourthly, an elaboration of this last type of explanation which emphasizes the different requirements for control over labor at the workplace that characterize different types of work organization; thus it is not primarily the low wages of immigrants but their willingness to work at certain kinds of job, which explains their obtaining employment in the face of growing unemployment (Sassen-Koob, 1980). Finally, analyses of immigration policies (Keely, 1979) and of the role of the state in regulating the labor supply (Bach, 1978). In sum, the push of unemployment, the pull of an existing immigrant community, and the need for cheap labor in declining and backward industries are elements for an explanation about high immigration in a period of high unemployment in the U.S.

But the developments of the last fifteen years in international and domestic aspects of the U.S. economy point to a need for refinement of existing explanations and specification of additional variables. Important contributions in this direction, and ones I will draw on, can be found in the studies on the relation between U.S. investment in Mexico and Mexican immigration (Cornelius, 1980; Fernandez Kelly, 1983); U.S. investment in Puerto Rico and emigration (Centro de Estudios Puertorriqueños, 1979); U.S. investment in the Caribbean Basin and emigration (Ricketts, 1983); immigration and foreign policy (Keely, 1979) and characteristics of the international system as they affect migration (Portes and Walton, 1981). This body of scholarship brings to the fore the active participation of the U.S. through investment and other development programs in creating linkages that contributed, directly or indirectly, to emigration. The clearest historical example is Puerto Rico where by the late 1940s the impact of U.S. investment and modernization of the economy had resulted in the formation of a vast supply of migrant workers (Centro de Estudios Puertorriqueños, 1979). The book attempts to continue this theoretical and empirical work, but the focus is somewhat less on migration and somewhat more on economic restructuring processes in sending and receiving areas.

The foremost concern is not a full explanation of emigration. Nor is the focus one that can account for the various stages in international migrations. Rather, the concern is with capturing the particular moment in the process of labor migration that links it with fundamental processes in the contemporary phase of the world economy. The overall theoretical stance is that to specify the place of labor migration in a particular historical period, within the general history of capitalist development, we need to identify the modes of articulation with the leading economic dynamic of that period. This is not to deny the many general conditions at work in all migrations nor the different individual reasons for migrating. The specificity of labor migration in the current historical period lies not in these general conditions or individual motivations but in its articulation with the internationalization of production, a dynamic which assumes concrete forms in particular locations. The aim is to document the existence and the details of this articulation, the subject of Chapters 4 and 5, and how the existence of an immigrant workforce itself contributes to new conditions for the internationalization of production, the subject of Chapter 6. The next two sections discuss the main argument briefly. In Chapter 2 I return to a discussion of these general theoretical and historical issues.

## THE GROWTH OF DIRECT FOREIGN INVESTMENT AND THE UPROOTING OF PEOPLE

The generalization of market relations and the development of modern forms of production have historically had a disruptive effect on traditional work structures. This process, discussed at length in Chapter 2, assumes new forms in the current phase of the internationalization of production. In Chapter 4 I will focus on the particular expression of this broader process in the main immigrant sending countries today. The argument, briefly, is as follows.

The expansion of export manufacturing and export agriculture, both inseparably related with direct foreign investment from the highly industrialized countries, has mobilized new segments of the population into regional and long-distance migrations. I am using the term "mobilize' somewhat freely to refer to a variety of processes. First, the transformation of subsistence workers into wage-labor, either directly, e.g., through large-scale employment in commercial agriculture, or indirectly, through rural to urban migration due to small farmers' displacement by commercial agriculture. Even if these rural migrants fail to find a job in the city, they have been mobilized into an urban reserve of wage-labor. Second, the recruitment practices of foreign plants, notably world market factories and plants in Export Processing Zones, have led to a large-scale movement of young women into waged labor (UNIDO, 1980; Lim, 1980; Wong, 1980; Grossman, 1979). Electronics plants, especially semi-conductor assembly plants, require highly disciplined workers. Young women in patriarchal societies are probably among the more controllable workers (Safa, 1981; Grossman, 1979), at least initially.

One key process mediating between the introduction of these modern forms of production and the formation of labor migrations is the disruption of traditional work structures. The mechanisms involved are quite different in the case of export manufacturing from those in commercial agriculture. The development of commercial agriculture, which is almost completely for export, has directly displaced small farmers who are left without means of subsistence. This forces them to become wage-laborers in commercial agriculture or to migrate to cities. Sometimes the move from sharecropper or subsistence farmer to rural wage-laborer becomes a move to another country, e.g., Colombians in Venezuela agriculture or Mexicans in U.S. agriculture. Sometimes this move becomes a move to an urban job in another country, e.g., Dominicans to New York City.

In export manufacturing this disruption is mediated by a massive recruitment of young women into newly created jobs. The mobilization effect has been particularly strong due to the high degree of concentration of the employment effects of direct foreign investment in manufacturing in a few countries. The "new industrialization" has generated domestic and international migrations *within* the regions which eventually may overflow into long-distance migrations. These migrations have been found to contribute to the disruption of traditional, often unwaged, employment structures. This disruption reduces the possibility of returning if laid-off or unsuccessful in the job search. The available evidence shows a large mobilization of young women into waged labor, women who under other conditions would not have entered waged employment. This has an additional disruptive effect on traditional employment structures, notably household production for internal consumption or local markets. The feminization of the new proletariat has also been found to contribute to male unemployment and, in several cases, to male emigration. It does so both directly and indirectly. There is now a female labor supply competing for jobs with men, a supply that did not exist only a few years ago. An indirect emigration inducement among males results from the disruption of traditional work structures: with the massive departure of young women there is a reduction in the possibilities of making a living in many of these rural areas. Eventually this disruption of traditional work structures adds to the pool of unemployed. Finally, the widespread practice of firing the new, mostly female, workers after a few years also adds to a pool of potential emigrants. These women, left unemployed and westernized, may have few options but emigration.

Though these developments are not necessarily a function of foreign investment *per se*, it seems important to emphasize the presence of foreign investment. First, because in the absence of such investment the large-scale development of export manufacturing and export agriculture could not have occurred. Here I want to emphasize that foreign investment stands for a variety of arrangements, some involving direct ownership, others consisting of subcontracting with domestic producers, and yet others being simply foreign buying groups. The key is that these developing countries could not have penetrated the export market in the absence of these arrangements with foreign investors which *have* access to those markets. Second, because the presence of such investment creates cultural–ideological and objective links with the countries providing this capital. And these are of course largely the highly industrialized countries which have also been major recipients of immigration from the less developed countries. Besides the long recognized westernization effect of large-scale foreign investment in the less developed world, there is the more specific impact on workers employed in production for export or in services in the export sector. These workers are using their labor power in the production of goods and services demanded by people and firms in the U.S. or any other highly developed country. The distance between a job in the off-shore plant or office and in the *on*-shore plant or office is subjectively reduced. Under these conditions emigration may begin to emerge as an option actually felt by individuals.

Foreign plants are a factor establishing linkages with the U.S., especially cultural ones. The workers mobilized into wage-labor on plantations or world market factories probably are only a small share of those that make use of these linkages. But they are part of the linkage for potential emigrants. On the other hand, those employed in services and office work necessary for the export sector are more likely to become part of the pool of emigrants. The ideological effect is not to be underestimated: the presence of foreign plants not only brings the U.S. or any other "western" country closer, but it also "westernizes" the less developed country and its people. Emigration to the U.S. emerges as an option. In an "isolated" country, that is one lacking extensive direct foreign investment, emigration would be quite unlikely to emerge as such an option.

This is a highly mediated process, one wherein direct foreign investment is not a cause but a structure that creates certain conditions for emigration to emerge as an option. Furthermore, it is important to differentiate those workers actually employed in foreign plants, offices and plantations and those representing the supply of potential emigrants. They are often not the same individuals.

Under these conditions, the origin of the foreign capital may matter less than the types of production it goes into. Thus, the large increase in direct foreign investment by all major industrialized countries will tend to have similar effects. It is in this context that the 1965 Immigration Act and the continued image of the U.S. as a land of opportunity acquire their full impact. Whether West German, Dutch or U.S., foreign investment may well have the effect of promoting emigration to the U.S.

Continued vitality of the U.S. as an immigration country and the absence of alternatives acquire particular significance in the context of a continuing growth of direct foreign investment and its expansion to additional countries. The general trend is for all the major industrial countries to increase investment in less developed countries. Though most of this investment is concentrated in a few countries, there is also a trend towards significant levels of investment in "new" countries. Accepting my analysis of the effect of direct foreign investment on the formation of a pool of potential emigrants and on the emergence of emigration as an actual option, it could be argued that this expansion of direct foreign investment by the major industrial countries will contribute to additional emigration to the U.S. Proposed changes in U.S. immigration laws would hardly affect these countries which probably have under-used entry quotas.

In brief, I examine how significant levels and concentrations of direct foreign investment are one factor promoting emigration through: (a) the incorporation of new segments of the population into wage-labor and the associated disruption of traditional work structures both of which create a supply of migrant workers; (b) the feminization of the new industrial workforce and its impact on the work opportunities of men, both in the new industrial zones and in the traditional work structures; (c) the consolidation of objective and ideological links with the highly industrialized countries where most foreign capital originates, links that involve both a generalized westernization effect and more specific work situations wherein workers find themselves making goods for people and firms in the highly industrialized countries.

What I posit is a generalized effect that contributes to the formation of a pool of potential emigrants and, at the same time, to the emergence of emigration as an actual option. This effect would seem to be present regardless of whether the direct foreign investment originates in the U.S. or in any of the other major advanced industrialized countries. The lasting image of the United States as a land of opportunity, which can only be reinforced by the current massive immigration, will tend to have the effect of making "emigration" identical with "emigration to the U.S."

## THE RISE OF GLOBAL CITIES AND THE NEW LABOR DEMAND

Transformations in the world economy, including that discussed in the preceding section, generate a new or significantly expanded role for major urban centers, particularly in the highly developed countries. The technological transformation of the work process, the shift of manufacturing and routine office work to less developed areas domestically and abroad, in part made possible by the technological transformation of the work process, and the ascendance of the financial sector in management generally with the decline of production focused management, have all contributed to the consolidation of a new kind of economic center, global cities from which the world economy is managed and serviced. That is to say, these trends have intensified the role of major urban centers as producers and exporters of advanced services, including finance and management and control functions. Alongside the growing decentralization of manufacturing and office work we see the growing concentration of high-level servicing, control and management operations.

While the redeployment of manufacturing and office work to less developed countries has contributed to conditions that promote emigration from these countries, the concentration of servicing and management functions in global cities has contributed to conditions for the demand and absorption of the immigrant influx in cities like New York, Los Angeles and Houston. *The same set of basic processes that has promoted emigration from several rapidly industrializing countries has also promoted immigration into several booming global cities.* The growth conditions in both types of areas will, doubtlessly, become exhausted. But in the meantime they will have created major transformations in the economic and population dynamics of the areas involved.

The consolidation of such global centers generates a restructuring of labor demand. The job supply is shaped by several key trends, notably (a) the growth of the advanced service sector, including the financial system, and (b) the shrinking of traditional manufacturing industries and their replacement with a downgraded manufacturing sector and high technology industries, in both of which sweatshops are mushrooming. The evidence shows that the result is an expansion of very high-income professional and technical jobs, a shrinking of middle income blue- and white-collar jobs, and a vast expansion of low-wage jobs. The expansion of the low-wage job supply is in good part a function of growth sectors and only secondarily of declining industries in need of cheap labor for survival. It is in this expansion of the low-wage job supply that we find the conditions for the absorption of the immigrant influx.

Immigration can be seen as providing labor for (1) low-wage service jobs, including those that *service* (a) the expanding, highly specialized, export-oriented service sector and (b) the high-income lifestyles of the growing top level professional workforce employed in that sector; (2) the expanding downgraded manufacturing sector, including but not exclusively, declining industries in need of cheap labor for survival, as well as dynamic electronics sectors, some of which can actually be seen as part of the downgraded sector. A third source of jobs for immigrants, is the immigrant community itself (Light, 1972; Chaney, 1976; Portes and Bach, 1980). These jobs include not only those that are a temporary arrangement until a job in the mainstream society can be found. They include also a large array of professional and technical jobs that service the expanding and increasingly income-stratified immigrant communities in the city (Cohen and Sassen-Koob, 1982). And they include jobs that produce services and goods for the subsistence of members of the community, and therewith contribute to lower the costs of survival – both for themselves and, ultimately, for their employers.

The redeployment of manufacturing and the associated international trade in specialized services, contain new business opportunities for major urban centers. There has been a sharp rise in the national and international demand for specialized services, induced both by the dispersion of manufacturing and clerical work and by the technological transformation of work. Thus this growth rests in part on the crisis of traditional manufacturing. While a city like Detroit just loses factories, New York and Los Angeles find new business opportunities in their own *and* Detroit's factory losses. Furthermore, unlike what is the case with other kinds of services, production of specialized services does not tend to follow population patterns. On the contrary, they are subject to agglomeration economies and hence tend towards strong locational concentration and production for export nationally and internationally. Since the highly specialized service sector is the most dynamic in the U.S. economy, its concentration in major cities also entails that these come to contain a disproportionate component of national economic growth.

I will analyze the restructuring of the job supply. The timing, magnitude and destination of the new immigration become particularly noteworthy when juxtaposed with the pronounced changes in the job supply in major urban centers. I will be particularly interested in examining the generation of low-wage jobs in major growth sectors, the advanced services and the downgraded manufacturing sector. I use the term downgraded manufacturing sector to refer to both the downgrading of old industries, e.g., replacing unionized shops with sweatshops and industrial homework, and to the prevalence of low-wage, dead-end production jobs in new industries, particularly in the field of high technology. What is notable is that even the most dynamic and technologically developed sectors of the economy, such as the advanced services and high-technology industries generate a considerable supply of low-wage jobs with few skill and language proficiency requirements.

Two analytical distinctions important to my argument are (a) the distinction between job characteristics and sector characteristics, and (b) the distinction between sector characteristics and growth status. Thus, backward jobs can be part of the most modern sector of the economy and backward sectors can be part of major growth trends in the economy. Use of these two kinds of distinctions allows me to explain the presence of immigrants in technologically developed sectors of the economy and it allows me to posit that the downgraded manufacturing sector – also an important employer of immigrants – is part of major growth trends. Furthermore, these distinctions also lead me to a partial reconceptualization of what is often referred to as the informal sector. As Portes (1983) has discussed, the informal sector represents a survival strategy for the people involved and a mechanism to transfer surplus to the formal sector of the economy. I will argue further that the development of informal sectors in major cities in the U.S. (and Western Europe) is in good part a function of the characteristics of growth sectors in such cities; the existence of immigrant communities facilitates the development of an informal sector but does not cause it, for example, via importation of survival strategies typical of the Third World. Changes in the organization of production, particularly the growing importance of highly customized goods and services, promote the desirability and viability of small scales of production and labor-intensive work processes. These are conditions that will tend to induce informalization. And informalization can easily lead to a demand for immigrant workers.

In the empirical elaboration of the argument I will focus on New York and Los Angeles. These are the two major producers of financial and other advanced services in the U.S. They are also two major producers of a downgraded manufacturing sector and major recipients of the new immigration. And yet each of these cities is an instance of what are usually seen as two very different configurations in the 1970s: the declining Frostbelt and the ascendant Sunbelt. Within the national economy each does indeed contain distinct trends of decline and growth associated with each of these regions. However, in the context of the major developments in the world economy discussed in Chapter 4, what comes to the fore is their role as centers for the servicing and management of the vastly decentralized manufacturing sector and for the globalization of economic activity generally. This role would also explain why both have been major recipients of direct foreign investment in banking and other advanced services over the last few years, as I will discuss in Chapter 6. Western European and Japanese manufacturing is becoming decentralized in ways akin to those of the U.S., including redeployment to select less-developed countries *and to the U.S.* This generates a similar need for centralized management and servicing. New York City and Los Angeles seem to fill part of these functions alongside major centres in Western Europe.

# 2

# The use of foreign workers

The use of foreign labor, whether slaves or immigrants, has been a basic tendency in the development of industrial economies. In most accounts of capitalist development, the struggle by employers to recruit and maintain an adequate labor supply has been overshadowed by the problems of realization, most particularly, market expansion. However, a central precondition for the realization of the surplus-generating possibilities of a geographic location is the formation of a politically and economically suitable labor supply. In the study of centrally planned economies, the securing of an adequate labor supply has been more prominent than in that of free market economies.

This chapter has a dual purpose. First, to document how past and present dynamic growth situations tend to require drawing on "foreign" labor supplies. This is significant because today, at a time of growing unemployment, the general belief is that labor is always in surplus. In fact, labor shortages and the need to bring in workers from other areas have been common features in several recent high-growth situations, such as the post World War II reconstruction in Western Europe, the vast industrialization programs in OPEC members after 1973, and the U.S. Sunbelt region in the mid-1970s. Furthermore, socialist economies also experience labor shortages in growth areas and have relied on various types of foreign labor, e.g., Algerian migrant workers in East Germany and Finns in the Soviet Union.

The contradiction between the existence of labor shortages and the existence of large unemployment worldwide is due to various factors which generate differentiation within the labor supply and in the demand for labor. Among these factors are the price of labor, the expectations of workers, the need for certain types of economic system to secure cheap and *docile* workers, and the technological transformation of the work process in the last ten years that has not only upgraded some jobs but also downgraded many more jobs, making them unattractive to workers with middle-class aspirations.

Second, this chapter examines how historically the introduction of modern forms of production generates conditions conducive to emigration. The generalization of market relations has had a strong dissolution effect on traditional waged and unwaged work structures thereby promoting the formation of migrant labor. I will discuss the main forms historically assumed by this process. In Chapter 4 I will argue that the development of export-oriented manufacturing in several countries of South-East Asia and the Caribbean Basin constitutes yet another historical example illustrating the introduction of modern forms of production and the generalization of the labor market, two fundamental conditions in the generation of labor migration.

This chapter sketches the historical background pertinent to the particular forms assumed by certain processes in the contemporary phase. It also presents a comparative analysis of traits common to all immigrant labor and concludes with a brief discussion of the main labor migrations taking place over the last two decades to help place the case of the U.S. today in a historical and comparative perspective.

### HISTORICAL BACKGROUND

Labor scarcity has historically been a central problem enterprises have had to solve to realize an area's surplus-generating potential – a fact easily forgotten today in countries experiencing high unemployment. Any situation in which the characteristics of the labor supply threaten existing or foreseeable levels of accumulation can be defined as one of labor scarcity (Portes, 1978: 471–482; Sassen-Koob, 1978: 516–518). Included in this definition are absolute shortages such as those observed in the Arab oil-exporting countries today, and relative scarcities such as those in many advanced industrialized countries in the 1960s where successful working-class organization and welfare state policies had strained the supply of cheap and powerless labor. Specific tendencies in industrial economies have generated specific types of labor scarcities. For example, rapid industrialization creates a need for a direct, quantitative increase in the labor supply which is only partly offset by labor-saving technologies. On the other hand, declining profits generate a need for cheap labor in core countries to offset the victories of organized labor.

The use of foreign labor has taken many forms, varying with a country's place in the international division of labor and the particular mode of specialization prevalent at a given time in the world system. For example, the use of Chinese contract labor on Caribbean plantations in the nineteenth century differs significantly from the use of Irish immigrant labor in England at the same time. These were different labor-supply systems resulting from different surplus-generating processes, each of which played a distinctive role in the division of labor. In the Caribbean, the basic mechanism for world accumulation was the transfer to the metropolitan countries of value produced in the colonies by the development of export-oriented production, e.g., plantations (Amin, 1974; Beckford, 1972; Centro de Estudios Puertorriqueños, 1979). In England, on the other hand, the surplus generated was not exported but transformed into further economic activity and the associated expansion in labor demand. This accelerated large domestic migrations to the cities and Irish immigration (Jackson, 1963).

Furthermore, the use of foreign labor in surplus-generating processes with similar characteristics (e.g., industrialization) may have a different politico-economic role depending on the mode of international specialization prevalent at the time. For example, the rapid industrialization of both the United States at the turn of the century and the Arab oil-exporting countries today generated a pronounced need for foreign labor. But industrialization and labor immigration in the United States occurred at a time when the world economy was still in the process of formation and the struggle for hegemony among the leading countries was moving them into a new phase of the international division of labor. Industrialization in the oil-exporting countries today is taking place under conditions of technological dependence and an unusually high incidence of imports of basic inputs. Furthermore, in the current phase of international specialization, a certain level of industrialization exists in most countries and no longer ensures any kind of pre-eminence.

Using location in the international division of labor as a criterion, one may distinguish four types of instances in the development of world capitalism which have historically generated significant levels of labor imports. Each of these instances subsumes a variety of concrete historical stages in the development of the international division of labor. Hence, periodization is, to a degree, subordinated for the sake of a more analytic conception of the international division of labor. To group migrations belonging to different historical stages into one category clearly has shortcomings. On the other hand, in light of the prevalence of accounts of single migration streams in the immigration literature, it seems useful at this point to identify common roots among apparently highly divergent processes. The purpose here is to provide a general background for the subsequent detailed discussion of labor migrations.

The first type of instance may be characterized by the association of labor imports with the expansion of the capitalist mode of production into less- or un-"developed" areas. The basic mechanism of accumulation in this case is the international transfer to the metropolitan centers of value produced in the Third World (Emmanuel, 1972; Amin, 1976: 133 ff.; Centro de Estudios Puertorriqueños, 1979). One way of accomplishing this is the development of export-oriented production, most typically mines and plantations and, today, highly labor-intensive manufacturing industries. Mines and plantations entailed the *sudden* introduction of large-scale production in areas where pre-capitalist modes of production had been prevalent or exclusive. Mobilization of the necessary labor force thus required an equally sudden transformation of subsistence producers into wage-laborers, slaves, or peons (Schapera, 1947). This accounts, in part, for the violence of the process of capitalist penetration into the Third World. In areas where the surplus-generating possibilities exceeded the local labor supply and there were economic or technological constraints upon the substitution of labor by capital, the new enterprises imported workers. There follow some examples, since I will not return to this case.

In Ceylon (now Sri Lanka) the labor force required for coffee, and later, tea production was formed by importing hundreds of thousands of South Indians. Nearly one million were imported in the 1840s and 1850s alone (Halliday, 1977: 156–157). The labor supply needed for sugar production in the Caribbean Basin was first formed through the import of at least one-half million workers from India who typically came on five-year contracts with free round-trip transportation (Williams, 1970: 348). Similarly, in Brazil, slave labor was imported to the mines and plantations and was later replaced by wage labor; Europeans, particularly from Southern Italy, were offered free transportation and a subsistence plot if they agreed to be wage laborers on coffee plantations (Furtado, 1963: chapters 20–24). African plantations and mines frequently resorted to seasonal migrant workers recruited from distant tribes, a precursor of today's widespread international migrations of workers within Africa (Lasserre-Bigorry, 1975; Amin, 1974a; Arrighi and Saul, 1973; Wolpe, 1975; Wilson, 1976).

In the second type of instance, labor imports are associated with capital expansion and, unlike the first case, a significant level of capital accumulation in less-developed regions. The large migrations to the United States in the late 1800s and early 1900s can be seen as a process called forth by accumulation rather than simply as expansion aimed at value transfers to the metropolitan centers (Thomas, 1973). The association between labor imports and capital expansion is even clearer in the case of oil-exporting countries today. The construction and operation of a production apparatus financed by oil revenues could not take place without large-scale labor imports covering the whole occupational range. However, the association between labor imports, accumulation, and a changed place in the international division of labor is more difficult to establish in the case of the oil exporting countries today than it is for the United States at the turn of the century. One reason for this difference is that the decision to launch an accelerated industrialization program has required the re-injection of oil revenues into the international economic system due to the need for the large-scale imports of inputs. Eventually, this has led to a renewed dominance of these countries by international capital, only under a different form.[1] Unlike the mines and plantations described in the first instance, value transfers to the advanced industrial countries are here mediated by a program of national construction involving basic industry. On the basis of this changed role in the accumulation process, I have tentatively included the case of the oil-exporting countries in the second instance, characterized by the association of labor imports with accumulation in less-developed countries.

In the third type of instance, labor imports are associated with intense capital accumulation in developed countries.[2] Examples of this include the large immigrations of Irish workers into the industrialized cities of Britain – estimated to have reached 700,000 by 1850 (Jackson, 1963: 11) – and the migrations of Southern and Eastern Europeans into Switzerland, old Germany, and France throughout the 1800s and early 1900s (see, e.g., Cinanni, 1968: 29).[3] After World War II, reconstruction generated a large demand for labor which, in most Western European countries, could only be satisfied through labor imports. However, even in the cases of acute labor shortages, such as those in Switzerland, Luxembourg, and the Federal Republic of Germany (henceforth West Germany), an important factor determining the desirability of labor imports as a solution to labor shortages was its profitability due to cost-reducing and anticyclical effects.[4]

In the fourth type of instance, labor imports are associated more directly with the reproduction of capital's dominance over labor in developed countries. Labor imports by Western European countries after World War II as well as several aspects of immigration policy and practice in the U.S. during the last few decades are examples of this type of international labor migration.[5] Such imports (1) increase the level of profits of certain firms and, more generally, of capital as a whole by lowering the cost of labor and the cost of reproduction of the labor force; and (2) operate as an anticyclical mechanism by facilitating the export of unemployment through repatriation of immigrants or lack of unemployment compensation; this anticyclical effect is also furthered by the downward pressure on fluctuations in the demand for goods and services by that share of the labor force represented by immigrants due to the low dependency ratios and minimal consumption levels typical among immigrants.

These, then, are the four types of instances in which labor imports have historically played a significant role in the constitution of the labor supply needed for the world accumulation process. As I indicated earlier, these are not historical stages. At a given time, different types of foreign labor-supply systems were prevalent in different locations of the world economy. For example, slavery became an important labor supply system in Brazil at a time when it was being replaced by other types of labor in the U.S. On the other hand, the same type of foreign labor supply system may be prevalent in different locations of the world economy at different times, e.g., the use of Indian contract labor in the Caribbean during the last century and the use of Caribbean contract labor in the U.S. and Venezuela today.

MIGRATION AS A GLOBAL LABOR SUPPLY SYSTEM

International labor migrations did not evolve as an important labor-supply system until the consolidation phase of the world capitalist economy (Portes, 1978; Zolberg, 1978; Centro de Estudios Puertorriqueños, 1979). The earlier phases of capitalist penetration and incorporation of new regions into a single world economy under European hegemony had generated different types of labor-supply systems. The most important types relied on (1) forced movements of people from one area of the periphery to another, and (2) the subjugation of indigenous and hitherto autonomous populations and their forced transformation into laborers through such means as slavery, *mita*, peonage, *encomienda*, and tribal contract labor.[6] Some of these persist today in areas not completely transformed by the generalization of market relations.

Colonizing migrations belong to the early stages of capitalist penetration.[7] They are distinct from forced-labor supply systems as well as from the international labor migrations that evolved at a later stage. Unlike both of these, colonizing migrations originated in developed countries and colonists were viewed as a valuable resource. Although there are important differences among colonizing migrations (Omvedt, 1973), they have a common root in the process of capitalist penetration into previously unincorporated, autonomous regions of the world that was in full motion by the sixteenth century.

In this early stage, when Western Europe was engaged in state building and colonial expansion, population was seen as a scarce resource. The ideological context was one of belief in the absolute value of population. States enforced strong anti-emigration policies (Hansen, 1961; MacDonagh, 1961) oriented toward a form of primitive accumulation regarding population: "keeping the indigenous population within the sovereign's possessions, maximizing its size, while acquiring a surplus from elsewhere in the system or even outside of it at the lowest possible cost" (Zolberg, 1978: 246). European mercantilism considered emigrations a resource loss. Even J. B. Say, the foremost follower of the Scottish economists in France, made an exception to the free-market model when it came to emigration. Throughout the seventeenth, eighteenth and well into the nineteenth centuries, this view on population was captured in axioms such as Rodin's "Il n'est force ni richesse que d'hommes"; Sir Joshua Child's "The riches of city or nation [lie] in the multitude of its inhabitants"; and Sarmiento's "Gobernar es poblar."

Population was indeed a valuable and scarce resource in the context of slow demographic growth, labor-intensive production, labor-intensive warfare, and the increasing economic and strategic importance of settling uncolonized areas. The population in Western Europe did not even meet the labor needs generated by internal industrialization, let alone the massive need for workers in the colonies. The latter had to be met through large-scale population shifts from one area in the periphery to another. European states contributed only a small share of the total labor needs of the colonial empires, and then only for selected areas. Britain, the dominant power, had the greatest need for labor. It could not have consolidated its empire without recourse to millions of workers from the Third World. This explains the massive population shifts organized by Britain: millions of West Africans to the Caribbean, millions of Tamil-speaking Dravidians to Ceylon (now Sri Lanka), and hundreds of thousands of Chinese and Indians to the Caribbean, Indians to East Africa, and so on.

The incorporation of most areas of the world into the capitalist system resulted in the disintegration or subordination of non-capitalist forms of subsistence (Amin, 1974; Wallerstein, 1974; Centro de Estudios Puertorriqueños, 1979). Although in colonial areas this disintegration was less thorough than in Western Europe, it was sufficient to move large masses of people into the labor market. Here we find the conditions for the creation of a supply of potential migrant workers. Capitalism transforms land into a commodity. Because land was the basis for precapitalist modes of subsistence, its transformation into a commodity created a mass of landless peasants with little alternative to becoming part of the rural or urban labor reserve. This was especially pronounced in the colonial areas where the disintegration of precapitalist modes of subsistence did not arise out of the expanded reproduction of capital *in situ*. As a result, the transformation of displaced peasants and farmers into wage labor that took place on such a large scale in Western Europe and the United States occurred only minimally in colonial areas.

The generalization of capitalist relations and the corresponding transformation of land into a commodity gave a "voluntary" quality to the resulting migrations.[8] This was in contrast to the forced population transfers of the earlier stage. The disintegration of autonomous modes of subsistence resulted in the creation of labor reserves willing to be mobilized into the labor market. There was no longer a need for the direct, physical subjugation and mobilization of workers. The new social structure accomplished this by robbing them of their means of subsistence. This process was not fully completed until the twentieth century.[9]

The consolidation of a world system through the subordination of large areas of the world in the form of a periphery also brought about a shift in the flow of labor. Henceforth, the major international labor flows originated in the less-developed countries and went to satisfy the labor needs of the industrializing countries. The flow was no longer from one colonial area to another, as was the case in the earlier phase of penetration and colonization. After the early phase of forced-labor mobilization, the reserves from which immigrant labor was drawn expanded gradually to encompass more and more parts of the world. The major Western European countries first imported labor from their immediate peripheries: Irish went to England; Poles to Germany; Italians and Belgians to France (Castles and Kosack, 1973; Cinanni, 1968; Hechter, 1975). Then this periphery was expanded to include all of Eastern and Southern Europe – the main sources of labor for Western Europe and eventually the United States. As these reserves were exhausted or their flows interrupted due to wars, China, Mexico, and North Africa emerged as important labor suppliers. In the last two decades, the Caribbean Basin and a growing number of countries in South America, Africa, and Asia have become major labor suppliers.

An important new pattern of labor flows has been added since the 1960s to the continuing flow from developing countries to developed countries.[10] The export of jobs from the developed countries to the developing countries in the form of export processing zones, has brought about new domestic and international labor flows *within* the developing countries. Without the development of the new industrial zones, some of these internal migrations would not have occurred. I will return to this subject in Chapter 4.

The shift from mobilization of forced-labor and colonizing migrations to international labor migrations reflects the complex internal differentiation of the world system. The consolidation of the world economic system has paralelled the strengthening of the nation-state as the basic political unit. Since the late nineteenth century, the state has regulated the entry and exit of labor. Zolberg (1978) convincingly argues that more variance in migration flows can be accounted for by the geopolitical interests and actions of states than by individual migrants' motivations and invidious comparisons between country of origin and destination.

A state's position on migration partly reflects its location in the world economy (Hansen, 1961; Plender, 1972; Thomas, 1973). The most developed country, Britain, had the most liberal position. Thus, while Britain relaxed its anti-emigration stance after the Napoleonic Wars (1812–1815) and introduced the most liberal policy, other European states such as France, some of the German states, and Russia maintained strong anti-emigration policies. France, for example, had sound reasons to be opposed to emigration. Industrialization and the generalization of the labor market were not as fully developed there as elsewhere in Western Europe.[11] Full-time farming remained widespread. Small families, however, were a condition of its viability given the small size of holdings. Slow demographic growth was further compounded by France's continuing need for soldiers in its attempt to create a new colonial empire in North Africa and Eastern Europe. France's internal economic structure, the loss of its colonial empire in North America and Asia, and heavy war involvement created interests different from those of Britain (Savage, 1979; Zolberg, 1978).

Furthermore, even within the well-integrated North Atlantic region controlled by Britain, restrictions on the movement of goods and people were more commonplace and effective than the *laissez-faire* view suggests (MacDonagh, 1961). Britain did not suddenly abandon its mercantilist position on emigration, but at least three factors contributed to its decline: (1) a 15 percent population growth shown in the 1811 census; (2) continued internal migration supplying labor to the new urban industrial centers; and (3) the growing influence of the political economists who viewed emigration and settlement as a way of creating foreign markets for British goods.[12] Nonetheless, attempts to control emigration continued through regulations, preferential fares, and restrictions.

In the United States, immigration policy fluctuated considerably throughout the nineteenth century (Hansen, 1961; Plender, 1972; Zolberg, 1978). By 1819, the economic boom of the early nineteenth century had collapsed and the government resorted to a law that had never previously been enforced to restrict immigration. When the economy recovered it stopped enforcing the law and immigration grew rapidly in the 1830s and 1840s. However, by 1850 immigration was once again closed. The economy began expanding again after the Civil War, but an economic boom in Europe at the same time absorbed a growing share of European migrants. This led the American government to offer incentives to immigrants. The homesteading program, made possible by further expropriation of Indian lands, not only drew settlers but also created a supply of industrial workers from the ranks of would-be settlers who could not acquire land. Labor shortages in this period were so severe that Congress passed a law authorizing employers to pay passage for prospective immigrants. Several states established recruitment agencies in Europe, and a treaty with China for the import of labor was signed in 1868.

The replacement of earlier labor-supply systems by international labor migrations was a gradual process corresponding to the gradual transformation of what is today the Third World. In the middle of the 1800s, the labor market in the North Atlantic region was more generalized than in other areas of the world. While free labor replaced slavery in areas under British control, slavery actually increased in areas such as Latin America. There, slave imports rose from an average of 22,450 a year for the period 1701–1810, to an average of 29,700 a year for 1811–1870 (Curtin, 1969). Various forms of labor-supply systems, ranging from slave labor to free labor, were instituted in different parts of the world. Common to most was the active participation of the state. Nevertheless, the forms of labor supply dominant in the capitalist core eventually became dominant in the Third World, confirming Amin's (1974) proposition that the rhythm of expanded reproduction at the center determines the tendencies of the world system as a whole.

### THE STATE AND IMMIGRATION

At first glance, the strengthening of states and the concomitant enforcement of borders seems to counter the needs of a consolidated world economy for massive international labor migrations. In fact, national boundaries do not act as barriers so much as mechanisms reproducing the system through the international division of labor. The capitalist world economy consists of a multiplicity of political units, the nation-states. This ensures that no single political regime can gain full control over the world economy. "Capitalism as an economic mode is based on the fact that the economic factor operates within an arena larger than that which any political entity can fully control . . . This gives capitalists a freedom of maneuver that is structurally based" (Wallerstein, 1974: 348). National boundaries are one way of facilitating international specialization and higher returns on accumulated capital, including human capital. Both are central tendencies in capitalist development (Amin, 1974; Emmanuel, 1972).

The enforcement of national borders contributes to the existence of a large number of countries in the form of a periphery and the designation of its workers as a labor reserve for global capital. Border enforcement is a mechanism facilitating the extraction of cheap labor by assigning criminal status to a segment of the working class – illegal immigrants. Foreign workers undermine a nation's working class when the state renders foreigners socially and politically powerless. At the same time, border enforcement meets the demands of organized labor in the labor-receiving country insofar as it presumes to protect native workers. Yet *selective* enforcement of policies can circumvent general border policies and protect the interests of economic sectors relying on immigrant labor. This points out the contradictory role of the state in the accumulation process, especially evident in the consolidation of the liberal state (Petras, 1980; Weinstein, 1968).

While the generalization of the labor market emerging from the consolidation of the world capitalist economy creates the conditions for international migrations as a world-level labor-supply system, the strengthening of the nation-state creates the conditions for immigrant labor as a distinct category of a nation's labor supply. That is to say, immigrant labor is not just any labor. It is a component in the labor supply with a distinct role in the labor process characterized by: (1) the institutional differentiation of the processes of labor-force reproduction and maintenance; and (2) a particular form of powerlessness, associated with formal or attributed foreign status, that meets the requirements of types of work organization based on direct rather than structural control over the workforce.

## *The reproduction of the labor force*

The process of reproduction takes place in the country of origin; that of maintenance at least partly in the receiving country. Together they allow the receiving country to externalize renewal costs (Burawoy, 1976; Sassen-Koob, 1978). This institutional differentiation constitutes the invariant characteristic of any system of immigrant labor. While both the conditions which produce a particular migration and the traits of individual migrants may change, the system itself need not change. Similarly, although the conditions producing and reproducing the system of migrant labor may vary over time, the traits of individual migrants may remain the same (e.g., rural, unskilled, young, and so forth). Finally, although migrants' traits may be the same, their place in the receiving country may vary. For example, a growing number of Mexican immigrants are now employed in urban jobs in the north-central region of the United States, though they may have traits similar to those of Mexicans employed in agriculture in the Southwest. An analytical distinction between the individual migrants, the conditions producing and reproducing the system of migrant labor, and the system itself can in this way be maintained.

Institutional differentiation helps lower the cost of the reproduction of the labor force. This macrosocial effect requires a view of capital as a whole – as a historical category – rather than of individual enterprises. Confirming this cost-lowering effect is difficult. Except in the case of highly trained immigrants, there are no estimates of the monetary value involved in labor migrations.[13] The "brain-drain" is a small part of all international labor migrations and must be distinguished from the overall supply of immigrant labor which typically has a low human capital component. In the case of immigrant labor, variables other than the human capital represented by individual migrants have to be used. Macrosocial variables such as government expenditures for social services and infrastructure are useful. Some of the best data come from countries with high levels of control over the recruitment, employment and repatriation of immigrant workers. For that reason, I have used data on Western Europe, particularly Switzerland and Western Germany.

Labor importing countries in Western Europe have realized substantial savings on social services and infrastructure as a result of their access to foreign labor (Böhning and Maillat, 1974; Salowsky, 1972). Before closing immigration in the early 1970s, West Germany and Switzerland especially screened immigrants carefully. Recruits had to pass strict medical examinations and possess a certain level of education which, though below average in the importing countries was high for sending countries and required significant outlays by the state (Castles and Kosack, 1973; Rist, 1978). Many immigrants were skilled or semiskilled, and many of these were recruited off jobs in their native country (Böhning, 1975a, 1976; Cetin, 1974; Krane, 1975; OECD, 1974; Paine, 1974; Poinard and Roux, 1977; Schiller, 1974; Simon, 1973). As a result, some labor-exporting countries such as Algeria, Yugoslavia, Morocco, Greece, and Portugal enacted protective legislation under pressure from local employers who were losing workers they had often trained on the job. In short, besides shifting the costs associated with reproducing a share of its labor supply to the labor-sending country, the labor-importing countries have been quite selective in their recruitment and therewith also benefited from the private and public investments in training in sending countries.

The evidence for Western Europe points out that immigrant labor offers several important advantages to a country. Foreign workers demand fewer social services than national workers. Immigrants often occupy vacant workplaces and housing, and their presence does not require additional expenditures by the government or private capital. This is especially true in the initial phases of immigration (Böhning, 1976; Jones and Smith, 1970; Kindleberger, 1967). The generally low dependency ratios of immigrant workers and their below-average consumption exert relatively little pressure on the production of goods and services.[14] Immigrant workers produce more in relationship to what they consume than native workers. Furthermore, some of the foreign workers can be repatriated when they are no longer needed or when their physical or mental health prevents them from working. The costs associated with unemployment, workers' disability, and medical care can at least be partly exported. Moreover, social discontent can be exported (Freeman, 1979). In short, the possibility of repatriation and the below-average demands of immigrants generally exempt the receiving country's economy from the need to build the kind of infrastructure and service organizations that would be required by an equal number of national workers. This issue, however, is complicated by the presence of children born to foreign workers and the number of these workers who become more or less permanently settled (Rist, 1978), a subject I will return to in Chapter 5.

## The organization of the labor process

Employers not only seek to obtain labor, but to obtain labor that can be used under specific conditions of organization of the labor process. The ways labor has been used have varied historically and have generated distinct components within the overall labor supply. Low-wage labor, in its many forms, is one such component. In industrialized economies, low-wage labor tends to be employed in firms or sectors of firms which have shift work, obsolete and hazardous equipment, and job insecurity. These conditions embody a form of control over the workforce that presupposes the powerlessness of the workers. The continuing creation of such jobs is particularly significant in advanced industrialized economies where organized labor has attained considerable power and where the more oppressed native workers have become politicized, are unwilling to take highly undesirable jobs even if they pay minimum wage, and have access to welfare benefits as an alternative to low-wage jobs. In this context, immigration can be seen as a labor-supply system particularly suited to the needs of firms where the organization of the labor process entails low wages and powerless labor. Such firms are a sizeable component of advanced industrialized economies (Edwards, 1979; Melman, 1965; Piore, 1978; Sassen-Koob, 1984b; Bluestone, Harrison and Gorham, 1984). It is important to emphasize that both backward and very modern and highly dynamic growth sectors in advanced industrialized economies generate a vast array of such low-wage jobs. As I will examine in Chapter 5, the evidence for the U.S. points to an increase in low-wage jobs since the early 1970s.

The use of immigrant labor reduces the cost for employers directly through lower wages and indirectly through lower costs for the organization of production. Their status as foreigners (often as temporary labor), their lack of familiarity with union politics, and their frequent segregation from native workers on the job and in neighborhoods, all combine to make immigrants unusually dependent on their employers and difficult to recruit to working-class struggles according to some analysts (Castles and Kosack, 1973).

Given the prevalent view of immigrants as cheap labor, it is important to point out that not all immigrants are at the bottom of the wage scale and that it is not simply through their low wages that they have a cost-lowering effect on production. Firms in the competitive sector of capital derive additional benefits from (1) labor-supply flexibility (e.g., night shifts and ease of hiring and firing) and (2) organizational flexibility (e.g., the use of hazardous equipment in substandard work spaces). These two types of benefits may be quite significant for firms that operate on narrow profit margins, are subject to wide fluctuations in demand, and depend for their survival on meeting demand whenever it emerges. The importance of these two types of flexibility, in addition to low wages, is evident in the northeastern United States where firms pay taxes even on illegal workers (Piore, 1979) and a large share of illegal workers are estimated to receive minimum wages or above (NACLA, 1979; North and Houstoun, 1976; Sassen-Koob, 1980). Thus, if we only consider wages, immigrants are not always much cheaper than low-wage national workers; it is also their powerlessness which makes them profitable. The availability of immigrant labor reduces the pressure on backward sectors of the economy to change techniques of production or to improve working conditions unacceptable to national workers (Böhning, 1975; Böhning and Maillat, 1974; Castells, 1975; Castles and Kosack, 1973; Oppenheimer, 1974; Piore, 1978; Sassen-Koob, 1980; Wachter, 1978). *And* it reduces the pressure to upgrade jobs in modern sectors of the economy (Sassen-Koob, 1984a; 1984b), a subject I return to in Chapter 5.[15]

In Western Europe, the availability of an abundant, cheap, and highly flexible labor supply has been a key factor in the development of a capital-intensive production apparatus. The supply of foreign labor prevented slowdowns, bottlenecks, and wage increases during the reconstruction period after World War II, all of which would have stimulated inflation (Balke, 1966). It also allowed employers to postpone costly capital investment, as, for example, in the automobile industry in France. Eventually, many immigrant workers were employed in capital-intensive firms in the monopoly sector, belying the notion that they are only to be found in backward sectors of the economy. For their willingness to work nights and weekends allowed these firms to operate at full capacity. Western Europe profited from the availability of immigrant workers not only because of their cheapness, but also because they satisfied an absolute need for labor (except in France and England) and constituted a flexible labor supply.

It is not sufficient to show that immigrants are more susceptible to direct personal control to explain why they are more desirable to certain types of employers than native workers. First we must show that control is a significant variable in the organization of the labor process. This is difficult because the literature on work structure views the labor process as an almost inevitable consequence of techniques of production, themselves generated by some overall process of technological development (Nelson, 1975). Such a view tends to ignore the struggle for control at the workplace. More attention should be given to this variable, as there is growing evidence that the organization of work is the product, not only of a technical process, but also of a social process (Baxandall *et al.*, 1976; Braverman, 1974; Burawoy, 1981; Edwards, 1979; Marglin, 1974; Montgomery, 1979; Stone, 1974; Work Relations Group, 1978). Studies of the coal and steel industries in particular show how the organization of the labor process resulted in part from the struggle between managers and workers over how much such organization would reflect or constrain their interests (Montgomery, 1979; Stone, 1974; Work Relations Group, 1978). This struggle for control cannot be reduced to overt conflicts on the shop floor, but must be viewed as a strategic struggle for control between the historical categories of capital and labor.

Different types of organization of work use different systems to control workers:

(1)   The transfer of skills from craftsmen to machines historically has meant a loss of control by workers over the process whereby labor power is transformed into actual labor (Braverman, 1974; Edwards, 1979; Montgomery, 1979; Stone, 1974). In production work, the standardization of tasks and their performance by machines generated a type of control that could be described as "technical" (Edwards, 1979) insofar as it was mediated by the rhythms of machines (e.g., the assembly line). In the context of large-scale capital-intensive production, however, this technical control has resulted in a new kind of control by workers. Industrial unions were the institutionalized outcome of this control.

(2)   Large firms also developed structural forms of control in white-collar work. Those components of the work process that could not be routinized, either through mechanization or standardization, were incorporated into an organization of work that ensured the standardization of the workers themselves. This was achieved by imposing specific work behaviors and attitudes that led to workers internalizing the firm's goals.

(3)   Immigrants, especially in the United States, are often employed in firms where the system of control rests not on techniques of production and elaborate organizational arrangements, but on the powerlessness of the workers. Control is not structural, but immediate and personal. Employers can respond to workers' dissatisfaction, complaints, and rebellion by firing them. Given these means of controlling workers, the powerlessness of immigrants is particularly significant (Sassen-Koob, 1980, 1981b).

The selective enforcement of immigration policies further accentuates what is distinctive about immigrant labor. Several studies on Mexican immigration to the United States have documented how the state creates a profitable supply of cheap, powerless labor, through such selective enforcement (Bach, 1978; Briggs *et al.*, 1977; Burawoy, 1976; Bustamante, 1976; Cardenas, 1978; Jenkins, 1978; Portes, 1977, 1978). Bach (1978: 539) observes that overemphasizing the role of policy enforcement in studying the exploitation of Mexican immigrants assumes that correct policies and correct enforcement will eliminate exploitation: "The conditions of exploitation of the Mexican immigrant cannot be erased so easily." These conditions are rooted in the process of reproduction of capitalist social relations in general and the state's participation in this process.[16]

Several trends are discernible in contemporary international labor flows. Some of these represent older trends in a new historical form; others seem to be novel. First, the advanced industrialized countries continue to employ immigrant labor as they did in the nineteenth and early twentieth centuries. But the number of developing countries supplying labor is growing and immigrant workers are claiming a larger share of urban service jobs. Second, rapid industrialization in the oil-exporting countries has generated a major new international labor flow. Third, labor import and export policies suggest immigrants are increasingly being as a commodity. I will discuss each of these trends in turn.

(1) Most advanced industrialized countries use a considerable number of immigrant workers. In 1982, immigrants constituted 7 percent of the employed labor force in the major Western European countries. In the smaller countries, immigrants range from between 1.5 and 4 percent of the labor force in countries such as Denmark and the Netherlands, and from 17 to 33 percent in Switzerland, Luxembourg, and Liechtenstein (SOPEMI, 1980; Direction de la Documentation Française, 1986). Despite several recessions and the closing of immigration, there are an estimated 11 million immigrants in the major receiving countries, half of whom are working. These figures are an underestimate because they exclude seasonal and frontier workers and illegals (SOPEMI, 1980). These figures also exclude political refugees and displaced persons after World War II.

The United States, Canada, and Australia have increased their intake of immigrants since the middle of the 1960s. Legal immigration to the United States increased to 500,000 entries a year in the 1980s, up from 265,000 in 1960.[17] The 1970 U.S. Census recorded 9.6 million immigrants, representing 4.7 percent of the population. The 1980 Census recorded 13.9 million immigrants, representing 6.2 percent of the population (U.S. Dept of Commerce, Bureau of the Census, 1981c). These figures underestimate the impact of immigrant workers on concentrated, regional labor markets, and they exclude undocumented immigrants, estimated to range from three to seven million, a large share of whom are probably employed.

Several new patterns are discernible since World War II (see Table 2.1). The labor-supplying peripheries for Western Europe and North America have shifted and expanded to incorporate new countries. In the case of Western Europe, these new sending countries are Yugoslavia, Turkey, Greece, Algeria, Tunisia, and Morocco. On the other hand, major nineteenth-century labor exporters such as Sweden, Denmark, and Belgium have also become labour importers in the last few decades, while Spain and Portugal have consolidated their position as major labor exporters. Italy has remained the major labor supplier since the late nineteenth century, with the exception of the period between 1926 and World War II when the fascist regime restricted emigration in the mercantilist tradition. East Germany, whose territory includes many of the labor-supplying German states in the nineteenth century, has become a labor importer. Furthermore, some of the traditional labor exporters now have a significant number of immigrant workers, mostly undocumented; the presence of North African workers in Spain, Italy, and Greece is the most notable example.

In North America, there has been a major shift to non-European immigrants since the 1960s. Asian and Caribbean countries now provide half of all the immigrants to Canada (Hawkins, 1977). In the United States, the labor-supplying Third World has expanded to include a growing number of South American, Caribbean, and Asian countries. Two recent changes in immigration flows to the United States are significant. First, low-wage countries have replaced high-wage countries as the main source of immigrant labor. In 1950, 60 percent of legal immigrants were from Europe and less than one-seventh from Asia and Latin America (excluding Mexico). By 1970, these shares were reversed (INS 1981). Second, there has been a marked increase in immigration. Between 1961 and 1970, there were 1.2 million more immigrants admitted than between 1950 and 1960; and between 1970 and 1980, 5 million more.

In the main labor-importing countries of Western Europe, immigrant labor has consolidated its place in the secondary sector and expanded its role in the tertiary sector. In the initial phase after World War II, immigrants were recruited mostly for agriculture and construction. Today, they are concentrated in the secondary and tertiary sectors. The cases of Switzerland and West Germany are

Table 2.1 *Foreign workers$^a$ in the main labor-receiving countries of Western Europe*

| Country | 1976 | 1979 | 1979 As % of Total Labor force |
|---------|------|------|--------------------------------|
| West Germany | 2,027,100 | 2,025,100 | 9.3 |
| Austria | 171,000 | 175,200 | 6.4 |
| Belgium | 306,300 | 310,100 | 8.0 |
| Denmark | 39,400 | 42,867$_b$ | 1.5 |
| France | 1,642,800 | 1,591,900 | 7.5 |
| Luxembourg | 49,100 | 50,400 | 33.4 |
| Netherlands | 180,500 | 196,400$_d$ | 4.0 |
| United Kingdom | 1,665,000$_c$ | 929,000 | 3.0 |
| Sweden | 235,500 | 231,999 | 5.3 |
| Switzerland | 518,000 | 490,700 | 17.3 |

$^a$ Excludes seasonal and frontier workers
$^b$ Estimate made October 1979 using the 1976 figure and annual flow data for subsequent years
$^c$ This is an estimate by the European Economic Community Commission. Most immigrants working in the U.K. are from Commonwealth members.
$^d$ Based on 1979 Labor Force Survey by the Department of Labor.
*Source:* SOPEMI (1977, 1979, 1980); Commission des Communautés Européennes (1977); Lebon and Falchi (1980)

interesting in view of the fact that they tightly control recruitment (see Table 2.2). This suggests that the levels at which immigrants are employed actually correspond to the need for foreign labor. A few years after the immigrant labor force was stabilized, almost 73 percent of immigrants in West Germany (1975) and 67 percent in Switzerland (1972) were in the secondary sector, with the rest mostly in the tertiary sector. Immigrants comprised 13 percent of all secondary sector workers in West Germany and almost 30 percent in Switzerland.

This pattern is less clear in the United States. Since the 1960s, when legal immigration has been predominantly from low-wage countries, there has been a pronounced growth of immigrant labor in low-wage service jobs. A good indicator of this trend is Mexican immigration, because it has provided cheap labor to the United States since it began in the twentieth century. Originally employed mainly in agriculture, most Mexicans today hold secondary and tertiary sector jobs.[18]

The growing concentration of immigrant workers in the urban tertiary sector is a significant trend that has not received sufficient

Table 2.2 *Distribution of total and foreign labor force by sector: Switzerland (1972) and West Germany (1975)*

| | Switzerland | | | | West Germany | | | |
|---|---|---|---|---|---|---|---|---|
| | Total workers | | Foreign workers[a] | | Total workers | | Foreign workers | |
| Sector | number | % | % | As % of total workforce | number | % | % | As % of total workforce |
| I Agriculture, Hunting, Forestry, Fishing | 220,000 | 7.1 | 2.5 | 7.7 | 1,823,000 | 7.3 | 1.0 | 1.1 |
| II Mining, Quarrying, Manufacturing, Electricity, Water, Gas, Construction | 1,440,000 | 46.8 | 66.9 | 29.7 | 11,408,000 | 45.8 | 72.8 | 13.0 |
| III Transport, Communication, Catering, Finance, Trade, Services (Domestic and other) | 1,418,000 | 46.1 | 30.8 | 14.5 | 11,567,000 | 46.9 | 26.2 | 4.6 |
| Total | 3,078,000 | 100.0 | 100.2 | 21.6 | 24,798,000 | 100.0 | 100.0 | 8.2 |

[a] Excludes workers with permanent permits, of whom there were 254,191 in 1972. These are included in the figure for the total workforce.
*Source:* Switzerland: OECD (1974): 376–377), Switzerland (1973: 104, 108, 40–42); West Germany: OECD (1978), SOPEMI (1977)

study. This trend may be an indicator of certain limits to the historical transformation of the international division of labor. The service sector is labor intensive, but unlike other labor intensive components of industrialized economies, many services cannot be exported to countries with large reserves of cheap labor. The growing concentration of immigrants in the service sector of developed countries complements the growing export of unskilled and semi-skilled manufacturing jobs from the developed countries to the Third World (Sassen-Koob, 1981b), a subject I return to in Chapters 4 and 5.

It can be argued that the recent, large-scale capital flight from the northeastern United States and the recent, large-scale immigration of workers from the Third World to the same area are two processes with a common origin. Organized labor's struggle in the old northeastern industrial centers resulted in higher wages, a measure of political power, and a welfare apparatus that supports unproductive labor and provides an alternative to low wages. These factors helped raise the cost of labor and the cost of the reproduction of the labor force in the Northeast. Those components of the economy that could move did so. Those that could not used the internal reserves of low-wage labor and, when these became politicized in the 1960s, gained recourse to immigrants. These same social conditions in the Northeast explain why legal as well as illegal immigrants there earn higher average wages than those in the South of the United States. It suggests that the socioeconomic context – as expressed by the costs of the reproduction of the labor force – has a greater effect on immigrant wages than immigrant status. Immigrants are part of the working class in the receiving country and are subject to the same conditions that shape wage levels of national workers. The powerlessness of immigrants, rather than low wages *per se*, and the consequent possibility of using them for undesirable jobs and of exercising considerable control over them makes immigrants a distinct category within the overall labor supply. Similarly, the export of jobs is not necessarily directed to countries with the cheapest labor in absolute terms, but to countries where labor can be controlled, such as Indonesia and the Philippines.[19]

(2) The main obstacle to large-scale industrialization in Arab oil-exporting countries after 1970 was an acute labor shortage (Halliday, 1977; International Labour Office, all sources; Legum, 1978). Massive immigration to these countries took place throughout the 1970s and continues today (see Table 2.3). The country studies

Table 2.3 *Foreign labor force in Arab labor-importing countries, 1975*

| Country | Total labour force | Nationals (%) | Employed foreign workers (%) |
|---------|--------------------|---------------|------------------------------|
| Saudi Arabia | 1,600,000 | 51.6 | 48.4 |
| Kuwait | 303,288 | 30.3 | 69.7 |
| Qatar | 88,346 | 18.8 | 81.2 |
| Bahrain | 75,753 | 60.4 | 39.6 |
| United Arab Emirates | 301,500 | 14.9 | 85.1 |
| Libya | 786,450 | 57.7 | 42.3 |
| Total | 3,155,337 | 47.1 | 52.9 |

*Source:* ILO (1978a,b,c,d,e,)

sponsored by the International Labour Office (ILO) show that, in 1975, the proportion of foreign workers in the labor force was 39 percent in Bahrain, almost 70 percent in Kuwait, 42 percent in Libya, 81 percent in Qatar, 48 percent in Saudi Arabia, and 85 percent in the United Arab Emirates.[20] The bulk of these workers came from other Arab nations and from India, Pakistan, Bangladesh, South Korea, and the Philippines.

Although there are no accurate figures, it is generally accepted that the size of the foreign labor force has continued to increase in the Arab oil-exporting countries. Officially, the number of foreign workers in Saudi Arabia in 1980 was 813,000. Yet the *Financial Times* (April 28, 1980) reported that Saudi government officials informally put the number of foreign workers at 1.5 million – representing 75 percent of the labor force (see Table 2.4). There are estimated to be one million Yemenis in Saudi Arabia. In Kuwait, illegal residents were estimated to number 300,000 by 1979, far above the official count. Similar discrepancies between official figures and estimates of the foreign population and foreign labor force can be found in all Arab oil-exporting countries. Governments are concerned about this large foreign presence and have imposed tighter controls, launched drives to apprehend illegals, and deported foreign workers who strike or try to organize.[21] Yet the continuing need for foreign workers is well illustrated by the case of the United Arab Emirates, where severe restrictions on visas for foreigners coincided with the declaration of a huge industrial complex in Dubai as a free zone where Arab and Asian workers need no visa or contracts (Legum, 1978).

Table 2.4 *Saudi Arabia: employment of foreign workers by economic sector,*
*1975*

| Sector | Total | Nationals (%) | Foreign (%) | Foreign as (%) of all |
|---|---|---|---|---|
| Agriculture and fishing | 585,600 | 51.7 | 7.1 | 9.4 |
| Mining and petroleum | 27,000 | 1.5 | 1.5 | 43.0 |
| Manufacturing | 115,900 | 2.1 | 12.2 | 81.4 |
| Electricity, gas and water | 20,350 | 0.7 | 1.7 | 64.6 |
| Construction | 239,300 | 3.5 | 26.3 | 85.0 |
| Wholesale and retail trade | 192,100 | 5.9 | 17.0 | 68.5 |
| Transport, storage and communication | 103,850 | 7.1 | 4.0 | 29.8 |
| Finance and insurance | 12,100 | 0.5 | 0.9 | 57.4 |
| Community and personal services | 503,700 | 27.0 | 29.3 | 45.0 |
| Total | 1,799,900 | 100.0 | 100.0 | 43.0 |

*Source:* ILO (1978)

Besides construction, several other sectors employ large numbers of
foreign workers – notably manufacturing, wholesale and retail trade,
and many services, including government administration and education. Saudi Arabia is a case in point (Table 2.4). Eighty-five
percent of all workers in construction were foreigners, as were more
than 80 percent of those in manufacturing and 70 percent of those in
wholesale and retail trades. Labor shortages are so pronounced in
these countries that foreigners claim a significant share of civil service
jobs – one third in Oman (ILO, 1977a) and almost 80 percent in
Qatar (ILO, 1978a).

The main labor exporters in the Middle East have felt the
repercussions. By 1975, labor exports represented the equivalent of 28
percent of the labor force in Jordan, 27 percent in North Yemen, 4
percent in Syria and up to 10 percent in Egypt (ILO, 1978). In one
decade, Jordan has gone from labor surplus to labor shortage; it now
imports workers from Syria, Egypt, and Pakistan.[22] In Egypt, labor
exports are one of the main sources of foreign exchange (Keely,
1980).[23]

This major new labor flow generated by accelerated industrialization reflects the transformation in the articulation of the oil-
exporting countries with the world accumulation process. This
transformation cannot be explained simply by the rise in the

international price of oil. Before the current phase, the transfer of value from the oil-exporting countries to the center was direct, in the form of low-priced oil. Now, this transfer is mediated by national industrialization. Oil revenues are being re-injected into the international circuit through the long-term constitution of economies whose production patterns will incorporate imports to an extent inconceivable before the current phase, especially in the Arab oil-exporting countries. Accelerated industrialization has led to large-scale imports of raw materials and machinery, thereby transferring a large share of oil revenues back to capital in the developed countries.[24] Upper-class luxury consumption could not have generated such high levels of imports.

(3) Compared with the earlier phase of international migrations, especially at the turn of the century, there is a growing tendency to treat migrants as commodities. This expresses itself in the inclusion of labor in government-run export sectors and in migration policies. South Korea is the outstanding example. In its economic transactions with Arab oil-exporting countries, South Korea has included the export of workers as a component of its export projects. The labor shortage in the Arab countries was the initial rationale. However, South Korea has now formalized this inclusion and negotiated deals with countries such as Ecuador which do not have a labor shortage. The Philippines tried developing a similar tactic (Keely, 1980). And China announced in July, 1980, that it would export labor and expected to "underbid" its competitors. Labor transfers to the Arab countries have been profitable for many private agencies specializing in this trade, especially in India, Bangladesh, and Pakistan. But these countries have not quite reached the level of formalization and government supervision attained by South Korea.[25]

South Korea has a higher level of economic development than the countries to which it exports labor. No developing country sending labor to developed countries has attained this level of control over its labor outflow or systematically incorporated labor in its international economic exchanges. Relevant here is Emmanuel's (1972) analysis of international trade: price is determined not by the commodity being traded, but by the location of selling and buying countries in the world economy.[26] The South Korean government can make labor exports a profitable enterprise; the Jamaican cannot.

Immigration policies in Western Europe and Arab oil-exporting countries increasingly treat immigrants as a commodity. Western

European countries try both to stabilize the resident immigrant population through family reunion policies and minimize permanent residence and naturalization of new immigrants. In the Arab oil-exporting countries, policies minimize permanent residence and maximize rotation of the immigrant labor force. This is much less the case in the classic immigration countries, such as the United States and Canada, but even here there is a growing tendency towards stabilization through family reunion and justification of immigration in terms of labor requirements.

Switzerland and West Germany are extreme cases of this commodification. Residence regulations in these countries were liberal in the nineteenth century, but became increasingly restrictive in the twentieth century. Since then, extremely tight mobility restrictions on immigrants have been implemented (Kaufman, 1975; Klee, 1975). In Switzerland, the minimum period necessary to obtain citizenship was increased from two to six years after World War I. After World War II it was increased to twelve years. Immigrants have no legal claim to a residence permit. In 1963, the government launched a stabilization program which permitted dependents of already established immigrants to enter but restricted the entry of non-dependents to those filling specific labor shortages. Finally, in 1970, immigration was all but closed. West Germany also followed a path of increased restrictions aimed at minimizing any claims to permanent residence. It finally ended immigration in 1973. However, dependents and "needed" immigrant workers continue to arrive, with a noticeable increase in the late 1970s. The minimum residence period for naturalization is eight years, though this does not give the immigrant a legal claim.[27] There are also restrictions on immigrant mobility within these two countries. In 1968, foreign workers in Switzerland were not allowed to change employers, occupations, or cantons of residence for five years after their arrival. After the closing of immigration in 1970 this period was reduced to one year. West Germany imposes similar restrictions. A work permit may stipulate that special permission for a change of job has to be obtained for up to five years after arrival. Foreign workers can be forced to accept new jobs which pay less than their previous jobs or even less than unemployment insurance. Though both Switzerland and West Germany have explicitly announced throughout the years that they are not immigration countries and that labor imports are a temporary measure, the immigrant population has increased over the last two decades and become a fairly permanent feature of the labor force.[28] Family reunion policies for permanent residents partly recognize this fact. Other European countries also have imposed restrictions on foreign workers, but have been less extreme than Switzerland and West Germany.

The classic immigration countries view immigrants, potentially at least, as permanent residents and citizens (Keely, 1979). But Western Europe and the Arab oil-exporting countries have sought to maximize rotation of the immigrant labor force. In these countries, immigrants are viewed as a production factor that can be repatriated when no longer needed. The recognition of a *permanent need* for at least some of the foreign workers in Western Europe is what seems to underlie family reunion policies and regulations aimed at integrating permanent residents socially and politically. Exemplary in this regard is Sweden, which has sought to extend all political rights to foreign workers, at least at the local level.

### CONCLUSION

International migrations evolved as an important labor-supply system with the consolidation of the world economy. The labor needs generated by the earlier phases of capitalist penetration and incorporation were satisfied largely through the forced mobilization of labor from one colonial area to another. The generalization of the labor market and the incorporation of large regions of the world in the form of a periphery were the structural processes underlying international labor migrations.

The consolidation of the world economic system also corresponds to the formation of nation-states and enforcement of borders, two developments which would seem to run counter to the needs of a world system and to pose obstacles to international flows. But in the world capitalist system, the multiplicity of nation-states becomes a factor in the reproduction of the system, particularly through the international division of labor.

While the consolidation of the world economic system creates the conditions in which international migrations emerge as a massive labor-supply system, the formation of states creates the conditions for immigrant labor as a distinct category within the overall labor supply. This distinctiveness rests on (1) the institutional differenti-ation of the processes of labor-force reproduction and maintenance;

and (2) a particular form of powerlessness which meets the control requirements of a type of organization of the labor process which, though usually defined as backward, is a significant component in most highly industrialized countries – most notably, in the service sector.

The forms that immigrant labor has assumed over time varied, depending on a country's place in the international division of labor and the mode of specialization prevalent at the time in the world system. In the contemporary phase, two features characterize labor migration: the growing use of immigrant labor in the tertiary sector of developed countries and the growing use of foreign and native migrants in the secondary sector of the developing countries. This reflects the recomposition of capital at the world level. The requirements of capital accumulation have led to the development of novel ways of realizing surplus. Among these are the export of manufacturing jobs to the Third World (in the form of export processing zones) and large-scale industrialization in the oil-exporting countries. This has generated major international migrations within the Third World. On the other hand, unlike other labor-intensive components of industrialized economies, service jobs cannot easily be exported. Thus, the growing concentration of immigrant labor in the service sector of highly industrialized countries may be pointing to constraints in the historical transformation of the international division of labor, insofar as most service jobs must be performed *in situ*. This growing concentration of immigrant labor in service jobs in developed countries can be viewed as the correlate of the export of jobs to the Third World.

What is important for my analysis is that the introduction of modern forms of production and the generalization of market relations has a dissolution effect on traditional waged and unwaged work structures. This both contributes to the formation of a pool of migrants and minimizes the possibilities of their returning to the areas of origin. In Chapter 4 I will examine what is perhaps a new form of the same process discussed in a historical perspective here, the development of labor-intensive export-oriented manufacturing in several countries of South-East Asia and the Caribbean Basin. Manufacturing for export is playing the same role in these areas as the development of commercial agriculture did in several major countries of Latin America in the generation of large rural migrations to the cities. The conditions for the absorption of the migrant influx assume a specific form in the contemporary phase. Labor-intensive manufacturing for export has generated considerable concentrations of jobs in the new industrial zones. And the transformation of the economies in highly industrialized countries has generated considerable concentrations of low-wage service jobs particularly in the large cities. For a number of reasons, discussed in Chapters 4 and 5, the current internationalization in the conditions for the absorption of the new migrations contains both a continuation of old forms and the development of new ones.

# 3
# The new immigration

Immigration to the United States has changed from a preponderance of high-wage countries of origin in the 1950s to one of low-wage countries of origin in the 1970s. This recomposition cannot be taken for granted, especially since the family reunion emphasis of the 1965 Immigration Act was expected to bring in the relatives of those already here, i.e., mostly Europeans. Secondly, the data show that there has been a massive increase in annual entries, even excluding undocumented immigrants. From 265,000 in 1960, annual entries reached 570,000 in 1985 and about 1 million if we include all entries, a level approximating the peak period at the turn of the century. Thirdly, the data show a tendency toward concentration in a limited number of large metropolitan areas: New York City is the major recipient of immigrants from the Caribbean Basin, including several South American countries, while Los Angeles, San Francisco and, again, New York City are the major recipients of Asians.

Thus the new Caribbean Basin and Asian immigration can be seen as (a) backing up two low-wage immigrations that began earlier – Mexicans to Los Angeles and other West Coast cities and Puerto Ricans to New York City; and (b) geographically complementing the large and continuing flow of Mexicans into the Sunbelt.

The new Caribbean Basin and Asian immigration to the United States represents yet another component in the long history of the formation and reproduction of the low-wage labor supply. Historically the formation of the low-wage labor supply has occurred through the incorporation of a wide diversity of population segments: rural migrants, youth, women. Only in certain periods was immigration a central mechanism for the provision of low-wage workers. A number of developments which coalesced in the early 1960s had the effect of reducing the supply of native low-wage labor. Notable among these were (a) the end of the massive domestic rural-to-urban migrations which had provided the bulk of low-wage labor in the

1940s and 1950s, and (b) the politicization of traditional low-wage workers such as blacks, Puerto Ricans, Chicanos, women and youth during the 1960s and into the 1970s. This reduction happened in a context of an expansion in the supply of low-wage jobs.

The growth in the supply of low-wage jobs is a central trend in the restructuring of economic activity in the U.S. which began in the mid-1960s and became fully evident in the late 1970s. While Mexican immigration continued to supply low-wage, willing workers to the Southwest and Midwest throughout the 1960s, this was not the case in other areas, notably the Northeast. Furthermore, the politicization of Puerto Ricans in the Northeast and Chicanos in major West Coast cities along with the expansion of welfare benefits significantly reduced the supply of native low-wage workers in these areas.

Clearly these developments do not fully explain the timing and destination of the new Caribbean and Asian immigration. But they add a historical background that is one variable in the explanation. The reduction in the supply of domestic low-wage workers during the 1950s and 1960s acquires its full significance for immigration in the context of (a) the increase of low-wage jobs in both major growth sectors and declining sectors during the 1970s and continuing today (see Chapter 5) and (b) the post-World War II development of major linkages, particularly through investment and foreign policy measures, between the United States and the countries that eventually became the major suppliers of immigrants to the United States in the 1970s (see Chapter 4).

### BACKGROUND: FORMATION OF THE LOW-WAGE LABOR SUPPLY

The geographic and occupational replacement of the earlier Eastern and Southern European immigrants by Southern Blacks beginning during World War I eventually became part of a much larger domestic movement, the massive rural migrations to the cities in the 1940s and 1950s. These migrations were 80 percent white. It is also in the 1940s that the implementation of the Mexican "bracero" program takes place and we see the development of the associated large-scale undocumented Mexican migrations which continue to supply low-wage labor today.

The phase of massive domestic migrations to the cities had come to an end in the 1960s, substantially reducing an important source of

low-wage labor. The 1960s is also the period of heightened politicization of other groups traditionally supplying low-wage labor –
women, youth, blacks, Chicanos, and Puerto Ricans. In this same
period, we see the passage of a major new Immigration Act and the
development of a major new phase in U.S. immigration history, the
new Caribbean Basin and South-East Asian immigration. In this
section I will briefly discuss these factors in the history of the
formation of a low wage labor supply in the U.S.

Immigrants and Blacks have a long-standing relationship in the
labor market, one rooted in their common condition as a low-wage
labor supply. This relationship has been characterized by displacement, replacement and complementarity in different time periods and
in specific labor markets. An early instance of this relationship
occurred in the mid-1800s, before the Civil War, when immigrants
began to displace Northern Blacks from jobs they had held, at times
almost exclusively. There were colonies of free Black workers in the
Northeastern cities, especially New York, Philadelphia and Baltimore. Frederick Douglass comments that these Northern Blacks
were "elbowed out of employment by some newly arrived emigrant
. . ." and that these White men were becoming "house-servants,
cooks and stewards . . . porters, stevedores . . . brick-makers, white
washers and barbers . . . coachmen . . .," all occupations formerly
performed mostly by Blacks (quoted in Fishel and Quarles, 1970:
143).

However, only with the large Black migrations to Northern cities
due to the closure of immigration during World War I did this
relationship assume a clear and widely recognizable form. The war
halted the large inflow of Southern and Eastern Europeans which
had provided the vast supplies of cheap labor needed by expanding
industries in the North. Labor recruiters sent by Northern employers
initiated these migrations of Blacks (Drake and Clayton, 1962: 58;
Spero and Harris, 1968: 140–182, 264–267, 257, 337–338).[1] Labor
flows initiated by labor recruiters answer in part some of the questions
that have been raised as to why the Black migrations to the North
started when they did and why they did not flow westward where
racism was much weaker (Myrdal, 1962: 185–191). But once
established, such migratory channels typically attain a certain
autonomy and recruiters are no longer necessary (e.g., Sassen-Koob,
1978: 516–518). In 1920, half of all Blacks living in the North had
been born in the South and by 1930 this share had grown to 57

percent (Bureau of the Census, 1960: 41–44). On the other hand, immigration which had averaged 1.2 million entries in each of the two years preceding the war declined to 300,000 a year in 1914–1917 and to 100,000 a year in 1918–1919, and remained well below 100,000 annually in the two subsequent decades.[2]

The role of immigrants and later Blacks as a supply of low-wage labor in the North can be seen in the data on occupational concentration. In 1910 immigrants represented less than 21 percent of the labor force, yet they were 61 percent of all nonfarm laborers and service workers and 31.6 percent of operatives (Wool and Phillips, 1976: 45–54, tables 2.3, 2.4, 2.5). By 1930 almost 56 percent of all Blacks were nonfarm laborers, service workers, operatives and other semiskilled workers, mostly concentrated in the northern cities. Although the actual figures involved were small, the rate at which these occupational shifts in the Black population took place is significant. If the northward migration rate of Blacks had continued at the pre-1915 level, the number of Blacks living in the North by 1920 would not have been attained until after 1970. Furthermore, 57 percent of the native White population in the Eastern North was urban in 1920, and the share for Blacks resembled that of immigrants, with 79 percent for each (Forman, 1971: 15–16). Finally, Black migrants went to the same area, the Eastern North, the destination of 80 percent of the "new immigration" from 1880 to 1920. This was the area in need of laborers, service workers and operatives which first drew on immigrants and later on rural Southern Blacks. Between 1900 and 1910, for every 15 foreigners added to the population in this region, one Black was added, a ratio which not only contracted, but was actually reversed in the next decade, when for every new immigrant there were three new Blacks.

This geographic and occupational replacement of immigrants by Blacks continued throughout the 1940s and 1950s but increasingly as a component of a much larger process, the massive rural migrations to the cities which were overwhelmingly White. These domestic migrations dwarfed international migrations to the U.S. Thus, while immigration reached one million in the 1940s and 2.5 million in the 1950s, rural migrants numbered respectively 10.6 and 9.6 million in those two decades (INS, 1972: Table 1; USDA, 1973: Table 6). To this has to be added the rapid growth of the Puerto Rican population, significant beyond its numbers because it was concentrated primarily in New York City. In 1940 Puerto Ricans in New York City numbered 70,000; by 1960 they reached 613,000 in that city, with an additional 250,000 nationwide (cited in Glazer and Moynihan, 1963: 93–94; Bureau of the Census, 1953b). Furthermore, the Mexican contract labor program initiated during World War II as an emergency measure was continued long beyond the initial expiration date and provided several hundred thousand farmworkers annually until 1964. This contract labor program also indirectly created the conditions for illegal immigration which grew throughout these decades and continued after the closure of the labor program (Samora, Bustamente, and Cardenas, 1971: 18–20, 33–46; Bustamante, 1972; Cardenas, 1976). Mexican immigrants, Puerto Ricans, Blacks, and a large share of rural migrants provided low-wage labor.[3] Except for Mexicans, immigration supplied much less low-wage labor than at the turn of the century since in 1950, 60 percent of the immigrants were Northern and Western Europeans and only 8 percent were Asians and Latin Americans (excluding Mexicans) (INS, 1977: Table 14). Moreover, the share of immigrants in the labor force declined markedly: while they constituted 21 percent of workers in 1910, this lessened to only 8.2 percent in 1950, and with a much smaller share of low-wage occupations than in 1910.[4]

It is worth noting that as the numbers of rural migrants to the cities declined substantially in the 1960s, immigration both increased markedly and included more low-wage countries of origin (INS, 1977: Table 14; USDA, 1973: Table 6). Thus, rural migrants declined almost by half from 9.6 million in 1951–1960 to 5.9 million in 1961–1970 while immigrants increased by 1.2 million over their level in 1951–1960. As the large cities in the North began to experience a decline in the sources of cheap labor that had emerged in the earlier decades – southern Blacks and rural migrants – immigration once again began to provide cheap labor especially in the late 1960s and throughout the 1970s.

During the 1960s the decline in the earlier sources of cheap labor was substantially offset by the entry into the labor force of the baby-boom generation and of adult White women. Between 1960 and 1970 the share of young White men in the lowest-level occupations (nonfarm and farm laborers, personal service jobs such as restaurant workers, janitors, certain kinds of operatives and private household workers) increased from 18.1 percent to 31 percent, and for young White women from 12 to 13.4 percent (Wool and Phillips, 1976: 142, 183), which means that the major occupational growth at this level was accounted for by young White men. In terms of numbers, young White men added 720,000 workers to this occupational level, an increase of 73 percent over the previous decade; young White women added 100,000, an increase of 50 percent; and adult White women added 250,000, an increase of 21 percent. These shifts were accompanied by a particularly sharp increase in the educational level of workers at this occupational level, with a net gain of 1.2 million high school graduates. Similar shifts occurred for young White workers in somewhat less lowly paid occupations, which are nonetheless considered low-wage jobs, such as operatives in the garment and leather industries, hospital attendants, transport operators and so on (Wool and Phillips, 1976: 153–154). These shifts show clearly that along with an educational upgrading in the labor force of those aged 16–24 years, there has been a substantial occupational downgrading. In their detailed study, Wool and Phillips (1976: 102ff.) found that the share of workers in higher-level occupations declined for each new educational cohort, with corresponding increases of their shares in lower-level occupations. That is to say, more persons with a given educational attainment are in lower-level occupations than was the case in 1960. Controlling for race, the trend is accentuated for Whites and slightly reversed for non-Whites – although non-Whites are still overrepresented in low-level occupations.

A number of trends, some already emerging in the 1970s and others expected in the next decade, point to new patterns in the composition of the low-wage labor supply in the late 1970s and 1980s. First, youth and women account for a much smaller share of labor force growth than they did in the two earlier decades. Young workers (16–24) will increase by only 18 percent while those aged 25–34 increased by 55 percent between 1970 and 1980. Teenagers (16–19) actually experienced very sharp decline from a growth rate of 46.4 percent in 1960–1970 to 9.1 percent in 1970–1980, a decline further intensified during 1980–1985 when the full impact of the smaller birthrate will be felt. The sharp decline in new labor force entrants, besides its direct quantitative effect, will also have consequences in terms of the flexibility of the labor supply. The data for 1960–1970 show that young workers were willing to take low-wage jobs even though their educational attainments had risen; their declining share may well mean a labor supply less adaptable to the ongoing demand for low-wage workers. Furthermore, the Bureau of Labor Statistics also expects a decline in the growth rate of female labor force participation as compared with the 1960s rate. This decline along with the struggle for women's equality further reduces the supply of low-wage labor in the late 1970s and early 1980s.

Second, although the share of non-White workers is expected to increase from 10.7 percent in 1970 to 11.6 percent in 1985, due to a smaller decline in the non-White birthrate, their declining participation rate in the lower level occupations starting in the 1960s will continue (Wilson, 1978: 123–143). The trend seems to be towards an increased participation in higher-level occupations and a declining rate of entry into lower-level occupations. This is accompanied by a sharp reduction in labor force participation rates among young workers, particularly those with less than 12 years of education and therefore most likely to enter low-wage occupations (Wool and Phillips, 1976: 138–141, 245–246). Thus, although non-Whites are still overrepresented in the lowest-level occupations, between 1960 and 1970 there were 630,000 non-Whites who actually left these occupations; among Whites a million youths and adult women accepted such jobs at the same time that 280,000 adult men departed (Wool and Phillips, 1976: 182–183; Wilson, 1978: 126–134).[5] Overall, the relative occupational standing of non-Whites was 52.7 percent compared to that of Whites in 1960, and 66.3 percent in 1970 (Wool and Phillips, 1976: 132–134). These various gains by non-Whites are severely qualified by the growing hopelessness at the bottom levels which leads workers to drop out of the labor force or never enter it.

In sum, these trends underlie the Bureau of Labor Statistics projection for 1985 of a shortage in low-wage service workers and of a tight situation for nonfarm laborers and operatives. Furthermore, the recomposition of the economic structure has created a significant supply of low-wage manufacturing and particularly service jobs (Sassen-Koob, 1981b). This is especially the case in major cities, such as New York and Los Angeles, the destination of most of the new Caribbean and Asian immigration.

The rapid growth in immigration, both legal and illegal, since the late 1960s can be expected to provide a large share of low-wage labor. Immigrants in the previous two decades had substantial shares in higher level occupations, not surprisingly given the prevalence of European countries of origin up to 1960. However, the figures on legal immigrants underestimate the total share of foreign-born workers in low-wage jobs because they exclude information on the undocumented, many of whom are in such jobs. I will return to this subject in Chapter 5.

## A NEW PHASE IN U.S. IMMIGRATION

There has been a remarkable transformation in the levels of entries and national composition of immigration since 1965 compared with the two preceding decades. As recently as 1960, Europe accounted for over two-thirds of all entries. By 1985, Europe's share had shrunk to one-ninth. Asia, Latin America and the Caribbean now provide the vast majority of all immigrants. It is worth noting that not only Europe's share but also its actual numbers had declined, from almost 140,000 entries in 1960 to 63,000 entries in 1985. This halving in actual numbers further adds to the impression of a new phase in immigration.

The fastest-growing nationality group in terms of legal admissions is Asian. From 25,000 entries in 1960, levels rose to 236,000 in 1980 and to 264,700 in 1985. While these figures include refugee adjustments, much of this increase is due to higher immigrant entry levels. This becomes evident when we consider the main countries in Asia sending immigrants: the Philippines, South Korea, and India. Furthermore, even in a year like 1982, when total Asian entries reached an all-time high of 313,000, Vietnamese accounted for 72,000 entries, a level that had declined to 39,000 by 1983.

The single largest foreign language population in the U.S. is still the Hispanic, which includes both citizens (native-born and naturalized) and immigrants. In addition there are sound grounds to accept the estimate that the largest undocumented population is also of Hispanic origin. However, given a common misconception, it is important to emphasize that the fastest-growing resident foreign-language population is Asian, not Hispanic (see tables 3.1 and 3.2).

Entries over the last fifteen years describe a bimodal curve: a large increase after 1965, a decrease in the first half of the 1970s, and a new increase in the second half of the 1970s. This pattern holds for each of the major nationality groups, notably Hispanics and West Indians, and partly for Asians. Total entries of Hispanics (South and Central Americans, excluding Mexico) reached about 170,000 from 1965 to 1969, declined to 149,000 from 1970 to 1974, and rose to 368,000 from 1980 to 1985 (INS, 1981; 1984; 1985). In the case of West Indians, entries reached 351,000 from 1965 to 1969, declined to 318,000 from 1970 to 1975 and rose to 445,000 from 1980 to 1985. There was no decline in the case of Asians: entries reached 258,000 from 1965 to 1969, rose to 574,000 from 1970 to 1974 and reached 1,612,000 from

Table 3.1 *Immigrants admitted by selected origin, 1960, 1980, 1985*

| Selected origins | 1960 | 1980 | 1985 |
|---|---|---|---|
| Europe | 138,426 | 72,121 | 63,043 |
| Asia | 24,956 | 236,097 | 264,691 |
| Africa | 2,319 | 13,981 | 17,117 |
| Latin America and the Caribbean | 66,440 | 186,077 | 209,718 |
| Mexico | (32,684) | (52,096) | (61,077) |
| Caribbean | (14,047) | (73,296) | (83,281) |
| Central America | (6,661) | (20,968) | (26,302) |
| South America | (13,048) | (39,717) | (39,058) |
| Total immigrants admitted[a] | 265,398 | 530,639 | 570,009 |

[a] Also includes origins not listed here.
*Source:* Immigration and Naturalization Service, "Tabulation of Immigrants Admitted by Country of Birth" (1981 and 1985, unpublished; 1984 Statistical Yearbook of the INS)

Table 3.2 *Immigrants admitted by area: Caribbean, Latin American, and Asian, 1955–1985*

| | West Indies | Central America[a] | South America | Asia | Total |
|---|---|---|---|---|---|
| 1955–1959 | 78,557 | 26,825 | 42,278 | 98,856 | 246,516 |
| 1960–1964 | 120,337 | 43,658 | 100,131 | 117,140 | 381,266 |
| 1965–1969 | 351,806 | 51,344 | 119,219 | 258,229 | 780,598 |
| 1970–1974 | 318,680 | 44,159 | 104,676 | 574,222 | 1,041,737 |
| 1975–1979 | 413,715 | 73,794 | 155,745 | 879,178 | 1,522,432 |
| 1980–1985 | 444,828 | 144,094 | 223,683 | 1,612,396 | 2,425,001 |
| Total | 1,727,923 | 383,874 | 745,732 | 3,540,021 | 6,397,550 |

[a] Excludes Mexico
*Source:* INS, Tabulation of Immigrants Admitted by Country of Birth, 1954–1979, (1981, unpublished); 1984 Statistical Yearbook of the INS; 1985 INS, Tabulation of Immigrants Admitted by Country of Birth (unpublished)

1980 to 1985. This same pattern holds for single nationality groups, particularly the attainment of the highest levels of entries in the last five years (see tables 3.3 and 3.4).

The countries providing the largest single flows confirm the overall regional distribution. The top ten countries are Latin American and Asian. Considering legally admitted immigrants from 1972 to 1979, we can see that Mexico with over half a million is by far the largest single sender of immigrants, followed by the Philippines with

Table 3.3 *Changing entry levels of Colombian and Dominican immigrants, 1955–1985*

|  | Dominicans | Colombians |
|---|---|---|
| 1955–1959 | 4,525 | 7,568 |
| 1960–1964 | 26,644 | 27,118 |
| 1965–1969 | 57,441 | 39,474 |
| 1970–1974 | 63,792 | 29,404 |
| 1975–1979 | 75,224 | 42,117 |
| 1980–1985 | 121,908 | 62,892 |

*Source:* INS, Tabulation of Immigrants Admitted by Country of Birth, 1954–1979, 1985 (unpublished); 1984 Statistical Yearbook of the INS

Table 3.4 *Changing entry levels of Filipino and Korean immigrants, 1955–1985*

|  | Filipino | South Korean |
|---|---|---|
| 1955–59 | 10,522 | 4,990 |
| 1960–64 | 15,573 | 9,521 |
| 1965–69 | 57,563 | 18,469 |
| 1970–74 | 152,706 | 93,445 |
| 1975–79 | 186,659 | 148,618 |
| 1980–85 | 263,482 | 198,341 |

*Source:* INS (1981) Tabulation of Immigrants Admitted by Country of Birth, 1954–1979 (1981, unpublished); 1984 Statistical Yearbook of the INS; INS, Tabulation of Immigrants Admitted by Country of Birth, 1985 (unpublished)

290,000, South Korea with 225,000, China (Taiwan and People's Republic) 160,400, India with 140,000, Jamaica with 108,400, and so on. All the countries sending over 100,000 immigrants were Caribbean Basin or Asian, with the single exception of Italy. Two European countries, the United Kingdom and Germany, and Canada sent about 80,000 each during the 1972–1979 period. Finally, traditional European emigration countries, Portugal and Greece, each sent about 80,000 during this period.

When we control for sex, a rather clear pattern emerges (see Table 3.5). The new immigration countries (the Philippines, Korea, Jamaica, Dominican Republic, Colombia, China, and the smaller ones) mostly have more females in their flows. The traditional

Table 3.5 *Top immigration flows from Asia, Latin America, and Caribbean by sex, 1972–1979[a]*

|  | Percent female | Total both sexes |
| --- | --- | --- |
| Mexico | 49.0 | 530,378 |
| Philippines | 59.9 | 289,429 |
| Korea (South) | 60.8 | 225,339 |
| China (Taiwan and People's Republic) | 52.8 | 160,454 |
| India | 48.1 | 139,834 |
| Dominican Republic | 52.5 | 118,147 |
| Jamaica | 51.8 | 108,454 |
| Colombia | 56.2 | 59,829 |
| Trinidad and Tobago | 52.7 | 49,492 |
| Haiti | 52.3 | 44,721 |
| Hong Kong | 52.0 | 40,438 |

[a] Includes only flows with over 40,000 immigrants admitted in 1972–1979. Excludes Vietnam and Cuba because most of them came as refugees, often years before their status was changed to immigrant, but are counted in year in which that change took place.
*Source:* Immigration and Naturalization Service, unpublished tabulations

immigration countries, such as Italy, Portugal, and Greece, have mostly males. Some of the Latin American countries that have not had strong emigration to the U.S., such as Argentina and Uruguay, also have a predominance of males in their flows. Males also dominate the migration from Africa and Asia, except for the countries of South-East Asia, which are also the main immigrant-sending countries. Controlling for age, we see that women dominate the 20–29 age group. In the 20–24 age group women outnumbered males by almost 100,000 (Houstoun, Kramer and Barrett, 1984: 935–937).

In many ways the predominance of females is a continuation of a pattern that began in the 1930s. But we need to specify the particular conditions underlying the overall trend. Thus Houstoun, Kramer, and Barrett (1984) point out the weight of the influx of so-called war brides in explaining the prevalence of women in certain nationality flows at a given period. Countries where a significant number of American servicemen are stationed tend to generate considerable female immigration, e.g., most of the women coming to the U.S. from Germany are brides of American servicemen. A second important consideration is the family-reunion emphasis; it has had a generalized effect on most immigrant nationalities of raising the share of women. However, the information on age suggests that while a majority of women may enter as dependents, the high incidence of young

working-age women points to potentially high labor-force participation rates.[6]

A third trend we need to consider in understanding the current
immigration phase is the increase in the supply of female immigrant
*workers*. This category, while small compared with the others (various
kinds of dependent) is growing and indicates independent migration
of women, including women who may be wives and mothers but leave
their families behind. Women represented 45.6 percent of all legally
admitted immigrants in 1972–1979 under the category of skilled and
unskilled workers in short supply (Sixth Preference) (Houstoun *et al.*,
1984: 945). It is also worth pointing out that in an old migration like
the Mexican, historically dominated by men, women have become an
increasingly large share, reaching almost half of all legal immigrants;
a similar trend is taking place in the undocumented Mexican
migration (Warren and Passel, 1983). Finally, women represented
over half of the 290,000 admitted in the non-preference immigrant
category; the non-preference category consists of the spaces that
become available when the preference quotas are not fully used.
What is of interest here is that (a) it was the third largest numerical
category among immigrants admitted from 1970 to 1979 under the
preference system; (b) it covers relatives not included under the
preference system, investors, and workers. That is to say, it could be a
significant vehicle for women to immigrate independently.

There is a pronounced tendency, both in the past and today, for
immigrants to be concentrated in certain areas, a fact which will tend
to add to their labor-market impact. In the early 1900s New York,
Pennsylvania and Illinois attracted most of the immigrants (Immigration Commission, 1911: 105). Until 1975, New York was still the
largest recipient, followed by California, now the main destination for
immigrants due to the large Mexican and Asian influx (INS, 1978:
75). Together, these two states receive almost half of all new
immigrants; New Jersey, Illinois, Florida and Texas together receive
about one-fourth of all new immigrants admitted annually in recent
years (INS, 1978: 75). About 40 percent of all immigrants live in the
ten largest cities which together account for less than 10 percent of the
total U.S. population and where immigrants represented a share
considerably higher than their total share in the U.S. population
(INS, 1978: 76–85). Between 1966 and 1976, New York City received
about one-fourth of all new arrivals, followed by Los Angeles. If we
add the immigrant population of New Jersey, which in the last years

Table 3.6 *Residential distribution of immigrants: leading states, 1972–1979*

| | All immigrants | | Females | |
| --- | --- | --- | --- | --- |
| | number | % | number | % |
| California | 812,928 | 22.6 | 430,596 | 22.6 |
| New York | 751,519 | 20.9 | 384,431 | 20.2 |
| Florida | 236,680 | 6.6 | 129,773 | 6.8 |
| Texas | 232,322 | 6.5 | 120,115 | 6.3 |
| New Jersey | 223,559 | 6.2 | 118,964 | 6.2 |
| Illinois | 213,479 | 5.9 | 108,936 | 5.7 |
| Massachusetts | 107,744 | 3.0 | 55,732 | 2.9 |
| Pennsylvania | 80,141 | 2.2 | 42,891 | 2.3 |
| Michigan | 81,829 | 2.3 | 42,204 | 2.2 |
| Total | 2,740,201 | 76.2 | 1,433,642 | 75.2 |
| Other states | 752,003 | 23.7 | 471,781 | 24.8 |
| Total | 3,492,204 | 99.9 | 1,905,423 | 100.0 |

*Source:* Immigration and Naturalization Service, unpublished tabulations

has been the third or fourth largest recipient, then the New York metropolitan area is experiencing an even more disproportionate share of the total labor-market impact of immigration.[7] Controlling for sex, the same pattern emerges. Almost half of all immigrant women lived in California, New York, and New Jersey. Ten states accounted for over 75 percent of all immigrant women and men admitted from 1972–1979 (see Table 3.6).

There are two as yet minor trends that need to be brought into this description. One is the addition of several South-East Asian countries to the list of immigrant-sending countries. While the numerical levels of immigrants from Singapore, Malaysia, and Indonesia are very small, they are growing every year and represent a new development. The data point to the emergence of conditions that are promoting out-migration. This incipient trend acquires added significance if we consider that some of the major immigrant streams are coming from South Korea, the Philippines, China, and Hong Kong, where we find highly evolved export economies, a development which is only at an early stage in Indonesia and Malaysia. Indonesia would traditionally have had migration streams directed to the Netherlands: thus the emergence of a migration stream to the United States needs to be explained.

Secondly, quite a few of what are today major migrations began as middle-class migrations but eventually created conditions that facilitate the migration of poorer strata as well as undocumented immigration. Thus such migrations (for example, that of South Koreans), perceived as consisting of mostly well-off persons, have by now become increasingly working-class migrations with significant numbers of undocumented immigrants and including growing numbers employed in sweatshops. Undocumented Filipino women have been found in growing numbers. And even cases of groups of undocumented Indonesians were identified in Southern California working at extremely low wages. In brief, what emerges from these instances is that a growing component of the new Asian migration is a labor migration.

IMMIGRANT WORKERS: BASIC CHARACTERISTICS

The supply of immigrant workers is drawn from three segments of the total alien population: legal immigrants, illegal immigrants, and nonimmigrant aliens. Workers in the first two segments are commonly referred to as immigrant workers. The third segment includes a variety of statuses, some entitling work permits and others not. Workers in this third segment range from international artists and scholars to contract farm labor. The rate of labor-force participation in each of the three segments varies considerably. The rate for immigrants increasingly resembles that of natives while that for the undocumented is commonly believed to be extremely high because they come here to work. Among nonimmigrant aliens, participation rates vary greatly according to the subclasses in this segment. The differences among these three types of alien workers are substantial enough to require a detailed discussion of their characteristics to adequately understand their labor-market impact.

The 1970 Census recorded 9.6 million immigrants, of whom 6.2 million had become citizens and 3.4 million permanent residents (see Table 3.7). Both in numbers and as a percentage (4.7 percent), this is a significantly lower level than that of earlier decades, for example, 1920 when immigrants numbered 13.9 million and constituted 13.2 percent of the total population (U.S. Bureau of the Census, 1976b; 1973: Table 17). The 1980 Census counted 13.9 million immigrants, representing 6.2 percent of the total population (U.S. Bureau of the Census, 1982d).

Table 3.7 *Foreign born in the U.S., 1970 and 1980*

|  | 1970 | 1980 |
|---|---|---|
| U.S. total population (a) | 203,302,031 | 226,504,825 |
| Foreign born (b) | 9,619,302 | 13,956,077 |
| (b)/(a) | 4.7% | 6.2% |

*Source:* U.S. Bureau of the Census, *1980 Census of Population and Housing: Advance Report* (Washington, D.C.: U.S.G.P.O., 1981c); U.S. Bureau of the Census, *1980 Census of Population and Housing: Provisional Estimates of Social, Economic, and Housing Characteristics (Supplement and Report); States and Selected Standard Metropolitan Statistical Areas* (Washington, D.C.: U.S.G.P.O., 1982d)

The large increases in annual entries of Asians and Hispanics over the last 15 years are reflected in the 1980 composition of the U.S. population. The share of persons of Hispanic origin counted by the Census increased by 62 percent from 1970 to 1980 and that of Asians by 100 percent. Their considerable concentration in particular geographic areas and occupations makes the impact of their growth rates significant even though their shares in the total population are rather small. Furthermore, the tendency for illegal immigrants to reside in areas with large concentrations of legals further maximizes the labor-market impact of this immigration.

The 1980 census counted 14.6 million persons of Hispanic origin and 3.5 million Asians (including Pacific Islanders), representing respectively 6.5 percent and 1.5 percent of the total population of 226.5 million (U.S. Bureau of the Census, 1981b and Table 3.8, this volume). Their geographic concentration, particularly high for Asians and non-Mexican Hispanics, renders their numbers far more significant than their shares in the total U.S. population would suggest. Over 60 percent of Hispanics reside in three states alone: California, Texas and New York. The Northeastern region with 2.6 million has a much smaller Hispanic population than other regions, but it is quite distinct in that it is not Mexican. The largest share is made up of immigrants from South America and the Caribbean Basin. This is for the most part a very recent immigration that may surpass the Puerto Rican component if we include undocumented immigrants. New York with 1.6 million and New Jersey with half a million accounted for the largest share of Hispanics in the

Table 3.8 *Population by race and Spanish origin, 1980*

| | Total | White | Black | American Indian, Eskimo, and Aleut | Asian and Pacific Islander | Other | Spanish origin | As % of total |
|---|---|---|---|---|---|---|---|---|
| United States | 226,504,825 | 188,340,790 | 26,488,218 | 1,418,195 | 3,500,636 | 6,756,986 | 14,605,880 | 6.4 |
| Regions | | | | | | | | |
| Northeast | 49,136,667 | 42,328,154 | 4,848,786 | 78,182 | 559,759 | 1,321,786 | 2,604,260 | 5.3 |
| New England | 12,348,493 | 11,585,633 | 474,549 | 21,597 | 81,005 | 185,709 | 299,164 | 2.4 |
| Middle Atlantic | 36,788,174 | 30,742,521 | 4,374,237 | 56,585 | 478,054 | 1,136,077 | 2,305,110 | 6.2 |
| North Central | 58,853,804 | 52,183,794 | 5,336,542 | 248,505 | 389,747 | 695,216 | 1,276,400 | 2.1 |
| East North Central | 41,669,738 | 36,138,962 | 4,547,998 | 105,881 | 302,748 | 574,149 | 1,067,790 | 2.5 |
| West North Central | 17,184,066 | 16,044,832 | 788,544 | 142,624 | 86,999 | 121,067 | 208,610 | |
| South | 75,349,155 | 58,944,057 | 14,041,374 | 372,123 | 469,762 | 1,521,839 | 4,473,170 | 5.9 |
| South Atlantic | 36,943,139 | 28,647,762 | 7,647,743 | 118,656 | 260,038 | 268,340 | 1,193,820 | 0.3 |
| East South Central | 14,662,882 | 11,699,604 | 2,868,268 | 22,454 | 41,041 | 31,515 | 119,315 | 0.8 |
| West South Central | 23,743,134 | 18,596,691 | 3,525,363 | 231,013 | 168,083 | 1,221,984 | 3,160,094 | 13.3 |
| West | 43,165,199 | 34,884,785 | 2,261,516 | 719,385 | 2,081,368 | 3,218,145 | 6,252,040 | 14.4 |
| Mountain | 11,368,330 | 9,958,545 | 268,660 | 363,169 | 98,416 | 679,540 | 1,441,480 | 12.6 |
| Pacific | 31,796,869 | 24,926,240 | 1,992,856 | 356,216 | 1,982,952 | 2,538,605 | 4,810,565 | 15.1 |

*Source:* Bureau of the Census, 1980 Census of Population, Supplementary Report (1981b: Table 3)

Table 3.9 *Main nationalities of Asian population in the U.S., 1970–1980*

|  | 1970 | 1980 | Percent increase |
|---|---|---|---|
| Chinese | 435,062 | 806,027 | 85.3 |
| Filipino | 343,060 | 774,640 | 125.8 |
| Japanese | 591,290 | 700,747 | 18.5 |
| Korean | 69,130 | 354,529 | 412.8 |

*Source:* U.S. Bureau of the Census, 1973, 1981b

Northeast. While they were only 5.3 percent of the total population in the Northeast, they represented 9.4 percent in New York State and 19.9 percent in New York City.

A comparison of the Hispanic and Asian populations, the other high-growth immigration, indicates that the size of the latter is significantly lower but the rate of growth much higher[8] (see Table 3.9). The Asian population doubled its numbers from 1970 to 1980, and the INS reports that 1.5 million Asians were admitted legally between 1970 and 1980. The Chinese increased by 85.3 percent from 1970 to 1980, and are now the largest single Asian group, followed by the Filipino with 774,600 – an increase of 125.8 percent over their 1970 level. One of the highest growth rates between 1970 and 1980 is that of the South Koreans, 412.8 percent. Their numbers went from 69,100 to 354,500. Finally, the Japanese, the largest single Asian nationality in 1970, are now third in size. These growth rates are unusually high, especially against the overall U.S. population increase of 11.4 percent and the fact that these figures exclude a share of illegals.

The 1980 Census data on economic characteristics records a median income of $14,711 for Hispanics and $22,075 for Asians (including Pacific Islanders). Median income for Whites is $20,840 and for Blacks, $12,618 (see Table 3.10). The figures for Hispanics and Asians are problematic in that they most likely exclude considerable numbers of low-wage individuals and families in the illegal population.[9] The share of persons with incomes below the poverty level follows the same pattern of extreme disadvantage for Blacks and relatively better status for Asians than Hispanics. Thus, 30.2 percent of the Blacks were below the poverty level, compared with 13.9 percent of Asians and 23.8 percent of Hispanics. Asians had the highest share of women in the labor force, over 50 percent

Table 3.10 *Economic characteristics by race and Spanish origin, 1980*

|  | White | Black | Asian and Pacific Islander | Spanish origin |
|---|---|---|---|---|
| *Total labor force* | *89,339,672* | *10,573,445* | *1,751, 494* | *5,944,156* |
| Employed | 84,134,204 | 9,300,661 | 1,665,706 | 5,421,433 |
| Unemployed | 5,205,468 | 1,272,784 | 85,788 | 522,723 |
| *Female labor force* | *37,458,881* | *5,210,640* | *801,792* | *2,366,949* |
| Employed | 35,297,665 | 4,625,693 | 758,397 | 2,127,752 |
| Unemployed | 2,161,216 | 584,947 | 43,395 | 239,197 |
| Median income ($) | 20,840 | 12,618 | 22,075 | 14,711 |
| Mean income ($) | 24,279 | 15,721 | 25,681 | 17,360 |
| Persons, poverty status determined | 184,431,365 | 25,661,955 | 3,610,970 | 14,343,741 |
| Income in 1979 below poverty level | 17,301,567 (9.3%) | 7,752,010 (30.2%) | 503,089 (13.9%) | 3,409,754 (23.8%) |

*Source:* U.S. Bureau of the Census, *1980 Census of Population and Housing: Provisional Estimates of Social, Economic, and Housing Characteristics*, [March] 1982d

compared with 40 percent among Whites, 50 percent among Blacks, and under 30 percent for Hispanics. Noteworthy is the fact that the similarity in female labor force participation rates among Blacks and Asians produces such different median incomes.

The two largest single concentrations of Hispanics are in Los Angeles and New York City; of Asians, in Los Angeles, San Francisco, and New York City. The next largest concentrations are significantly smaller. Los Angeles has 2 million Hispanics and New York City 1.4 million. San Francisco has 326,000 Asians and 400,000 Hispanics. The composition of the Hispanic and Asian populations by national origin is markedly different in New York City and Los Angeles. Mexicans are the overwhelming majority in Los Angeles and Puerto Ricans in New York City with the new Hispanics an increasingly close second. Japanese are the largest single group in Los Angeles and Chinese in New York City (see Tables 3.11 and 3.12).

The general trend in the 1970 Census data is for foreign-born workers to follow with a slight disadvantage the occupational distribution of persons of native parentage and of second generation immigrants. The latter were more highly represented among professional, technical, managerial and administrative occupations than were natives. They also had higher shares in sales, clerical and craft jobs, and smaller shares in operative and service jobs than natives. The

Table 3.11 *Population by race: Los Angeles–Long Beach SMSA[a], 1980*

| Race | | Spanish origin | |
|---|---|---|---|
| Total | 7,477,503 | Total | 2,066,103 |
| White | 5,073,617 | Mexican | 1,650,934 |
| Black | 943,968 | Puerto Rican | 36,662 |
| American Indian, | | Cuban | 44,289 |
| Eskimo, Aleut | 48,120 | Other Spanish | 334,218 |
| Asian | 417,209 | | |
| Japanese | 116,543 | | |
| Filipino | 99,043 | | |
| Chinese | 93,747 | | |
| Korean | 60,618 | | |
| Asian Indian | 18,562 | | |
| Vietnamese | 28,696 | | |
| Pacific Islander | 17,641 | | |
| Other | 976,948 | | |

[a] Standard Metropolitan Statistical Area.
*Source:* U.S. Department of Commerce, Bureau of the Census, *1980 Census of Population: General Population Characteristics, California*, 1982b

Table 3.12 *Population by race: New York City, 1980*

| Race | | Spanish origin | |
|---|---|---|---|
| Total | 7,071,639 | Total | 1,406,024 |
| White | 4,294,075 | Mexican | 22,577 |
| Black | 1,784,337 | Puerto Rican | 860,552 |
| American Indian, | | Cuban | 60,930 |
| Eskimo, Aleut | 11,824 | Other Spanish | 461,965 |
| Asian | 229,789 | | |
| Chinese | 124,764 | | |
| Asian Indian | 40,945 | | |
| Filipino | 23,810 | | |
| Korean | 23,257 | | |
| Japanese | 13,730 | | |
| Vietnamese | 3,283 | | |
| Pacific Islander | 1,712 | | |
| Other | 749,902 | | |

*Source:* U.S. Department of Commerce, Bureau of the Census, *1980 Census of Population: General Population Characteristics, New York*, 1982c

impression is that the occupational distribution of second generation immigrants is slightly more advantageous than that of natives. When we control for race and language among natives, this advantage becomes substantial with respect to Blacks and Spanish-speaking workers. Similarly, the occupational distribution of the foreign-born, though less advantaged than that of second-generation immigrants, is significantly better than that of Blacks and Spanish-speaking natives. This suggests that the flow of immigrants in the 1940s, 1950s, and early 1960s did not produce a large supply of low-wage workers.

These differences are reflected in the 1969 family income of each class. The highest median family income, $11,356, was earned by second-generation immigrants, followed by that of natives, $9,327, and finally that of the foreign born, $9,026 (Bureau of the Census, 1973: Tables 8 and 9). Median family income for blacks ($6,035) and the Spanish-speaking ($7,248) was substantially lower than that of all other natives and of first- and second-generation immigrants. Similarly, the unemployment rates of first and second generation immigrants are lower than those of natives, and markedly lower than those of native Blacks and Spanish-speaking.

After 1970, the same overall trends recorded by the Census appear to continue according to the available data. The best available data for non-Census years on the labor-market characteristics of immigrants are those compiled by the INS at time of entry. There are, however, serious problems with the data (Tomasi and Keely, 1975: 57–72). The INS obtains data for management purposes, not scholarly ones. Furthermore, the data are based on information provided by the entrants themselves; this leaves room for distortions since entrants are unlikely to give damaging, or what they perceive to be damaging, information. Thus women may claim their occupation as domestics rather than secretaries because the latter is an obstacle to entry while the former is not; men may upgrade their skills for similar reasons. Finally, North and Weissert (1973) found that INS data consistently underestimate, possibly by as high as 20 percent, the share of workers among immigrants. This particularly affects women, who tend to enter as dependents and homemakers and probably were not, and did not expect to be, in the labor force in their home countries; once in the U.S., however, economic need and the trend towards growing female labor-force participation led them to take jobs. This underestimate of female labor-force participation may be particularly significant in view of the kinds of jobs a good share of these women will take and the high unemployment rates among native women in those jobs.

A comparison of the 1970 Census data on the occupational distribution of immigrants with INS data for 1970 immigrant entrants shows that at the time of entry a much higher share of immigrants listed themselves as professionals, technical, craft and household workers than did the resident immigrants (INS, various years: Table 10A). Among the 1970 entrants, almost 30 percent gave professional or technical occupations and about 18 percent, craft occupations, as compared to, respectively, 15.5 and 14 percent of resident immigrants. On the other hand, fewer than 6 percent gave service occupations upon entry as compared with 13.7 percent of resident immigrants. North and Weissert (1973) did a follow-up study on the 1970 immigrant cohort and found that by 1972 their occupational distribution had changed towards a pronounced similarity with that of resident immigrants recorded in the 1970 census (1973: Table 35). Thus by 1972 only 17.8 percent were in professional and technical occupations and 14.5 percent in crafts; on the other hand, 13.3 percent were in services.

Post-1970 INS data on the occupational distribution of immigrants at entry show a fairly similar distribution to that of the 1970 immigration cohort. For example, in the 1976 occupational distribution at entry (INS, 1978: 10A) there were more professionals and technicians (30 percent), and more household workers (4.5 percent), fewer service workers (8.9 percent), fewer nonfarm laborers (7.8 percent), fewer operatives (13.4 percent), and fewer clerical workers (9.6 percent), than would have been expected after some years of residence in the country given the structure of labor-market demand. The differences between the occupational distribution at entry and after several years in residence reflect in part the differences in the social and economic structure between emigration countries and the U.S.

The available 1970 INS entry data and the North and Weissert (1973) follow-up study suggest two trends: one is that the occupational distribution at entry is bimodal, with concentrations of high-level and low-level occupations; the other trend is that once in the U.S., the degree of bimodality diminishes significantly with a shift of the more highly trained entrants (professions and crafts) to lower-level occupations (clerical and operatives) and low-wage entrants (household and farm work) toward relatively better-paid

Table 3.13 *Occupational distribution of the foreign born, 1950–1979*
*(percentages)*

| Years of entry | Professional/ managerial | Clerical sales | Craft workers | Other blue-collar | Service workers | Farm workers |
|---|---|---|---|---|---|---|
| 1975–79 | 18.1 | 11.2 | 6.6 | 35.4 | 21.3 | 7.2 |
| 1970–74 | 20.3 | 15.6 | 11.6 | 31.0 | 17.8 | 3.7 |
| 1965–69 | 24.0 | 24.0 | 12.9 | 24.7 | 18.3 | 3.1 |
| 1960–64 | 30.4 | 20.9 | 12.0 | 21.4 | 13.0 | 2.3 |
| 1950–59 | 29.0 | 19.2 | 13.8 | 23.3 | 13.0 | 1.8 |
| Pre-1950 | 27.1 | 25.4 | 13.5 | 16.6 | 15.4 | 2.0 |

*Source:* U.S. Department of Commerce, Bureau of the Census, 1979 (November); 1983b (April)

occupations (services and nonfarm labor). Clearly, the basic factor at work is not so much immigrants' failure or success to carry out their intended occupations, but the characteristics of the occupational structure in the U.S. and the kinds of labor needs it generates.

Comparing the occupational distribution of foreign-born workers from 1975 to 1979 with earlier periods reveals a decrease in professional, managerial, clerical, sales and crafts jobs and an increase in noncraft blue-collar jobs and services (Current Population Survey). Thus in the period 1950–1959, 29 percent of the foreign born held professional and managerial jobs. This share had declined to 18 percent for the period 1975–1979. Similarly, while 19 percent held clerical and sales jobs in the earlier period, this share declined to 11 percent in the later period. On the other hand, while 16.6 percent held noncraft blue-collar jobs in the earlier period, this share had increased to 35.4 percent in the later period. A similar though much less pronounced increase was registered in the share of service jobs. More detailed studies on particular nationalities, to be discussed below, tend to confirm these overall trends toward a marked concentration in blue-collar and service jobs (see Table 3.13).

The 1980 Census data confirm this bimodality in the occupational distribution of immigrants. Secondly, it shows that immigrants, especially women, have increased their share of jobs in manufacturing. Thirdly, immigrant women, to a larger extent even than native women, tend to be concentrated in a limited number of occupations.

Using 1980 Census data and controlling for sex and native/immigrant status, some sharp differences emerge. If we consider the five states in which most immigrants reside (California, New York, Texas, Florida, and Illinois), the sharpest difference in occupational distribution is between native and immigrant women in operative jobs: only about 8 percent of native women compared to 20 to 25 percent of immigrant women held such jobs (Bach and Tienda, 1984; Tienda, Jensen, Bach, 1984). Nowhere does the occupational distribution of men contain this large a divergence between natives and immigrants. A second large difference among the women is in clerical jobs: 37 to 40 percent of native women held such jobs compared with 25 to 30 percent of immigrant women.

About half of all immigrant women are concentrated in two occupations, operatives and services, with variations by nationality. Nearly 70% of all Hispanic immigrant women in these five states held operative, service or laborer jobs. The figure for Asians was lower; but among Asians arriving in the 1970s it reached 40 percent, a level that is higher than is generally assumed. On the other hand, the figure of all women workers holding these jobs in the U.S. was 29 percent (U.S. Department of Commerce, 1983). At the other extreme, fewer immigrant women than native women held professional jobs, 9 to 10 percent compared to 14 to 16 percent.

The evidence by industry shows a similarly high concentration in certain sectors (Bach and Tienda, 1984; Tienda *et al.*, 1984). The share of women in transformative industries (mainly garments, textiles and food) ranged from 24 to 35 percent in those same five states. This was about 10 to 15 percent higher than the share of native women. The second largest concentration was in social services, from 22 to 27 percent compared with 32 to 37 percent of native women. The differences between native and immigrant women are less pronounced in the other industry groups. From 23 to 30 percent of immigrant women are in the producer and distributive services, a share slightly lower than that of native women. As I will discuss at length in Chapter 5, the producer and distributive services are a key component of the economy and one of the most dynamic sectors. Thus the considerable presence of immigrant women in such jobs is of significance.

Comparing 1970 and 1980 Census data on the distribution of women by industry it is interesting to note that a larger share of immigrant women in 1980 than in 1970 were in extractive industries, producer services and social services. Within the transformative industries, a larger share of immigrant women held jobs in the food, machinery, and chemical branches. Comparing these national level trends with those for the five states with the vast majority of immigrants suggests divergent patterns: a disproportionate concentration of immigrant women holding jobs in the garment and textile industries are located in these states, while immigrant women holding jobs in the machinery and chemical industries are located outside of those leading states.

The data suggest that by 1980 the industrial distribution of immigrant and native women has become more dissimilar. Tienda, Jensen, and Bach (1984) estimated the index of dissimilarity for 1970 and 1980. In 1970, 12.8 percent of native or immigrant women would have had to change occupations for the two distributions to be equal; by 1980 the index had risen to 15.6 percent. A shift-share analysis revealed an increased allocation of immigrant women into low-wage occupations, notably those that have a declining share in the overall economy. Thus, while the national trend reflected a relative decline in the number of laborers and farm laborers, immigrant women increased their share of these jobs (Tienda *et al.*, 1984).

In evaluating the impact of immigrants on the labor market, certain facts have to be taken into account. First, spouses, children and other dependents of working immigrants may have a delayed impact on the labor market. This impact may be much more immediate in the case of women who would have been unlikely to enter the labor force in their home countries and had few expectations in that regard upon entry, but shortly after taking up residence find themselves holding a job. The delayed impact of dependents is particularly significant given the family reunion orientation of immigration policy and the fact that up to two-thirds of entrants are dependents. For example, in the 1970s over half of all entries were dependents, quite unlike the earlier waves of immigrants which consisted overwhelmingly of men directly entering the labor force (INS, 1978: 73). At the same time, this greater family emphasis in immigration also means that the immigrant family will contribute to consumption in a way that early waves of immigrants did not, and that a smaller share of immigrants' income is sent back home. There is then a growth inducement effect through immigrants' consumption.[10] Secondly, the labor-market impact of immigrants is not evenly distributed, given their tendency to be concentrated in certain areas. Thirdly, given the trend for illegal immigrants to follow the stream and concentrations of legal immigrants of the same nationality, cities such as New York and Los Angeles experience an additional labor-market impact due to the unrecorded concentrations of illegals.

## UNDOCUMENTED ALIEN WORKERS

There are three kinds of undocumented alien: (a) those who enter the country illegally, referred to as "entries without inspection" (EWIs) by the INS; (b) those who enter the country legally but abuse their visas, typically by overstaying and working without a proper visa; and (c) those whose documents are fraudulent. It is generally accepted by INS officials and immigration experts that the vast majority of undocumented aliens are in the first category, though the second one has been growing rapidly in recent years. The number of undocumented aliens is unknown and estimates vary from 3 to 12 million. While immigration scholars tend to agree on a much lower range of 3 to 6 million (Keely, 1979: 51; National Commission for Manpower Policy, 1978: 120), the INS generally uses the higher estimates, in part probably because it supports requests for agency expansion.

Estimates about the undocumented alien population are derived from the number of deportable aliens located. Their number, almost all of which represents apprehensions, has been rising steadily. In fiscal year 1964, 86,597 deportable aliens were located; in 1974, 788,145; and in 1984, 1,138,566. This represents an increase of over 1,300 percent between 1964 and 1984.[11] EWIs represent between 85 and 90 percent of deportable aliens located each year by the INS.

There are a number of problems with the data base from which estimates and descriptions of the total undocumented alien population are drawn. First, they are not based on individuals located but on workload figures, which signifies that an individual apprehended, for example, three times in the course of the year will be recorded as three aliens. Second, apprehensions follow a distinct pattern, a fact that is significant because the vast majority of deportable aliens located represent apprehensions. The INS has shown a preference for certain methods in its enforcement activities, especially those involving elaborate equipment such as sensors and helicopters with special detection devices. Consequently, the vast majority of apprehensions occur in the border areas and involve EWIs who are almost all Mexican and male.[12] Visa abusers are far less likely to be apprehended since they are concentrated in cities; hence apprehensions are far less likely to involve other nationalities and women since most undocumented immigrants in these categories are visa abusers. Third, the overrepresentation of Mexicans in apprehension data is further accentuated by the tendency of undocumented Mexicans to return home and re-enter the U.S. frequently, thereby increasing their chances to be apprehended. Apprehension data show that Mexicans travel home every six months on average (National Commission for Manpower Policy, 1978: 126–127; Cornelius, 1977; Bustamante, 1976). Similar data for visa abusers show a much lower frequency, though here too the amount of circulation back and forth is unexpectedly high; Eastern Hemisphere aliens averaged 1.8 trips over a cumulative period of $2\frac{1}{2}$ years and Western Hemisphere aliens, excluding Mexicans, 1.4 trips over the equivalent period (National Commission for Manpower Policy, 1978: 127). These averages may be skewed insofar as they describe apprehended aliens, and the chances for apprehension tend to increase with frequency of re-entry. This points to a fourth problem in the data base from which information about the undocumented alien population is drawn. The data on deportable aliens located do not permit estimates of the permanent and temporary stock of undocumented aliens in the country. Some of those apprehended have been in the country for twenty years without ever being detected. In their survey of a sample of INS apprehensions, North and Houstoun (1976) found that the average cumulative stay for apprehended aliens was 2.5 years. It is quite possible that there is a substantial stock of undocumented aliens who are long-term residents and whose characteristics are unlikely to be revealed through INS apprehension data given enforcement patterns.

Until recently the vast majority of undocumented aliens were Mexicans working in the border states, although there have been significant concentrations in the Midwest for many years (Cardenas, 1978).[13] In the last decade there has been a rapid growth in the undocumented alien population of the Northeastern cities, made up overwhelmingly of Caribbean and South Americans, and in the numbers of undocumented Mexicans in Midwestern cities. There is a substantial body of data on both old and new Mexican immigration (Galarza, 1964; McWilliams, 1968; Samora, 1973; Portes, 1978; Cornelius, 1983), but there is still little on the new Caribbean and South American immigration (Bryce-Laporte and Mortimer, 1981;

Dominguez, 1975; Chaney and Sutton, 1979; Kritz and Gurak, 1985 Papademetriou and Di Marzio, 1986).

The available evidence shows that undocumented immigrants are mostly male, young and unmarried or separated due to the move, with extremely high labor-force participation rates, considerably lower educational attainments than the average native worker and little knowledge of English. However, the increasing presence of Caribbean and South American aliens in the undocumented population is generating some significant shifts towards a larger share of women, older workers, families, higher levels of education, and greater knowledge of English. In their survey of a sample of INS apprehensions, North and Houstoun (1976: 82) found that 11 percent of Mexicans were with their spouses in the U.S. and 9.6 percent with their children while the corresponding shares for other Western Hemisphere aliens were 27.8 and 20.3 percent, and for Eastern Hemisphere aliens, 21.3 and 10.7 percent. A similar difference was found in educational attainment (1976: 117), with Mexicans averaging 4.9 years of school and the other two groups respectively 8.7 and 11.9 years. These educational levels among visa abusers may be below average since the more highly educated are far less likely to be apprehended if, as is possible, they are able to get somewhat better jobs. This is further suggested by the data on the legal South American, Caribbean and Eastern Hemisphere immigration which show high levels of education in contrast to that of legal Mexican immigrants.[14]

The shifts in the geographic and nationality distributions of the undocumented alien population have brought about substantial changes in the educational, occupational and income distributions of undocumented workers. Most significant is probably the occupational shift away from agricultural jobs in the border states to Northern and Northeastern urban jobs. INS data for a sample of almost 50,000 undocumented aliens apprehended in 1975 show that although half were employed in agriculture, fully one-fourth were in light industry, 5.6 percent in construction, almost 14 percent in services and 3 percent in heavy industry (National Commission for Manpower Policy, 1978: 136). Given INS apprehension patterns, agricultural employment is likely to be overrepresented in these figures. In the Northeastern cities, especially New York and Boston, there are significant concentrations of undocumented workers in services and light industry (Piore, 1979; Chaney, 1976; Chaney and

Sutton, 1979; Sassen-Koob, 1981; Papademetriou and Di Marzio, 1986). Income changes associated with this occupational shift are probably quite significant. Apprehension data show that wages in every industry are lower for undocumented workers but that there are, however, marked differences according to industry. Wages in heavy industry and in construction are much higher than in services and light industry and these in turn were higher than in agriculture (National Commission for Manpower Policy, 1978: 138). The lowest hourly wages recorded were those paid Mexican farmworkers close to the border, $1.74, which was well below all minimum wage levels in 1975.[15] Undocumented workers in nonfarm jobs averaged $2.83 per hour. Almost 54 percent of those in heavy industry earned between $2.50 and $4.49 per hour as compared with 27 percent in services and 30.2 percent of all undocumented workers. There are significant differences by area and by nationality as well. The lowest wages were paid in the Southwest and hence Mexicans recorded the lowest hourly wage, $2.34 as compared with $3.05 for Caribbean and South American undocumented workers and $4.68 for those from the Eastern Hemisphere. These income differences reflect occupational and educational differences as well as geographic location rather than nationality per se. The income figures probably underestimate the share of undocumented workers earning above minimum wage due to the overrepresentation of Mexicans in the sample and the smaller likelihood of apprehension for those in better-paying, urban jobs.

The available evidence suggests that the labor market has the same leveling effect on undocumented workers as it does on legal immigrants. Undocumented workers with relatively high educational attainment are pushed into jobs at a lower level than those held in their home country, while a share of those who had been farmworkers ended up in service and light industry jobs in the U.S. A larger share of undocumented workers have operative, nonfarm labor and especially service jobs than would be the case in their home countries.

NON-IMMIGRANT ALIEN WORKERS

In this highly varied class, there are two categories that are particularly significant in terms of labor-market impact: foreign students, who may number about 400,000 at any time and who are often willing to take low-wage jobs; the other consists of temporary contract labor, involving mostly Caribbean farmworkers, and numbering between 25,000 and 50,000 annually in the last decade (INS, 1978: 96–106). There is strong agribusiness interest in expanding the temporary contract labor program which already has led to displacements of native farmworkers by even cheaper Caribbean workers (NACLA, 1976).

CONCLUSION

There were periods in American immigration history when most immigrants came from high-wage countries and the occupational distribution of the foreign born as well as their median income were more advantaged than that of native Americans. One of these periods, of particular concern to my analysis, was that of the 1950s and early 1960s. During this period the vast majority of legal immigrants came from European countries; the occupational distribution of the foreign born showed that about one-third held professional and managerial jobs and their median income compared favorably with that of natives. But this is also the period of large migrations of low-wage workers from Puerto Rico and continuing illegal entries of Mexicans. And it is the period of large rural-to-urban internal migrations and the mobilization of new segments of the population, notably women, into the labor force.

On the other hand, the high-immigration periods in U.S. history tend to contain a disproportionate share of individuals from low-wage countries. One such period is that begun in 1965, when overall entries increased to levels that approached those of the turn of the century. The influx is overwhelmingly from Asia and Caribbean Basin countries. This is also the period when domestic rural-to-urban migrations came to an end and traditional low-wage labor supplies became politicized under the forms of a youth movement, a women's movement, a Black movement, an American Indian movement, a Chicano movement, and a Boricua movement. Furthermore it is the period when American unions had gained considerable power in several key industries, in part because of the massive growth trends fueled by the expansion of internal demand, the jump in U.S. exports to the whole world and the space race that characterized the immediate post-World War II period.

Indubitably, the passing of the 1965 Immigration Act was an important lever in the new migration from low-wage countries that followed. But it is a lever that could acquire such power only because it operated in a context that had mobilized linkages between the U.S. and new sending countries. This is particularly so if we accept the intention of this legislation to promote family reunion, besides lifting discriminatory barriers, which entailed the inflow of persons predominantly from countries that already had large immigrant communities in the U.S. that is, Europeans.

The available data on the occupational and income distribution of immigrants show that they are largely in low-wage jobs and that in this they diverge from immigrants of the 1950s. From 1950 to 1980 there was a decline in the share of immigrants with higher-level occupations. And from 1970 to 1980 the occupational distribution of immigrants and natives became more dissimilar. This is particularly so among immigrant women. Their share in operative and service jobs has increased and now accounts for 70 percent of all jobs among Hispanic women and 40 percent among Asian women who arrived during the 1970s. About a third of immigrant women are employed in manufacturing and another third in the producer and distributive services. The labor market impact of immigrants is accentuated by their regional concentration. In 1980 40 percent resided in the ten largest cities, compared with 10 percent of the total U.S. population. Recently proposed changes in immigration law would probably contribute to the low-wage labor input of immigration, especially through an expanded contract-labor program and a legalization program that would bar large numbers of undocumented immigrants from applying. In conjunction with the proposed sanctions on employers who knowingly hire undocumented workers, such a partial legalization program may well have the effect of consolidating a labor supply with few options but homework.

At the same time, the formation of a low-wage labor supply has a long history not only in the U.S. but in all industrialized countries. The characteristics of the low-wage labor supply and its locations in the economic structure may vary over time and from one context to another. Yet there always seems to be one. The current immigration from low-wage countries directed to low-wage jobs in the U.S. needs to be placed in this broader historical context. The specific structural and legal factors that shape the current flow cannot override this larger history.

# Appendix

A CASE STUDY: OCCUPATIONAL DISTRIBUTION OF NEW
HISPANICS IN NEW YORK CITY

The borough of Queens in New York City contains the largest single concentration of the new Hispanic immigration as well as significant numbers of the more traditional European immigrant nationalities, notably Greeks and Italians. In 1980 Cohen and Sassen-Koob conducted a survey of the six main nationality groups in the borough in order to obtain information about the new Hispanics and compare their socio-economic characteristics with those of other immigrant groups (Cohen and Sassen-Koob, 1982).

It was found that the new Hispanics (excludes Puerto Ricans) had far higher concentrations in factory and service jobs than the other ethnic groups in the Queens sample (see Table 3.14). Only 11 percent of Jews and about 30 percent of the major European immigrant groups as well as Puerto Ricans had such jobs compared with over half of the new Hispanics. Within the Hispanic population of our sample some additional differences emerge. While Puerto Ricans, Colombians and other Hispanics all three show a similar share of managerial jobs, about 11 percent, a significant difference emerges regarding professional jobs; only 3.8 percent of Colombians compared with over 13 percent each of Puerto Ricans and other Hispanics. The other major new immigrant group, the Asians, had almost 42 percent of members in this stratum. Colombians, on the other hand, had the highest share in crafts jobs, about 15 percent compared with 3.3 percent of Puerto Ricans, 7.7 percent of Blacks and between 6 and 9 percent for the major European groups. This would seem to confirm INS data showing a high share of highly skilled workers among the Colombian and other South American immigrants. But the highest concentration of new Hispanics is in operative and service jobs, half of all Colombians and 42 percent of other Hispanics.

Table 3.14 Occupational distribution by ethnicity, Queens (New York City), 1980
(percentages)

| | Blacks | Jews | Italians | Irish | Other European ethnics | Puerto Ricans | Colombians | Other Hispanics | Asians | Others |
|---|---|---|---|---|---|---|---|---|---|---|
| Management | 8.9 | 13.4 | 8.6 | 11.4 | 14.7 | 11.7 | 11.5 | 11.3 | 2.8 | 7.9 |
| Professional and technical | 24.6 | 31.0 | 18.0 | 31.4 | 21.5 | 13.3 | 3.8 | 13.6 | 41.7 | 22.8 |
| Sales | 6.0 | 8.8 | 7.0 | 1.0 | 5.1 | 11.7 | 3.8 | 3.4 | 8.3 | 7.9 |
| Clerical | 14.1 | 27.2 | 18.0 | 24.8 | 24.9 | 21.7 | 15.4 | 15.9 | 22.2 | 18.5 |
| Crafts | 7.7 | 4.2 | 6.2 | 5.7 | 9.0 | 3.3 | 15.4 | 12.5 | 0.0 | 13.6 |
| Operatives and laborers | 14.5 | 3.1 | 18.0 | 5.7 | 7.9 | 16.6 | 19.2 | 20.5 | 8.3 | 9.3 |
| Transport | 4.8 | 2.3 | 6.3 | 2.9 | 1.7 | 1.7 | 0.0 | 1.1 | 0.0 | 2.9 |
| Services | 19.4 | 10.0 | 17.9 | 17.1 | 15.2 | 20.0 | 30.9 | 21.7 | 16.7 | 17.1 |
| Total | 100.0 | 100.0 | 100.0 | 100.0 | 100.0 | 100.0 | 100.0 | 100.0 | 100.0 | 100.0 |
| Total N = (1,269) | (248) | (261) | (128) | (105) | (177) | (60) | (26) | (88) | (36) | (140) |

Source: Cohen and Sassen-Koob (1982)

Furthermore, the new Hispanics have an above average incidence of two-job households, about 30 percent compared with 15 to 20 percent among the other ethnic groups in the sample (see Table 3.15). Both Urrea Giraldo (1982) and Castro (1982) found a very high incidence of multiple-earners households among Colombians.

Generally, the available data suggest that the new Hispanic immigration is a labor supply for service jobs and a downgraded manufacturing sector. Furthermore, they are also a labor supply for clerical and low-level managerial jobs, especially in small firms (Urrea Giraldo, 1982). The fact that the occupational distribution of the new Hispanics in New York City diverges considerably from that in their country of origin at the time of departure also points to the extent to which the job supply in the receiving society determines their occupation. The evidence in this regard is probably most clear with respect to women (see Table 3.16). Castro (1982) found that while over 50 percent of the Colombian women in the Queens sample had jobs in manufacturing, only 12 percent of them had had such jobs in Colombia. A good share of the Colombian men now in low-level managerial positions had experienced considerable downward mobility (Urrea Giraldo, 1982); they represent considerable human capital for a low price to employers. In my earlier fieldwork study of Colombians and Dominicans in Queens (Sassen-Koob, 1979), I found a highly stratified situation. The upper-income segments had experienced what according to standard occupational measures would be considered downward mobility, from professional to clerical jobs; and the lower-income segments, upward mobility, from farm or operative to service work.

Comparing the occupational distribution of Hispanics generally and other major ethnic groups in the New York City SMSA (data for 1979) (U.S. Bureau of Census, 1980) with that of the new Hispanics in the sample, we can see that the latter have one of the highest concentrations in service jobs (see Table 3.17). Blacks have the highest concentration, due partly to the higher share of transport jobs they hold, 4.8 percent compared with about 1 percent among the new Hispanics in our sample. Secondly, all Hispanics and the new Hispanics in our sample have above average shares of manufacturing jobs. The considerable decline in the average industrial wage for factory workers in New York City over the last ten years suggests that manufacturing jobs are increasingly unattractive even when we exclude sweatshops and industrial homework as these figures do.

Table 3.15 *Selected household characteristics by ethnicity, Queens (New York City), 1980 (percentages)*

| | Blacks | Jews | Italians | Greeks | Other European ethnics | Puerto Ricans | Dominicans | Colombians | Other Hispanics | Asians | Others |
|---|---|---|---|---|---|---|---|---|---|---|---|
| Average years of education | 12.4 | 14.1 | 12.4 | 11.9 | 12.6 | 11.7 | 11.1 | 11.3 | 12.3 | 14.6 | 12.4 |
| Average family income (in $1,000s) | 21.0 | 25.3 | 21.8 | 22.6 | 22.7 | 23.5 | 22.8 | 19.7 | 20.4 | 22.7 | 20.9 |
| Two-job family | 13 | 21 | 17 | 18 | 14 | 21 | 32 | 29 | 32 | 33 | 20 |
| Retired | 9 | 12 | 17 | 3 | 20 | 1 | 0 | 0 | 0 | 5 | 7 |
| Total N = (1696) | (370) | (345) | (170) | (40) | (426) | (76) | (38) | (35) | (104) | (45) | (47) |
| Percentage of total | 22 | 20 | 10 | 2 | 25 | 5 | 2 | 6 | 2 | 3 | 3 |

*Source:* Cohen and Sassen-Koob (1982)

Table 3.16 *Occupational distribution by national origin and sex, Queens (New York City), 1980 (percentages)*

|  | Colombian | Puerto Rican | Other Hispanics | All Hispanics |
|---|---|---|---|---|
| White Collar, total | 100.0 | 100.0 | 100.0 | 100.0 |
| Male | 44.4 | 28.6 | 41.7 | 37.0 |
| Female | 55.6 | 71.4 | 58.3 | 63.0 |
| Blue Collar, total | 100.0 | 100.0 | 100.0 | 100.0 |
| Male | 62.5 | 66.7 | 55.2 | 59.2 |
| Female | 37.5 | 33.4 | 44.8 | 40.8 |
| Services, total | 100.0 | 100.0 | 100.0 | 100.0 |
| Male | 44.4 | 25.0 | 43.5 | 36.5 |
| Female | 55.6 | 75.0 | 56.5 | 63.5 |

*Source:* Cohen and Sassen-Koob (1982)

Comparing the occupational distribution of the new Hispanics in our sample with that of other major Hispanic groups nationally (U.S. Department of Labor, 1981a) we can note four major trends (see Table 3.18). First, all Hispanics, including our sample, have a higher share of blue-collar and service jobs compared with workers generally. Secondly, the new Hispanics in our sample had the highest share of service jobs, 34.6 percent, and Puerto Ricans, another major New York City based group, the next largest. Thirdly, the new Hispanics in our sample have, together with Cubans, one of the highest shares in white-collar jobs. Fourthly, the new Hispanics in our sample had a considerably lower share in manufacturing jobs than was typical for all other major Hispanic groups, though it was higher than that for workers generally. Again, here we have to note that the figure for manufacturing excludes what is probably a considerable share of jobs in sweatshops and industrial homework.

The 1980 Census data show a somewhat similar picture in that they reveal a severe disadvantage of Hispanics in New York City compared with other major cities and a high incidence of very low incomes. A comparison of selected characteristics of the Hispanic population in major SMSAs of 1 million or more population and 25,000 or more Hispanics shows New York City to rank second in size of the Hispanic population, but twelfth in family income, second in numbers of families below the poverty level, thirteenth in terms of the share of Hispanics 25 years of age and over with a high school degree

Table 3.17 *Occupational distribution of major ethnic groups, New York City, 1979, and Queens, 1980 (percentages)*

| Occupation | New York City (SMSA), 1979 | | | | | Queens (NYC), 1980 | |
| | All | Whites | Blacks | Hispanics | | Puerto Ricans | New Hispanics |
|---|---|---|---|---|---|---|---|
| White Collar | 60.8 | 64.0 | 50.2 | 35.7 | | 58.4 | 42.1 |
| Blue Collar | 20.8 | 20.9 | 20.7 | 38.6 | | 19.9 | 33.3 |
| Services[a] | 18.4 | 15.1 | 29.1 | 25.7 | | 21.7 | 24.6 |
| Total | 100.0 | 100.0 | 100.0 | 100.0 | | 100.0 | 100.0 |

*Source:* U.S. Bureau of Census, 1980, *Persons of Spanish Origin in the United States: March 1979;* Cohen and Sassen-Koob, 1982
[a]Transport is included in Services.

Table 3.18 *Occupational distribution of major Hispanic groups, United States and Queens (New York City), 1980*
*(percentages)*

| Occupation | United States, 1980 | | | | | | | Queens (NYC) 1980 |
| | All workers | Whites | All Hispanics | Mexicans | Puerto Ricans | Cubans | New Hispanics |
|---|---|---|---|---|---|---|---|
| White Collar | 52.2 | 53.9 | 34.2 | 29.2 | 38.8 | 44.7 | 42.1 |
| Blue Collar[a] | 28.1 | 27.7 | 41.6 | 44.7 | 39.0 | 39.5 | 33.3 |
| Services | 16.9 | 15.4 | 20.3 | 20.3 | 21.6 | 15.9 | 24.6 |
| Farm | 2.8 | 2.9 | 3.8 | 5.7 | 0.6 | 0.0 | 0.0 |

*Source:* U.S. Department of Labor, 1981a, *Geographic Profiles of Employment and Unemployment, 1980;* Cohen and Sassen-Koob, 1982
[a]Transport is included in Services.

Table 3.19 *Selected characteristics of Hispanics in SMSAs of 1 million or more population and 25,000 or more Hispanics, 1980*

| SMSA | Hispanic median family income | | Hispanics below the poverty level | | Hispanics, 25 yrs and over with a high school degree (%) | | Persons who speak Spanish in the home as a % of Hispanics, 5 yrs and over | | Hispanics 18 yrs and over who speak Spanish at home and speak English well or very well | | Size | Total Hispanics |
|---|---|---|---|---|---|---|---|---|---|---|---|---|
| | Rank | Value | Rank | Value | Rank | Value | Rank | Value | Rank | Value | Rank | |
| Los Angeles, Long Beach, CA | 7 | 15,447 | 6 | 21.2 | 10 | 39.1 | 11 | 82.4 | 11 | 60.1 | 1 | 2,066,103 |
| New York, NY–NJ | 12 | 10,347 | 2 | 39.3 | 13 | 35.4 | 2 | 96.4 | 8 | 64.0 | 2 | 1,492,559 |
| Chicago, IL | 4 | 16,551 | 8 | 19.5 | 11 | 36.1 | 6 | 91.7 | 10 | 61.0 | 3 | 580,467 |
| Miami, FL | 5 | 16,133 | 10 | 15.9 | 5 | 53.3 | 1 | 101.4 | 12 | 57.8 | 4 | 580,427 |
| San Antonio, TX | 11 | 13,284 | 5 | 26.9 | 9 | 40.5 | 7 | 90.8 | 2 | 83.0 | 5 | 481,378 |
| Houston, TX | 3 | 17,185 | 9 | 18.1 | 8 | 44.9 | 3 | 93.1 | 7 | 73.5 | 6 | 424,957 |
| Dallas, TX | 6 | 15,754 | 7 | 20.1 | 12 | 35.8 | 5 | 91.8 | 6 | 74.4 | 7 | 247,937 |
| Newark, NJ | 8 | 14,596 | 4 | 30.1 | 7 | 45.2 | 8 | 90.1 | 9 | 62.0 | 8 | 131,655 |
| Philadelphia, PA–NJ | 10 | 13,287 | 3 | 33.4 | 4 | 56.8 | 9 | 88.9 | 4 | 80.1 | 9 | 116,869 |
| Washington, D.C. | 1 | 22,834 | 13 | 10.6 | 1 | 74.5 | 1 | 101.4 | 3 | 82.9 | 10 | 93,686 |
| Boston, MA | 13 | 9,586 | 1 | 42.0 | 3 | 57.3 | 3 | 93.1 | 10 | 61.0 | 11 | 65,696 |
| Fort Lauderdale, Hollywood, FL | 2 | 19,174 | 12 | 12.2 | 2 | 62.5 | 4 | 92.7 | 5 | 78.2 | 12 | 40,345 |
| Cleveland, OH | 9 | 14,502 | 11 | 15.3 | 6 | 49.3 | 10 | 87.2 | 1 | 84.3 | 13 | 5,475 |

*Source*: Population Research and Analysis Human Resources Division, New York City Department of City Planning

(see Table 3.19). Los Angeles, which ranks first in size of the Hispanic population, shows only a slightly better performance on these socio-economic indicators. It is worth noting that although the composition of the Hispanic population in New York City and Los Angeles differs markedly, they rank rather similarly in terms of various socio-economic characteristics, and do so in the bottom half of these fourteen metropolitan areas.

# 4

# The globalization of production: implications for labor migrations

Why did high outmigration from various countries discussed in the preceding chapter occur at a time when these countries had high industrial growth rates and major increases in direct foreign investment while the U.S. economy was marked by growing unemployment and inflation? The overall levels of entries for Asian and Caribbean Basin immigrants kept growing in the 1970s, a decade when unemployment was particularly high in the U.S. and the recession was headlined in major newspapers throughout the world. During that same period the main immigrant-sending countries had growth rates of about 5 to 9 percent in GNP and even higher in manufacturing.

The high GNP growth rates in sending countries were in good part due to large increases in direct foreign investment from the major industrial countries. A growing share of such investment from advanced industrialized countries is going into industries producing for export. Export industries tend to be highly labor intensive, this being precisely one of the rationales for locating factories in low-wage countries. The evidence shows rather high employment growth, particularly in manufacturing, in several of the Asian and Caribbean Basin countries that have been major recipients of direct foreign investment for export-oriented production. These are also among the main immigrant-sending countries.

The coexistence of such high growth rates and of large emigration flows needs to be examined. The push factors traditionally used to explain emigration, most importantly lack of economic growth, are insufficient. In fact, foreign investment and job creation should have acted as a deterrent rather than inducement to emigration. This is further underlined by the fact of higher GNP growth rates in the sending countries than in the major receiving country, the U.S., and the redeployment of a share of American manufacturing and associated service jobs to these countries.

Here I posit that the coexistence of high growth and high

emigration in the same country can be seen as yet another version of the expansion of modern forms of production and their impact in the formation of a pool of migrant labor, the subject of Chapter 2. The large-scale development of commercial agriculture in Latin America and the Caribbean Basin has long been recognized as a key factor in the displacement of subsistence farmers and small producers. This displacement created both a supply of rural wage laborers and large-scale migrations to the cities. For a variety of reasons, in some of these countries the migrations became international: Mexicans to the U.S., Colombians to Venezuela, and Paraguayans to Argentina. The migration literature contains a number of studies on the role of modern forms of production in the formation of international labor migrations (e.g., Portes, 1979; Dinerman, 1982; Cornelius, 1981; Fernandez Kelly, 1983; Bonilla and Campos, 1982; Centro de Estudios Puertorriqueños, 1979). These focused exclusively on Mexico and Puerto Rico.

In this chapter I will examine how the large-scale development of export-oriented manufacturing in South-East Asia and the Caribbean Basin, including Mexico, has come to play the role traditionally held by export agriculture in the uprooting of people and the resulting labor migrations. I will analyze data and studies on South-East Asian and Caribbean Basin countries concerned with the development of export-processing zones and world-market factories, domestic and regional migrations and general employment trends. I will use this information on major developments in sending countries to examine the relationship between industrialization and emigration by way of the mobilization of new segments of the population into wage labor, the associated disruption of traditional waged and wageless work structures and the feminization of the new proletariat in export manufacturing industries. That is to say, I will explore the effect such industrialization has on conditions promoting the formation of a pool of potential migrants and the emergence of emigration as an option actually exercised by individuals. The period 1960–1980 is crucial for the examination of this relationship, particularly from 1965 to 1975 when these new types of growth emerged on a significant scale in several countries.

## INDUSTRIALIZATION AND EMIGRATION

We need to specify the links between the occurrence of rapid export-led industrialization and emigration, particularly emigration to the

U.S. The evidence clearly documents the existence of industrialization in sending countries and of immigration into the U.S. What is necessary is a conceptual and empirical elaboration of the linkages between these two processes. Because the analysis presented here is rather complex, is based on several distinct bodies of data, and at times must rely on inference, there follows a brief description of the main steps involved in the conceptual elaboration of the links between industrialization and emigration. Each of these steps requires brief review of the main findings relevant to an analysis of migrations in the major Asian and Caribbean Basin sending countries. These findings represent, in principle, one of several possible outcomes in an examination of the relation between industrialization and migration.

First, it is necessary to examine the characteristics of the new industrial growth in less developed countries and to place it in the context of the country's overall economic organization. A good part of these countries' economic expansion can only be accounted for by increasing exports. Access to the world market is a must given fairly limited internal markets. The development of a world market for these countries' exports is intimately linked to a significant growth in direct foreign investment (UNIDO, 1980; ILO, 1980; OECD, 1980). One distinctive trait about industrial growth in the major new immigrant-sending countries is the weight of production for export. While this is a particularly strong trend in the Asian and smaller Caribbean Basin countries, it is also present in Mexico and Colombia, two countries with rather developed industrial economies and large internal markets.

Secondly, it is necessary to examine the employment effects of these patterns of growth. Export-oriented agriculture requires a large supply of low-wage workers at crucial periods in the production cycle. Export-oriented plants are mostly labor intensive and are often concentrated in a given area for reasons having to do with servicing and transportation, a fact which may tend to accentuate the labor-demand impact. Finally, large agglomerations of firms producing for export generate a range of additional jobs, from packaging for shipment abroad to construction and operation of airports and harbors.

Thirdly, it is necessary to examine how these labor needs are met. Both export agriculture and export manufacturing have mobilized large numbers of people into wage labor. The large-scale development of commercial agriculture in Latin America and the Caribbean

Basin contributed to the creation of a rural wage-labor supply through the displacement of subsistence farmers and small producers. This displacement was also central in promoting rural unemployment and migration to the cities. On the other hand, because it is highly labor intensive, export manufacturing could conceivably have contributed to relieve the unemployment problem, particularly among prime-aged males. Instead, the evidence overwhelmingly shows that it has drawn new segments of the population into the labor force: mostly young women who under conditions of a more gradual industrialization would not have entered the labor force in so massive and sudden a way (Lim, 1980; Safa, 1981; Grossman, 1979; Fernandez Kelly, 1983).

Fourthly, it is necessary to examine the migration impact, if any, associated with such job creation and labor recruitment. Precisely because of the significant job-creation effect of export-manufacturing and its concentration in a few areas, the extent of the mobilization of new workers into the labor force has been considerable. This effect has been further accentuated by the high turnover rates resulting from the employment practices in the plants and the mental and physical fatigue associated with these jobs. In areas where the new industrial zones have been developed on a large scale, extensive mobilization of women into the labor force can contribute to the disruption of traditional work structures in communities of origin: the young men are left without mates and partners, the households are left without a key labor factor.

The disruption of traditional work structures resulting from an extremely high incidence of young female emigration has further contributed to increase the pool of unemployed. It has stimulated the departure of men and women who may not have planned on doing so. At the same time, the high turnover rates in the new industrial zones and the pronounced preference for very young women has contributed to growing unemployment among women. Incipient westernization among zone workers and the disruption of traditional work structures combine to minimize the possibilities of returning to communities of origin. In sum, these developments have induced the formation of a pool of migrant workers.

Finally, it is necessary to examine whether these conditions could promote the emergence of emigration as an option actually felt by individuals, particularly emigration to the U.S. At this point the reality of a strong foreign presence becomes significant. It is not only the concentration of foreign investment in a few areas; the foreign presence dominates the new industrial zones objectively and culturally, thereby creating linkages to the countries where the capital originates. The continued vitality of the image of the U.S. as a land of immigrants and the liberalization of American immigration policy after 1965 acquire added weight in this context.

The next four sections contain a more detailed elaboration of each of these aspects.

### FOREIGN INVESTMENT AS A MIGRATION PUSH FACTOR

Foreign companies and buying groups have dominated the development of export agriculture (George, 1977; Burbach and Flynn, 1980; NACLA, 1978). They also dominate the development of export manufacturing (UNIDO, 1980; OECD, 1980; ILO, 1981). The ways in which this has come about vary considerably, from direct ownership of plants and plantations to international subcontracting with domestic producers. In this context, the development of Export Processing Zones, in their many guises, represents merely an intensification of the basic patterns of export production – an arrangement that maximizes the subsidies to foreign firms through tax concessions, provision of infrastructure and disciplining of workers (UNIDO, 1980).[1]

Foreign investment *per se* does not always lead to the uprooting of people and the associated labor migrations. The concrete forms which such investment has assumed are of decisive importance. Nor is this uprooting always the result of the elimination of jobs accompanying capital-intensive methods of production. While this may be the case in commercial agriculture, it is not the case in manufacturing for export, which tends to be highly labor intensive. Finally, the evidence suggests that only significant concentrations of direct foreign investment in certain kinds of activities will have this uprooting effect. Since the case of commercial agriculture, which in developing countries is mostly export oriented, has received considerable study as a factor displacing people, I will limit most of my discussion to the case of manufacturing. Furthermore, since a large share of direct foreign investment in the main immigrant sending countries is in export manufacturing, I will pay particular attention to this development.[2]

It is important to distinguish between the weight of export production in the economies of these developing countries and the particular firms involved on the one hand, and the weight of such exports in the international trade of manufactures and in the imports of developed countries, on the other. For several developing countries and the firms involved, the development of labor-intensive production for export has been a key factor in their growth strategies. In terms of world trade and imports by developed countries, however, these exports represent a very minor fraction.[3]

Since I am concerned with identifying conditions promoting migrations in developing countries, it is the weight of this form of growth *in these countries*, rather than in world trade, that matters for my analysis. The issue is not whether export-production in developing countries represents a small or large share of all world trade. Similarly, the issue is not whether direct foreign investment in these countries represents a large or small share of all such investment in the world. Finally, I would not be concerned with such investment and export industries if these were evenly distributed among all developing countries in a manner that would make them a minor factor in their economies and one that could not generate a large-scale uprooting of people.

What makes the examination of interest in an analysis of conditions promoting emigration is the fact that direct foreign investment accounts for a significant share of economic activity in several countries, that much of it is production for export and, finally, that these countries are also among the main immigrant-sending countries and those with the most rapid growth in emigration.

## Major trends of direct foreign investment in less-developed countries

An examination of the magnitude, timing, origin and destination of direct foreign investment by the major industrial countries reveals several distinct patterns of importance to my analysis.

First, all major industrial countries have massively increased such investments over the last two decades. Most of this investment was in developed countries. However, the level of investment in developing countries has grown, particularly since the late 1960s, and the annual average growth rate in these countries during the 1970s surpassed that in developed countries. Total direct foreign investment (henceforth DFI) for all major industrial countries in developing countries increased from $35 billion in 1967 to $76 billion in 1976 (ILO, 1981: 2, 5). West Germany's DFI position went from $1.9 billion in 1970 to

Table 4.1 *OECD–DAC$^a$ countries' foreign direct investment$^b$ position in developing countries, 1970–1976*

| OECD–DAC countries | (Dollars in millions) | | Share of total (%) | |
|---|---|---|---|---|
| | 1970 | 1976 | 1970 | 1976 |
| Belgium | 765 | 1,255 | 1.8 | 1.7 |
| Canada | 1,659 | 2,960 | 3.9 | 3.9 |
| France | 3,832 | 5,254 | 9.0 | 6.9 |
| Germany (Fed. Rep.) | 1,942 | 5,970 | 4.6 | 7.8 |
| Italy | 1,245 | 2,446 | 2.9 | 3.2 |
| Japan | 1,218 | 4,970 | 2.8 | 6.5 |
| Netherlands | 2,247 | 3,503 | 5.3 | 4.6 |
| Switzerland | 875 | 1,657 | 2.1 | 2.2 |
| United Kingdom | 5,912 | 9,323 | 13.8 | 12.2 |
| United States | 22,300 | 36,990 | 52.2 | 48.6 |
| Others$^c$ | 717 | 1,872 | 1.7 | 2.4 |
| Total | 42,712 | 76,200 | 100% | 100% |

$^a$The Development Assistance Committee countries within the OECD
$^b$Includes only private direct investment; includes reinvested earnings
$^c$Australia, Austria, Denmark, Finland, New Zealand, Norway, and Sweden
Source: Based on OECD, *Investing in Developing Countries* (1978a); ILO, *Employment Effects of Multinational Enterprises in Developing Countries* (1981)

$5.9 billion in 1976; that of the Netherlands, from $2.2 billion to $3.5 billion; that of France, from $3.8 billion to $5.2 billion; and that of the United Kingdom, from $5.9 billion to $9.3 billion (see Table 4.1). In the case of the U.S., it increased from $22 billion in 1970 to $40 billion in 1976.

The average annual growth rates of DFI for all major industrial countries grew significantly (see Table 4.2). They were 7 percent from 1960 to 1968; 9.2 percent from 1968 to 1973; and 19.4 percent from 1973 to 1978 (UN Centre on Transnational Corporations, 1979: 5). In the case of the U.S., the average annual growth rate was 11.7 percent for developed countries from 1950 to 1966 and 6.2 percent for developing countries; from 1966 to 1973 these rates were, respectively, 10.7 percent and 9.7 percent, and from 1973 to 1980, 11.8 percent and 14.2 percent (these figures exclude the petroleum industry).

In absolute values, U.S. direct foreign investment (excluding petroleum) in developing countries grew from $3.5 billion in 1950 to $8.8 billion in 1966 and $42.4 billion in 1980 (see Table 4.3). Furthermore, according to a recent study (Van Den Bulcke *et al.*,

Table 4.2 *Average annual growth
rate of direct foreign investment
from developed[a] to developing
countries, 1960–1978 (in current
$U.S.)*

| | |
|---|---|
| 1960–1968 | 7.0% |
| 1968–1973 | 9.2% |
| 1973–1978 | 19.4% |

[a] These are the OECD–DAC countries (see
Table 4.1 for a description)
*Source:* Sassen-Koob (1983); Based on
OECD, *Recent International Direct Investment
Trends* (1981)

Table 4.3 *Average annual growth rates of U.S. direct investment position
abroad, by region, 1950–1980[a]*

| | Amount (millions $) | | | | Average annual growth rates (%) | | |
|---|---|---|---|---|---|---|---|
| | 1950 | 1966 | 1973 | 1980 | 1950–66 | 1966–73 | 1973–80 |
| Developed countries | 4,715 | 27,629 | 56,303 | 122,911 | 11.7 | 10.7 | 11.8 |
| Developing countries | 3,567 | 8,815 | 16,830 | 42,413 | 6.2 | 9.7 | 14.2 |

[a] Excluding petroleum industry
*Source:* Compiled from Obie G. Whichard, 1981a, "Trends in the U.S. direct investment
position abroad, 1950–79," and 1981b, "U.S. direct investment position abroad in 1980"

1979), between 1967 and 1975, American multinationals withdrew
30 percent of their investments from the original six European
Common Market countries through closures of production units or
reductions in the degree of capital participation in their subsidiaries
to below 20 percent and even 10 percent. This disinvestment was
particularly strong from 1971 to 1973.

Second, there is a marked degree of concentration both in the
origin and destination of DFI from the major industrial countries to
the developing countries. Though its share has declined slightly, the
U.S. accounts for almost half of all such investments. West Germany,
the United Kingdom, France and the Netherlands account for

another 31.5 percent of such investment. If we include Canada and Japan, these countries account for 90 percent of DFI. On the other hand, over 50 percent of DFI of the major industrial countries goes to the same five or six countries. The U.S. is also becoming a major recipient of DFI from all the main industrial countries, accounting for almost 31 percent of all direct foreign investment coming from the seven leading OECD industrial countries (excluding Japan; see tables 6.2 and 6.3, Chapter 6 below). This is a fairly recent development. Between 1961 and 1967 the U.S. accounted for only 2.8 percent of all such investment, and from 1968 to 1973, for 13.4 percent. In the last few years, Japan has become a major investor in the U.S., with a DFI position in the U.S. by 1980 of $4.2 billion (see Table 6.3, Chapter 6).

In my analysis the relation between the characteristics of DFI in a given country and that country's economy is of primary importance. The absolute value of DFI in a given country and the share that value represents in total DFI in developing countries is, clearly, a simpler measure; but it is inadequate.

Simplifying, one can identify two distinct patterns. One is DFI in some of the more industrialized developing countries where such investment is absorbed into an overall process of industrialization predominantly oriented towards import substitution, e.g., Brazil and Argentina, two of the major recipients of DFI in the developing world.

At the other extreme we can find countries where the absolute level of DFI may be much smaller but the overall impact on the country's economy and people, far stronger. The trend of the last decade toward increased DFI in production for export, particularly in manufacturing, has had a pronounced effect both in the smaller, less industrialized countries such as Taiwan and the Philippines and in larger, rather industrialized countries like Mexico. Export-led industrialization is becoming a new development strategy to replace import-substitution industrialization.[4]

*Export-led development*

Export-led industrialization has emerged as a development strategy over the last fifteen years in response to several different conditions. Central among these are the exhaustion of import substitution as a model for development given limited internal markets and the search for cheap labor by multinationals and other firms in view of rising labor costs in the highly industrialized countries. Countries with limited internal markets and large reserves of cheap labor were especially eager to attract foreign investment for export production. The impact of this type of production is, clearly, much weaker in countries which already have highly complex economies with significant levels of import substitution industrialization. On the other hand, in countries such as Colombia and Mexico, the concentration of export production in certain areas has been so high that, notwithstanding their complex and rather developed economies, the consequences for the population in those particular areas have been similar to those in countries with much less developed economies.

Export-oriented DFI is growing at a faster rate than import-substitution oriented DFI. This holds for all major industrial countries investing in the developing world. Furthermore, the rapid growth of international subcontracting as a basic investment strategy has also been recognized to be the outcome of the rapid expansion of export-oriented DFI (OECD, 1980: ILO, 1981: 54–55). Finally, even those countries where DFI in the 1960s was import-substitution oriented are now receiving rapidly growing export-oriented foreign investments. For example, in Colombia DFI flows amounted to about $25 million annually in the early 1970s; by 1979 they had reached $130 million, a rise largely attributed to production for export (Colombia Information Service, 1979). Similar trends can be observed in Mexico (see also Centro de Estudios Puertorriqueños, 1979).

There are various indicators of the growth in export-oriented DFI. One set is provided by the individual countries that are the major recipients of this type of investment, e.g., several South-East Asian countries where exports account for well over 50 percent of GNP and where DFI and international subcontracting are overwhelmingly in manufacturing for export (United Nations, 1978: 259; II–50; see Table 4.4).

The weight of export-oriented production in the South-East Asian and Caribbean Basin countries varies, depending on the overall level of economic development and the importance of import-substitution industrialization. The share of all exports in total GNP ranges from 8 percent in countries like Mexico and Colombia, to 16 percent in countries such as the Philippines, the Dominican Republic and Haiti,

Table 4.4 *Share of exports in GDP in selected developing countries, 1970–80*

| | 1970[a] | 1975[a] | 1980[b] |
|---|---|---|---|
| *Brazil* | | | |
| GDP (millions of $) | 79,200 | 84,880 | 250,000 |
| Exports (millions of $) | 2,740 | 4,330 | 20,000 |
| Share of exports in GDP | (3.4%) | (7.9%) | (8.4%) |
| *Colombia* | | | |
| GDP (millions of $) | 13,470 | 14,440 | 33,940 |
| Exports (millions of $) | 790 | 1,145 | 2,860 |
| Share of exports in GDP | (5.8%) | (7.9%) | (8.4%) |
| *Haiti* | | | |
| GDP (millions of $) | 1,010 | 1,060 | 1,540 |
| Exports (millions of $) | 39 | 42 | 210 |
| Share of exports in GDP | (3.8%) | (3.9%) | (13.7%) |
| *Mexico* | | | |
| GDP (millions of $) | 98,800 | 107,040 | 185,660 |
| Exports (millions of $) | 1,350 | 1,620 | 15,310 |
| Share of exports in GDP | (1.4%) | (1.5%) | (8.2%) |
| *Dominican Republic* | | | |
| GDP (millions of $) | 1,860 | 2,070 | 7,365 |
| Exports (millions of $) | 214 | 320 | 1,188 |
| Share of exports in GDP | (11.5%) | (15.5%) | (16.1%) |
| *Hong Kong* | | | |
| GDP (millions of $) | — | 10,350 | 21,200 |
| Exports (millions $) | — | 6,020 | 19,710 |
| Share of exports in GDP | — | (58.2%) | (92.9%) |
| *Philippines* | | | |
| GDP (millions of $) | — | 21,410 | 35,180 |
| Exports (millions of $) | — | 2,290 | 5,790 |
| Share of exports in GDP | — | (10.7%) | (16.5%) |
| *Taiwan* | | | |
| GDP (millions of $) | — | — | 40,020 |
| Exports (millions of $) | — | — | 19,810 |
| Share of exports in GDP | — | — | (49.5%) |
| *South Korea* | | | |
| GDP (million of $) | — | 33,900 | 56,460 |
| Exports (millions of $) | — | 6,080 | 17,510 |
| Share of exports in GDP | — | (18.0%) | (26.6%) |

[a] At constant 1970 prices
[b] At current prices

Source: UN, *Monthly Bulletin of Statistics, Sep. 1982*, 1982; UN, Economic and Social Commission for Asia and the Pacific, *Statistical Yearbook for Asia and the Pacific 1980*, 1982; UN, Economic Commission for Latin America, *Economic Survey of Latin America, 1980*, 1982; US Department of Commerce, International Trade Commission, *Foreign Economic Trends and Their Implications* (several issues), 1982

and reaches over half of GNP in several of the South-East Asian countries. In the city-state of Hong Kong, it rises to over 90 percent. A growing share of these exports consists of manufactures.[5]

## EMPLOYMENT IMPLICATIONS OF NEW GROWTH PATTERNS

The need to examine the relation between industrialization and emigration is further underlined by the relatively high growth rates in employment, value added and output registered by the major immigrant-sending countries. A good part of this growth can be accounted for only by growth in exports.[6] Access to the world market is a must given fairly limited internal markets. As I will discuss in greater detail below, for these countries gaining access to the world market is intimately linked to a significant growth in direct foreign investment – be it in the form of buying groups, direct investment in production or international sub-contracting (UNIDO, 1980; ILO, 1981; OECD, 1980). Of interest here is the fact that this growth in output has also resulted in significant levels of growth in employment, especially compared with the developed countries. Thus while annual employment growth rates from 1968 to 1975 were mostly negative for the developed countries in several traditional industries, they ranged from 5 to 10 percent in the developing world (see Table 4.5). This same pattern holds when we look at manufacturing as a whole – a situation where one could expect the developing countries to be at a disadvantage in the light of a comparative advantage criterion, i.e., the concentration of high-tech industries in developed countries. Both in terms of employment and value added the developing countries fared well. They were, however, at a disadvantage in labor productivity gains, a disadvantage that further points to job creation given overall growth in output.[7] (See Appendix to this Chapter, pp. 121–22.)

All trends hold when we disaggregate the information and focus on the major immigrant sending countries. Annual growth rates in Gross Domestic Product from 1965 to 1980 hovered around 6 percent for most of these countries, though with pronounced fluctuations over the fifteen-year period. Growth rates in manufacturing were slightly higher, although again with marked fluctuations (see Table 4.6 and Appendix). Finally, growth rates in employment, output and productivity, controlling for end use of product, were similarly high compared with those of developed countries (see Appendix).

Table 4.5 *Constant annual growth rates in employment, by branch of industry, for the economic groupings, 1968–1975 (percentages)*

| Branch | ISIC[a] | Developing countries | Developed market economies | World |
|---|---|---|---|---|
| Food, Beverages and tobacco | 31 | 4.8 | −0.4 | *2.3* |
| Textiles | 321 | 5.1 | −2.5 | *2.3* |
| Wearing apparel, leather, footwear | 322–324 | 8.7 | −0.3 | *3.4* |
| Wood and wood products, including furniture | 33 | 8.1 | −0.3 | *3.4* |
| Paper and paper products, printing and publishing | 34 | 6.3 | −0.0 | *1.0* |
| Chemicals | 35 | 8.9 | 1.0 | *3.3* |
| Non-metallic minerals | 36 | 7.9 | 0.2 | *3.3* |
| Basic metals | 37 | 14.4 | 0.5 | *2.9* |
| Metal products, machinery and equipment | 38 | 9.5 | 1.0 | *2.8* |
| Light manufacturing | | 6.2 | −0.4 | *2.8* |
| Heavy manufacturing | | 9.2 | 0.8 | *2.9* |
| Total manufacturing | | 7.0 | 0.4 | *2.9* |

[a] International Standard Industrial Classification

*Source:* UNIDO, *World Industry Since 1960: Progress and Prospects,* 1979, p. 239; Based on *Yearbook of Industrial Statistics, 1976 Edition,* vol. 1

Other indicators are the rapid increase in Export Processing Zones (or Free Zones) and the growth of imports by developed countries of goods assembled in developing countries.

The differences in employment growth between developed and major emigration countries become particularly marked when we examine certain industries, notably food, textiles, wood products, chemicals, basic metals and so forth. From 1968 to 1975, the developed countries showed mostly declines or slight increases in employment in these industries. In the developing countries there were significant growth rates in employment, ranging from 5 to 15 percent (see Table 4.7).

In sum, inadequate as they may be, the data indicate significant levels of growth in employment and output in manufacturing in the main immigrant-sending countries. These levels are considerably higher than those registered in the developed countries. Thus the question is how a situation of general employment growth created conditions promoting very high emigration levels. As I discussed

Table 4.6 *Annual growth rates of manufacturing production in major emigration countries, 1965–1980 (percentages)*

|  | 1960–70 | 71 | 72 | 73 | 74 | 75 | 76 | 77 | 78 | 79 | 80 |
|---|---|---|---|---|---|---|---|---|---|---|---|
| Colombia | 6.4 | 7.9 | 10.0 | 9.8 | 6.6 | 3.6 | 7.5 | — | 8.5 | 4.6 | 2.6 |
| Ecuador | 6.0 | 8.7 | 9.0 | 13.6 | 12.1 | 14.0 | 12.0 | — | 12.1 | 10.1 | 7.6 |
| Haiti | 4.4 | 6.0 | 7.1 | 7.2 | 9.8 | 4.8 | 8.5 | 0.6 | −0.8 | 10.8 | 6.5 |
| Dominican Republic | 13.6 | 17.0 | 12.9 | 7.5 | 9.1 | 6.1 | 6.1 | 3.2 | −0.6 | 5.1 | 5.5 |
| Mexico | 8.8 | 3.2 | 9.0 | 8.2 | 6.0 | 4.1 | 2.9 | 3.4 | 9.5 | 9.5 | 7.1 |
| Hong Kong | — | 10.8 | 11.6 | 9.6 | −17.0 | 6.7 | 21.8 | 11.8 | — | — | — |
| Philippines | — | 6.7 | 6.2 | 13.9 | 4.8 | 3.5 | 5.7 | 7.7 | 4.5 | 4.3 | 3.9[a] |
| Singapore | — | 18.7 | 16.7 | 16.2 | 3.8 | −0.2 | 9.5 | 9.6 | 11.6 | 14.5 | 13.5[a] |
| South Korea | 21.5 | 18.8 | 14.0 | 29.2 | 15.8 | 12.6 | 22.6 | 14.4 | 20.7 | 9.8 | −0.1 |

[a] First half ( = second quarter)
*Source:* ECLA, *Economic Survey of Latin America* (various issues), Santiago; ESCAP, *Economic and Social Commission for Asia and the Pacific* (various issues), Bangkok; World Bank, *World Tables*, Baltimore; The Johns Hopkins University Press, 1980; Banco de la República, *Revista del Banco de la Republica*, Bogata: (April) 1982; The Bank of Korea, *Economic Statistics Yearbook, 1981* Seoul, 1982

previously, a key variable in this process was the incorporation, often on a massive scale, of new segments of the population into wage-labor and the associated disruption of traditional work structures. In the next section I will examine the available data on employment characteristics in export-oriented manufacturing.

### THE FEMINIZATION OF THE NEW INDUSTRIAL WORKFORCE

Women have a distinct place in both the development of export agriculture and export manufacturing. Export agriculture has led, in certain areas, to male emigration and to what Elsa Chaney (1980) has called the feminization of small-holder farming. In other areas, export agriculture has led to the proletarianization of women who were once independent producers (Boserup, 1970; Nelson, 1974; Dauber and Cain, 1981; Petritsch, 1981). The particular socioeconomic and cultural configurations that contribute to these diverse patterns have received considerable attention in the anthropological and general development literature.

Overall, the data for the 1950s and 1960s show the prevalence of female rural-to-urban migration in Latin America and of male rural-

Table 4.7 *Annual growth rates[a] of output, employment and labor productivity in various branches of manufacturing, for major emigration countries, 1968–1974*

| Branch | ISIC | Colombia | Dominican Republic | Ecuador | Mexico | South Korea | Singapore |
|---|---|---|---|---|---|---|---|
| Food, Beverages, Tobacco | 31 | | | | | | |
|   Output | | 7.6 | 9.6 | 8.2 | 4.4 | 14.5 | 4.5 |
|   Employment | | 4.9 | 5.7 | 6.5 | 2.7 | 8.0 | 2.3 |
|   Productivity | | 2.6 | 3.7 | 1.6 | 1.7 | 6.0 | 2.2 |
| Textiles | 321 | | | | | | |
|   Output | | 8.0 | 3.8 | 9.2 | 8.5 | 21.8 | 24.2 |
|   Employment | | 7.0 | 3.8 | 3.6 | 4.4 | 7.2 | 24.1 |
|   Productivity | | 0.9 | 0.0 | 5.4 | 3.9 | 13.6 | 0.1 |
| Wearing apparel, leather, footwear | 322–324 | | | | | | |
|   Output | | 4.4 | 18.4 | 10.5 | 7.3 | 39.5 | 12.2 |
|   Employment | | 8.0 | 7.0 | 6.8 | 4.4 | 17.7 | 14.1 |
|   Productivity | | −3.3 | 10.7 | 3.5 | 2.8 | 17.7 | −1.1 |
| Wood and wood products, including furniture | 33 | | | | | | |
|   Output | | 8.4 | 10.7 | 13.4 | 5.0 | 7.0 | 5.5 |
|   Employment | | 5.9 | 15.7 | 3.3 | 1.0 | 3.3 | 10.2 |
|   Productivity | | 2.4 | −4.3 | 9.8 | 4.0 | 3.6 | −4.2 |
| Paper and paper products, printing and publishing | 34 | | | | | | |
|   Output | | 11.0 | 17.1 | 4.2 | 6.6 | 10.3 | 9.3 |
|   Employment | | 6.5 | 10.8 | 3.6 | 1.4 | 5.4 | 7.3 |
|   Productivity | | 4.2 | 5.7 | 0.6 | 5.1 | 4.7 | 0.9 |
| Chemicals | 35 | | | | | | |
|   Output | | 9.3 | 12.8 | 14.5 | 8.2 | 15.8 | 6.5 |
|   Employment | | 8.1 | 10.9 | 6.3 | 5.2 | 10.3 | 9.0 |
|   Productivity | | 1.1 | 1.7 | 7.7 | 2.9 | 5.0 | −2.3 |
| Non-metalic minerals | 36 | | | | | | |
|   Output | | 9.9 | 13.2 | 11.2 | 9.0 | 11.9 | 3.5 |
|   Employment | | 3.5 | 16.3 | 6.2 | 2.5 | 3.2 | 5.5 |
|   Productivity | | 6.2 | −2.6 | 4.7 | 6.3 | 8.4 | −1.9 |
| Basic metals | 37 | | | | | | |
|   Output | | 4.7 | 12.2 | 25.2 | 8.4 | 30.1 | 6.4 |
|   Employment | | 16.8 | 76.3 | 12.2 | 1.8 | 8.9 | 2.6 |
|   Productivity | | −10.4 | −36.3 | 11.6 | 6.5 | 19.5 | 3.7 |
| Metal products, machinery and equipment | 38 | | | | | | |
|   Output | | 11.4 | 35.8 | 13.2 | 9.1 | 34.3 | 25.8 |
|   Employment | | 6.9 | 20.9 | 7.1 | 6.3 | 17.0 | 34.6 |
|   Productivity | | 4.2 | 12.4 | 5.7 | 2.6 | 14.8 | −6.5 |

[a] Computed as compound rate of index numbers for 1968 and 1974
Source: UNIDO, *World Industry Since 1960: Progress and Prospects*, 1979, pp. 236–237

to-rural and rural-to-urban migration in Asia and Africa (Chaney, 1984; Nelson, 1974; Herrick, 1971; Byerlee, 1972; Orlansky and Dubrovsky, 1978; Petritsch, 1981).·This divergent pattern has been explained in part by the lesser role of women in agriculture in Latin America as compared with Africa and Asia (Boserup, 1970). There is disagreement in this respect. Several recent studies suggest that women's contribution to agriculture in Latin America has been underestimated due to deficiencies in data gathering (Recchini de Lattes and Wainerman, 1979). The absence of opportunities for paid employment in rural areas is probably a key factor inducing the greater female rural-to-urban migration (Orlansky and Dubrovsky, 1978).

The large-scale development of export manufacturing in several regions introduces a new variable into the inquiry. The available evidence strongly documents the overwhelming presence of women among production workers in export manufacturing (Lim, 1980; Safa, 1981; Grossman, 1979; Fernandez Kelly, 1983; Multinational Monitor, 1982; UNIDO, 1980; Salaff, 1981; Wong, 1980; Cho, 1984; Arrigo, 1980). Furthermore, there is a high incidence of manufacturing jobs among women in countries or regions within countries where export manufacturing is a key sector of the economy. In these cases there frequently is a growing incidence of manufacturing jobs alongside a declining incidence of service jobs. This trend diverges from what has been typical in the highly industrialized countries, both in the past and today, as well as from the prevailing pattern in Third World countries over the last two decades where service jobs have tended to proliferate.

This new pattern also diverges significantly from what most of the literature on female migration in the Third World found to be typical in the 1950s, 1960s and well into the 1970s. The general pattern discerned was that most women migrants to cities found employment in domestic service and in informal sector activities (Boserup, 1970; Schmink, 1982; Delaunoy, 1975; Shah and Smith, 1981; Orlansky and Dubrovsky, 1978; Recchini de Lattes and Wainerman, 1971; Youssef, 1974; Jelin, 1979). Furthermore, the evidence points to a displacement of women from manufacturing as the branches employing women become modernized, more capital intensive and operate on larger scales of production (Petritsch, 1981; Dauber and Cain, 1981; Tinker and Bramsen, 1976; Boulding, 1980; Parra Sandoval, 1975; Institute of Social Studies, 1979; Ahmand and Jenkins, 1980; Caughman and Thiam, 1980). The same pattern is evident in the development of heavy industry: as the latter becomes an increasingly significant component of a given country's or region's manufacturing base, the share of jobs held by women in manufacturing declines; for example, the share of women holding manufacturing jobs in Brazil declined from 18.6 to 11 percent from 1950 to 1970, a period during which heavy industry developed (Schmink, 1982: 6).

The prevalence of women in manufacturing together with the high incidence of manufacturing jobs among women in countries or regions where this type of production is prominent raises a number of questions about the nature of this development. One element for an explanation is the marked concentration of branches that historically have employed women – electronics, garments, textiles, footwear and toys. The expansion of these industries has induced major changes in the sex composition of internal migration flows in these areas. Women, not men, now predominate in rural-to-urban migrations in the Caribbean Basin and Asia (World Bank Staff, 1975; Standing, 1975; Arrigo, 1980; Kelly, 1984). For example, Standing (1975) notes a tendency to substitution of male labor within the non-agricultural sector in Jamaica over the last two decades, with the share of women in manufacturing increasing from 23–24 percent in the early 1950s to 35 percent in 1973 (Standing, 1975: 1).

These trends point to the need for certain distinctions to gain an adequate understanding of the place of women in export manufacturing, and more generally, in export-led development. We need to distinguish between so-called traditional and modern forms of manufacturing: the evidence shows that women's share of jobs declines as an industry modernizes. However, if we consider the developments in the new industrial zones, perhaps a better formulation would be one that distinguishes between labor-intensive and capital-intensive forms of production. This would incorporate both the earlier instances of female employment in certain industries and contemporary cases as diverse as electronics and garments. Furthermore, this distinction overcomes the inadequacy of conceiving of certain industries, notably garments, and certain forms of organization of the work process, notably sweatshops and industrial homework, as pertaining to the "traditional," non-modern sector. This notion can easily be read to mean that these forms will become increasingly insignificant as modernization takes place. On the contrary, the growth of labor-intensive manufacturing in Third World countries with rapid industrialization as well as the growing use of sweatshops and homework in highly industrialized countries, all point to the viability of these forms in "modern" or "modernizing" contexts. Such a reading of current developments carries considerable implications for an analysis of women's participation in paid employment. While earlier trends suggested both a tendency toward "modernization" in industry and a corresponding displacement of women from manufacturing, these new trends point to growing participation.

One of the better bodies of data on employment characteristics in export manufacturing is that covering Export Processing Zones. These zones represent an institutionalization of key patterns underlying export manufacturing.[8] Although they account for only a part of all such manufacturing, their traits tend to be typical. Thus the more exhaustive data on such zones can be used to obtain a profile of general employment conditions in export manufacturing.[9]

Although an increasing number of countries are developing EPZs, Hong Kong, South Korea, Singapore and Mexico have the largest share and the oldest zones. Indonesia, the Philippines, Taiwan, Malaysia, Colombia, El Salvador and Haiti represent a sort of second phase in the global development of such zones and export industries generally. A third phase is represented by countries in the Middle East (Syria, Egypt and Jordan) and Africa as well as in Asian countries such as Sri Lanka and India. This third phase can be seen as the penetration of export-oriented development into countries hitherto not particularly dominated by export-led industrialization as a development strategy or into countries with generally undeveloped industrial sectors where export industries may come to play an important role. In this regard these countries bear similarities to some countries in the second phase and, as in both cases, export industries may come to represent a significant share of total GNP.

Besides geographic concentration, zones have a very high industrial concentration. Electronics, textiles and garments account for up to 80 percent of all production in zones (UNIDO, 1980). These two types of industries represent very different characteristics of production, one with low levels of mechanization and the other with high levels of mechanization. Yet both are labor-intensive and need abundant supplies of cheap labor, one because it is technologically backward, the other because its technological sophistication has permitted the incorporation of tasks into machines and a fragmentation of the production process that allows the use of unskilled workers. Other industries located in zones are toys, footwear, leather, sports goods, plastic articles, miscellaneous light consumer goods products, assembly of scientific and medical instruments and of optical and photographic equipment. In one way or another they all represent a type of production or assembly that allows the use of unskilled labor even when the components being worked on are the result of high capital intensity and high levels of technical expertise.

About half of the total labor force in Asian zones is employed in electronics (Ho Kwon Ping, 1980: 18; Grossman, 1979; UNIDO, 1980; Lim, 1980; Safa, 1981). But there are variations among countries. Electronics dominates in Malaysia and Singapore and textiles and garments in South Korea and the Philippines. And new industries move in. Thus in 1975 virtually all firms in zones in the Philippines were in textiles and garments and footwear (UNIDO, 1980); beginning in 1976, electronics moved in (Snow, 1977).

In Central America and the Caribbean Basin there is a similar concentration in electronics. For example in 1975, almost half of all workers in factories producing for export in Mexico and El Salvador were employed in electronics. Textiles and garments accounted for another 26 percent. Figures for the Border Industrialization Program in Mexico reveal a similar pattern, only more accentuated. Thus in 1978, 60 percent of the BIP industries were in electronics and electrical assembly and 30 percent were in textiles and garments (Fernandez Kelly, 1983).

Electronics and garments and textiles dominate both in countries with well-established export industries, such as Hong Kong and Mexico, and in those where this is a more recent development, such as the Philippines, Taiwan, Malaysia, Thailand and Indonesia.

Besides geographic and industrial concentration, zones are also characterized by a very high concentration of women workers (Lim, 1980; Safa, 1981; Salaff, 1981; Wong, 1981; Fernandez Kelly, 1983; Grossman, 1979; Kreye, 1977). About 70 percent of all workers in zones are women and up to 80 percent of all production and assembly workers in zones are women. This level varies from country to country but is uniformly high. Women are 95 percent of all workers in zones in Malaysia (Lim, 1980) and in Mexico's Border Industrialization Program (Fernandez Kelly, 1983).

This high incidence of female employment rises even more if we look at the electronics and textiles and garments industries alone. In electronics, over 90 percent of all production workers and almost all assembly workers are women (Lim, 1980: 15). It is interesting to note that in an industry such as toys, which has been expanding its off-shore sector, 90 percent of all workers in plants in South Korea and the Philippines are women. The high incidence of female employment is not peculiar to the zones. It holds for export industries generally, particularly electronics, textiles and garments, and toys. It is estimated that American electronics firms employ over half a million workers in less-developed countries (NACLA, 1977: 15), with women accounting for over 90 percent of all workers (Lim, 1978: 122).

It is worth noting, for example, that in a rather developed state such as Singapore, the largest single concentration of women workers in the late 1950s was in services. By 1978, it was in production and related jobs. Although in absolute numbers service-sector employment has increased, its share of all jobs declined from 34.7 percent in 1957 to 14.9 percent in 1978, a result of the quintupling of production jobs, which accounted for almost 36 percent of all jobs in 1978 (Wong, 1980: 9). This is clearly a function of the expansion of export production. The conjunction of the weight of this type of production and the distinct employment patterns it promotes have generated an additional pattern that contrasts with what is typical in highly developed countries: there is no bimodality in the age composition of women workers. The labor force participation rates of women 20 to 24 years of age is very high, yet there is no resurgence in participation in women aged 40 and over (Wong, 1980: 8). A similar pattern holds for other countries with export-led development.

Available evidence shows no difference in wages between zones and the rest of the economy in these countries. Recent surveys on wages paid in EPZs as reported in the International Labor Office Yearbook (1982) show that semi- and unskilled workers earn an average of less than $0.50 per hour. Only a few countries are above this level: Mexico, Colombia, Panama, Jordan, Syria and Egypt. Average wage levels are between 16 and 57 times less than in the U.S. Furthermore, there are a variety of malpractices that contribute to lower wage levels, notably the fact that a high share of employees are classified as trainees for excessively long periods of time. High turnover hiring and firing practices further promote a high incidence of "trainees" and hence unusually low wages. These low wage levels are particularly remarkable in view of the relatively high productivity levels in export manufacturing where highly mechanized assembly plants predominate.

In some of the areas with high concentrations of export industries, the preference for young women and high turnover rates have created shortages of desirable workers. One possibility could be that this would lead to a gradual recruitment of more men into these jobs. However, the evidence suggests that the factories leave for areas with vaster supplies of young women (Lim, 1978; 1980; Pineda-Ofreneo, 1982; UNIDO, 1980), or bring in migrant women from neighboring countries, e.g. Malaysian, Thai and Filipino women in Singapore (Wong, 1981).

In brief, female labor-intensive employment is characteristic of both transnational subsidiaries and native firms producing for export.[10] As a consequence, in those countries where export industries are a large component of total industrial activity, this pattern of female employment in export industries has contributed to a feminization of the industrial proletariat and to an unusual pattern of women's employment characterized by a growing incidence of manufacturing rather than clerical and service jobs as "development" proceeds. Furthermore, a good share of the clerical and service jobs are directly related to export manufacturing as well.

The central role played by export manufacturing in female employment is a characteristic that distinguishes it from the historical evolution of women's entry into wage labor in what are today highly industrialized countries. It puts these Third World women in a highly vulnerable position given (a) the hiring and firing practices in many of these new industrial zones and (b) the disruption of traditional work structures and the westernization of these women, both of which minimize the possibilities of successful reincorporation in the work lives that preceded employment in the zones. We see here the conditions for the formation of a supply of women migrants. The liberalization of American immigration policy and the vast demand for low-wage workers in the U.S. acquire their full weight in this context.

## A new trend?

Besides a strong trend toward locating new plants in new areas with even cheaper labor and even more concessions on the part of host governments, there is also a slowly growing trend of retrenchment of existing facilities. In Puerto Rico this has been evident for many years, especially in garments and electronics. But it is now also beginning to happen in places such as Singapore and Hong Kong in the electronics industry. It is generally seen as the result of two factors: (a) competition among developing countries to attract foreign investment via offering more and more subsidies and concessions (UNIDO, 1980); and (b) a search for even cheaper and more docile labor, since the evidence suggests that there is a general trend toward rising wages and workers' struggles in the zones, notwithstanding the blocking of unionization and other workers' rights (CCA-URM, 1981; Pineda-Ofreneo, 1982; Lim, 1978; 1980). There is evidence (Sassen-Koob, 1987) that a third factor may be playing an increasingly important role. This is illustrated by what I have called the structuring of a new industrial zone in Southern California, which is emerging as an alternative to the zones in less developed countries. Very briefly, the reasons for this are: (a) the vast supply of cheap and powerless labor represented by immigrants from Mexico and, increasingly, from Asia; (b) the need to have certain assembly and production operations close to technical centers at particular stages of product development – that is to say, certain components in the electronics industry may be the first phase of a new product cycle; and (c) the desire to secure access to the American market which may make location of high-tech industries in Southern California with its vast supplies of cheap and technically proficient labor attractive to foreign companies, these being a major component in the accelerated growth of high-tech industry in the region. I return to these issues in Chapter 6.

## THE MIGRATION OPTION

Precisely because these countries have had large-scale direct foreign investment and considerable growth rates in employment, particularly manufacturing employment, traditional migration push factors seem inadequate to explain the high levels of emigration registered over the last decade and directed to areas with much lower overall growth rates. Apparently there are a number of intervening factors that along with considerable employment growth, transform the situation and promote emigration. While one can understand that the direct displacement of small farmers by commercial agriculture can generate out-migration, this is less clear in the case of labor-intensive manufacturing which creates jobs.

Do these developments induce emigration in the areas where they take place? That is to say, besides conditions inducing emigration among population sectors not affected by such developments, can we *infer* here the existence of a specific dynamic that facilitates emigration both as an objective process and as a culturally viable option? New and highly labor-intensive export manufacturing conceivably could contribute to solve the unemployment problem, particularly among prime-aged males. Instead, the evidence overwhelmingly shows that it has drawn new segments of the population into the labor force: mostly young women who under conditions of a more gradual industrialization would not so massively have entered the labor force. Large-scale creation of jobs concentrated in a few areas has rapidly and extensively mobilized young women into the labor force. This effect has been further accentuated by high turnover rates due to employment practices in the plants and the mental and physical fatigue associated with these jobs. This results in ongoing recruitment of new cohorts of young women.

The absence of expected outcomes and the creation of new, undesirable outcomes have to be taken into account when examining the employment implications of the development of export industries. First, the large-scale mobilization of young women into wage labor has had a disruptive effect on traditional waged and unwaged work structures. Second, employment in the new industrial zones has brought about a cultural distancing between the women and their communities of origin. Together these two processes pose objective and ideological barriers to these women's return to their family homes and the work they would traditionally perform there for the household or the local market. At the same time, long-term employment in export factories is highly unlikely. All the evidence points to average tenure being around five years. After that, for a number of reasons, women are laid off with little possibility of being employed in another firm, given the preference for women between sixteen and twenty-five years of age. These women, laid off and westernized, have few options. They add to the ranks of the unemployed. The disruption of traditional work structures due to the extremely high levels of young female emigration has further contributed to increase the pool of unemployed. It has stimulated male emigration and the emigration of women who may not have planned on doing so.

Under these conditions, emigration for both women and men may be the only option. At this point the fact of a strong foreign presence becomes crucially significant. The foreign investment presence is concentrated in a few areas and foreign firms also dominate the zones objectively and culturally. Finally, it is the fact that the workers employed in export manufacturing and associated services are applying their labor to goods or services that are geared to foreign countries. Year after year, day after day, these manual and service workers are engaged in activities that meet demand in the U.S., or West Germany, or Japan. In other words, they make things of use to people and firms in countries with much higher levels of development than their own. One could infer, then, that these workers may feel capable of using their labor power effectively in these developed countries as well.

The relation between urban and rural spaces in this process of mobilization of people into migration streams assumes a variety of forms. It cannot be reduced to a linear movement of displacement. Thus, even in areas where commercial agriculture has caused severe displacement of small farmers who are then forced to migrate to the cities, access to cash income through employment in commercial agriculture may make possible continued ownership of a plot of land. Owning such land, in turn, may contribute to lower their cost as wage-workers in commercial agriculture (Deere, 1976). Though under a different form, the rise in the use of homeworkers in rural areas to produce manufactured products for the export market may have the same effect in terms of facilitating continued ownership of a plot of land and even further lowering the cost of labor in export manufacturing (Pineda-Ofreneo, 1982). These developments will tend to counteract the disruption of traditional work structures resulting from commercial agriculture and export manufacturing. However, they do entail an articulation between these traditional work structures and modern forms of production. One concrete expression of this is a reduction in the share of workers' subsistence costs that needs to be met by wages. An extension of this development is represented by the remittances sent by migrants abroad which contribute to continued land ownership in the country of origin (Grasmuck, 1981; Pessar, 1982; Mines, 1978). Thus, the same conditions that promote the disruption of traditional work structures may eventually also generate possibilities, i.e., through access to money, for delaying or counteracting this disruption.

Besides this highly mediated effect on the formation of a pool of potential emigrants and the disruption of traditional, often unwaged, employment structures, the massive and concentrated foreign presence facilitates the emergence of emigration as an option. This would be far less likely in an "isolated" country, one lacking a massive foreign presence and the resulting structural and ideological links with "the West." It would then also follow that the emigration impact will be much stronger in countries without a large and complex industrial base where direct foreign investment can be a relatively measured, discreet presence. A growing share of direct foreign investment by the major industrial countries is going to smaller countries with less complex economies and increasingly into production for export. Under these conditions direct foreign investment becomes one of the central variables, along with those traditionally cited in the migration literature, contributing to the development of linkages that facilitate emigration flows.

In brief, what I posit is a generalized effect that contributes to the formation of a pool of potential emigrants and, at the same time, to the emergence of emigration as an actual option. This effect would seem to be present regardless of whether the direct foreign investment originates in the U.S. or in any of the other major advanced industrialized countries, including Japan. What matters are the characteristics of both foreign investment and the receiving economy. Thus the increased level of Western European and Japanese investments in export-oriented labor-intensive production contributes to these same two conditions: the formation of a pool of potential migrants and the emergence of emigration as an option.

Against this background, the changes in immigration legislation in 1965, together with the continued image of the U.S. as an immigration country, acquire their full significance. Under such conditions, Western European direct foreign investment could stimulate emigration to the U.S. by contributing to conditions that further emigration in the sending countries. Though Western Europe was a major target for labor migrations after World War II, it has not emerged as another "land of opportunity", an alternative to the U.S. The guest-worker orientation of its immigration policy may have had something to do with this, besides the more fundamental fact that the Western European nations were not built by immigrants as was the U.S. The closure of immigration in Western Europe can only reinforce this pattern.

The continued vitality of the U.S. as an immigration country and the absence of alternatives acquire particular significance in the context of continued growth of direct foreign investment and its expansion to additional countries. The general trend is for all the major industrial countries to increase investment in less developed countries. Although most of this investment is concentrated in a few countries, there is also a trend towards significant levels of investment in "new" countries. Accepting my analysis about the effect of direct foreign investment on the formation of a pool of potential emigrants and on the emergence of emigration as an actual option, it could be argued that this expansion of direct foreign investment by the major industrial countries will contribute to additional emigration to the U.S.

CONCLUSION

The generalization of market relations has historically had a dissolution effect on traditional work structures and promoted the formation of labor migrations. Chapter 2 discussed the historical development of conditions promoting labor migration. In this chapter I have focused on the particular forms assumed by these conditions in the main immigrant sending countries today. The expansion of export-oriented manufacturing and agriculture, both inseparably related to direct foreign investment by the highly industrialized countries, has mobilized new segments of the population into regional and long-distance migrations.

Direct foreign investment can be conceived of as a mediating structure, one that operates indirectly in a highly complex manner both ideologically and structurally. The 1,000 percent increase in DFI in developing countries from 1950 to 1980 (and mostly concentrated in a few of these) creates various kinds of linkages with the capital-sending country(s).

The employment effects of direct foreign investment are considerable and highly concentrated. The rather high levels of annual growth in employment, output and value added in manufacturing in the main immigrant-sending countries are significantly higher than in the developed countries. These employment effects, grouped by type of investment – export or import-substitution oriented – by country and by sector, can serve as an indicator of the impact of such investment on the mobilization of people into wage labor and into migration streams. The available evidence shows this impact to be pronounced in the case of countries where export-oriented investment is a major component not only of foreign investment but also of the country's GNP. The available evidence also indicates that the rates of immigration to the U.S. from these same countries increased significantly throughout the 1970s: for example, a 125 percent increase in legal Filipino entries from 1970 to 1980, a 400 percent increase in entries of South Koreans, a 250 percent increase in entries from Singapore and Malaysia (see Chapter 3). Finally, the available evidence also shows a growing trend toward direct foreign investment in export industries in more and more of the less-developed countries, a development which can be expected to promote new migration streams.

In brief, in this chapter I have examined how significant levels and concentrations of direct foreign investment are one, and only one, factor promoting emigration through: (a) the incorporation of new segments of the population into wage labor and the associated disruption of traditional work structures both of which create a supply of migrant workers; (b) the feminization of the new industrial workforce and its impact on the work opportunities of men, both in the new industrial zones and in the traditional work structures; and (c) the consolidation of objective and ideological links with the highly industrialized countries where most foreign capital originates, links that involve both a generalized westernization effect and more specific work situations wherein workers find themselves producing goods for people and firms in the highly industrialized countries.

# Appendix

Table 4.8 *Constant annual growth rates[a] of manufacturing employment, value added, and labor productivity, 1960–1976 (percentages)*

| Economic grouping | Employment 1960–1975 | Employment 1968–1975 | Employment 1975–1976 | Value added 1960–1975 | Value added 1968–1975 | Value added 1975–1976 | Labor productivity 1960–1975 | Labor productivity 1968–1975 | Labor productivity 1975–1976 |
|---|---|---|---|---|---|---|---|---|---|
| Developing Countries | 4.9 | 7.0 | — | 7.4 | 9.1 | 8.5 | 2.4 | 2.0 | — |
| Developed market economies | 0.9 | 0.4 | 0.0 | 5.7 | 4.1 | 8.9 | 4.8 | 3.7 | 8.9 |
| *World average* | *2.8* | *2.9* | *—* | *7.1* | *6.5* | *8.7* | *4.2* | *3.5* | *—* |

[a] Calculated using regression on time

*Source:* UNIDO, *World Industry Since 1960: Progress and Prospects*, 1979, p. 223; Based on UN, *Statistical Yearbook 1977; Yearbook of Industrial Statistics*, 1976 edition, Vol. 1, and data supplied by the United Nations Statistical Office

Table 4.9 *Annual growth rates of GDP in major emigration countries, 1965–1980[a] (percentages)*

| | Average, 1965–70 | 71 | 72 | 73 | 74 | 75 | 76 | 77 | 78 | 79 | 80 |
|---|---|---|---|---|---|---|---|---|---|---|---|
| Colombia | 5.8 | 5.8 | 7.8 | 7.1 | 6.0 | 3.8 | 4.6 | 4.9 | 8.9 | 5.1 | 4.2 |
| Ecuador | 5.6 | 8.3 | 9.8 | 12.7 | 9.9 | 8.4 | 6.8 | — | 5.4 | 5.4 | 5.3 |
| Haiti | 1.8 | 5.7 | 3.7 | 5.8 | 4.3 | 2.2 | 5.3 | 1.3 | 4.4 | 4.7 | 5.2 |
| Dominican Republic | 7.8 | 9.9 | 12.5 | 8.9 | 7.5 | 5.1 | 6.4 | 4.4 | 2.2 | 4.8 | 5.2 |
| Mexico | 6.9 | 3.4 | 7.5 | 7.5 | 5.9 | 4.2 | 1.7 | 3.2 | 8.1 | 9.0 | 8.4 |
| Hong Kong | 7.8 | 3.2 | 7.2 | 14.2 | 2.2 | 3.3 | 16.7 | 9.8 | 10.0 | 10.5 | 10.1 |
| Philippines | 5.4 | — | 4.8 | 8.7 | 4.9 | 6.6 | 7.5 | 5.6 | 5.8 | 5.8 | 4.7 |
| Singapore | 12.5 | 12.5 | 13.4 | 11.5 | 6.3 | 4.0 | 7.5 | 7.9 | 8.6 | 9.3 | 9.0 |
| South Korea | 11.1 | 9.0 | 7.4 | 17.1 | 8.8 | 8.8 | 14.6 | 10.0 | 11.3 | 7.4 | −4.5 |

[a] At constant factor cost

*Source:* ECLA, *Economic Survey of Latin America* (Various Issues, 1975, 1977, 1980), Santiago (1977, 1979, 1980); ESCAP, *Economic and Social Survey of Asia and the Pacific* (various issues, 1976, 1978, 1980); Bangkok; ESCAP (UN), 1977, 1979, 1981; Banco de la Republica, *Revista del Banco de al Republica*, Bogotá, April 1982, p. 94

Table 4.10 *Annual growth rates of output, employment and productivity in selected Developing Countries, by end-use, 1968–1974 (Percentages)*

| Country | Mainly non-durable consumer goods[a] | | | Intermediate goods[b] | | | Capital and durable consumer goods[c] | | |
|---|---|---|---|---|---|---|---|---|---|
| | Output | Employment | Productivity | Output | Employment | Productivity | Output | Employment | Productivity |
| Colombia | 7.7 | 6.6 | 1.0 | 9.6 | 6.7 | 2.7 | 9.9 | 7.7 | 2.1 |
| Dominican Republic | 9.9 | 5.8 | 3.9 | 13.1 | 13.3 | -0.1 | 30.6 | 29.1 | 1.1 |
| Ecuador | 9.2 | 5.8 | 3.2 | 12.2 | 6.0 | 6.0 | 13.4 | 7.0 | 6.0 |
| Mexico | 6.1 | 3.1 | 2.9 | 8.3 | 3.9 | 4.2 | 8.9 | 4.7 | 4.0 |
| South Korea | 20.9 | 8.8 | 11.1 | 14.8 | 7.8 | 6.5 | 33.7 | 15.6 | 15.7 |
| Singapore | 8.3 | 11.7 | -3.0 | 6.6 | 7.7 | -1.0 | 24.8 | 31.7 | -5.2 |

[a] ISIC 31, 32, 33, 342, 385, 390
[b] ISIC 35, 36
[c] ISIC 37, 381, 382, 383, 384
Source: UNIDO, *World Industry since 1960: Progress and Prospects*, 1979, p. 244

Table 4.11 *Export Processing Zones in operation in Asia, Africa, and Latin America, with year of commencement*

| Country | Export Processing Zone | Commence-ment of operation | Country | Export Processing Zone | Commence-ment of operation |
|---|---|---|---|---|---|
| ASIA | | | | | |
| Bahrain | Mina Sulman | 1972[a] | | | |
| Hong Kong | Hong Kong | 1965[b] | | Bupyong | n.a. |
| | Kwung Tong | | | Juan | n.a. |
| | Tsuen Wan/ | | | Juan | n.a. |
| | Kwai Chung | | Syria | Damascus | n.a. |
| | Sam Ka Tsuen | | Taiwan | Kaohsiung | 1966 |
| | San Po Kong | | | Nantze | 1970 |
| | Cheung Sha Wan | | | Taichung | 1971 |
| | Chai Wan | | | | |
| | Wong Chuk Hang | | AFRICA | | |
| India | Kandla | 1965 | Egypt | Port Said | 1976 |
| | Santa Cruz | 1974 | Mauritius | Plaine Lauzun | 1971 |
| Jordan | Aqaba Port | n.a. | | Coromandel | 1976 |
| Lebanon | Beyrouth | n.a. | Senegal | Dakar | 1976 |
| Malaysia | Prai | 1973 | Togo | Lomé | n.a. |
| | Prai Wharves | 1972 | Tunisia | Mégrine | n.a. |
| | Bayan Lepas | 1972 | | Ben Arous | n.a. |
| | Sungei Way | 1972 | | | |
| | Ulu Klang | 1974 | LATIN AMERICA | | |
| | Tolok Paligma | n.a. | Brazil | Manaus | 1973 |
| | Batu Berendam | 1972 | Colombia | Barranquilla | 1969 |
| | Tanjong Kling | 1972 | | Buenaventura | 1973 |
| Philippines | Bataan | 1973 | | Palmaseca | 1973 |
| Singapore | Singapore | 1967[c] | | Cúcuta | 1974 |
| | Bunkit Timan | | Domin. Rep. | La Romana | 1969 |
| | Jurong Town | | | S. Pedro de Macorís | 1973 |
| | St Michael's | | | Santiago | 1974 |
| | Tiong Bahru | | El Salvador | San Bartolo | 1975 |
| | Redhill | | Guatemala | S. Tomás de Castilla | 1975 |
| | Ayer Rajah | | Haiti | Port-au-Prince | 1974[d] |
| | Tangling Halt | | Mexico | Zona Frontera | 1966[d] |
| | Kallang Basin | | | Tijuana | |
| | Toa Bayoh | | | Mexicali | |
| | Ang Mo Kio | | | Nogales | |
| | Chai Chee | | | Ciudad Juárez (2) | |
| | Bedok | | | Ciudad Acuna | |
| | Indus Road | | | Piedras Negras | |
| | Woodlands | | | Nuevo Laredo | |
| South Korea | Masan | 1972 | | Reynosa | |
| | Iri | 1974 | | Matamoros (2) | |
| | Gumi | 1973 | Panama | Colón | 1975[e][f] |
| | Gurudong | n.a. | Puerto Rico | Mayagüez | 1974[f] |

[a] Freeport in operation since 1960
[b] Export-oriented industrialization since the beginning of the 1950s, production for the world market by foreign firms since the mid-1960s.
[c] Production for the world market by foreign firms since 1967.
[d] Start of production for the world market by foreign firms.
[e] Free port in operation since 1948
[f] Commercial activities since 1961
*Source:* Fröbel *et al.*, 1980: 308–309

Table 4.12 *U.S. imports under TSUS$^a$ items 806.30 and 807.00, 1966–1980 (in millions of U.S. dollars)*

| | 1966 | | | 1978 | | | 1980 | | |
|---|---|---|---|---|---|---|---|---|---|
| | Dutiable value | Duty-free value | Total value | Dutiable value | Duty-free value | Total value | Dutiable value | Duty-free value | Total value |
| **Developed Countries** | | | | | | | | | |
| Value | 774 | 119 | 893 | 4,959 | 493 | 5,452 | 7,080 | 578 | 7,658 |
| Percent of total | 96.1% | 80.4% | 93.7% | 69.4% | 19.1% | 56.0% | 69.0% | 15.4% | 54.7% |
| **Developing Countries** | | | | | | | | | |
| Value | 31 | 29 | 60 | 2,184 | 2,099 | 4,283 | 3,177 | 3,164 | 6,341 |
| Percent of total | 3.9% | 19.6% | 6.3% | 30.6% | 80.9% | 44.0% | 31.0% | 84.6% | 45.3% |
| **Grand total** | | | | | | | | | |
| Value | 805 | 148 | 953 | 7,143 | 2,592 | 9,735 | 10,257 | 3,742 | 13,999 |
| Percent of total | 100.0% | 100.0% | 100.0% | 100.0% | 100.0% | 100.0% | 100.0% | 100.0% | 100.0% |

$^a$Tariff Schedules of the United States

*Source:* Compiled from U.S. International Trade Commission, *Imports Under Items 806.30 and 807.00 of the Tariff Schedules of the United States, 1977–80,* 1981; *Import Trends in TSUS Items 806.30 and 807.00,* 1980; *Economic Factors Affecting the Use of Items 807.00 and 806.30 of the Tariff Schedules of U.S.,* 1970

Table 4.13 *Value of Haitian exports in assembly industries (in millions of $ U.S.)*

| | Products made of locally produced components | Products made of imported components | Total gross |
|---|---|---|---|
| 1967 | 1.5 | 2.3 | 3.8 |
| 1968 | 2.9 | 4.0 | 6.9 |
| 1969 | 2.7 | 5.8 | 8.5 |
| 1970 | 3.8 | 8.1 | 11.9 |
| 1971 | 4.5 | 11.9 | 16.4 |
| 1972 | 5.8 | 18.4 | 24.2 |
| 1973 | 6.5 | 32.1 | 38.6 |
| 1974 | 16.4 | 61.4 | 77.8 |
| 1975 | 12.4 | 58.0 | 70.4 |
| 1976 | 10.6 | 84.5 | 95.1 |
| 1977 | 13.3 | 91.0 | 104.3 |

*Source:* U.S. Embassy, Port-au-Prince, Commercial Section (unpublished data); Adapted from Leslie Delatour, "The Evolution of International Subcontracting Industries in Haiti" (Presented at UNCTAD Seminar, July 16–20, 1979, Mexico) [Mimeo]

# 5

# The rise of global cities and the new labor demand

The developments described in the preceding chapter contribute to explain the emergence of new migration streams to the United States. The developments addressed in this chapter contribute to explain the continuation of these migrations at increasing levels. That is to say, the preceding chapter identified conditions for the formation of a migrant labor supply in the sending countries, while the current chapter focuses on the conditions influencing the demand for an immigrant workforce in what have become key destinations of these migrations.

The new industrialization in several Asian and Caribbean countries is in good part the other side of what the U.S. experiences as deindustrialization. These shifts are one aspect of the territorial decentralization of economic activity generally. Decentralization and the technical transformation of work have contributed to the development of a new core economic base in highly industrialized countries. This new core consists of highly specialized services, the corporate headquarters complex, and high technology industries, and it promptly evokes images of high-level, specialized jobs. However, this is only part of the actual situation: the new economy has also generated a massive expansion in the supply of low-wage jobs.

For a number of reasons, these new trends are particularly accentuated in major urban centers, which are also the destination of the vast majority of new immigrants. They have intensified the role of major cities as producers and exporters of specialized services and of high-level managerial inputs. The technological transformation of the work process, the shift of manufacturing to less-developed areas domestically and abroad, in part made possible by the technological transformation of the work process, and the ascendance of the financial sector in management, have all contributed to the consolidation of a new kind of economic center – the global city from where the world economy is managed and serviced. That is to say, the domestic and international dispersion of manufacturing, clerical and service jobs could, in principle, have been accompanied by a parallel decentralization in ownership and control. This did clearly not take place. The pertinent literature generally analyzes the continued centralization of control and ownership in terms of the power of the large corporations. Insofar as the concern in this book is with jobs and labor demand, the question here is how does this continuation of centralized control over a geographically dispersed economic system translate into jobs. Rather than a focus on the power of the large corporation, this question brings to the fore what could be described as the *practice* of global control and specialized servicing: the activities involved in producing and reproducing such centralized control and specialized servicing. From this perspective, what matters in the examination of specialized service industries is not only the final output, e.g. a financial package or technical advice, but the whole range of jobs involved in the production of that final output, from the experts to the cleaners of the buildings where the experts work. The expansion of this sector has contributed to a growth of both very high-income and low-income jobs.

The locational concentration of this expanding sector of specialized services and corporate headquarters in major cities has emerged as an important source of low-wage jobs, both directly and indirectly. The direct effect is through the occupational structure of these sectors. The indirect effect is through the ancillary sectors and the consumption structure underlying the lifestyles of the new high-income professional/technical workers.

To this source of low-wage jobs we need to add (a) the ongoing growth of the consumer services sector catering to the population at large and (b) the growth of certain types of manufacturing, notably electronics, and certain forms of reorganized manufacturing, notably the proliferation of sweatshops and industrial homework. For various reasons, large cities tend to facilitate the growth of ancillary services, consumer services generally, and sweatshops. Thus also in these sectors we see a tendency towards locational concentration. The overall outcome is a large supply of low-wage jobs in major cities like New York and Los Angeles.

Of central importance to the argument I develop in this book are the following hypotheses which I examine in this chapter. First, the highly dynamic sectors of the economy directly and indirectly generate low-wage jobs, and these sectors tend to be concentrated in major cities. Second, the dynamic growth sectors in these cities are one key factor in the expansion of what could be described as an informal economic sector both in production and in retail business; an example is the increasing demand for highly customized products, from clothing and furniture to renovation of building interiors, which induces the proliferation of small, labor-intensive, full-service operations. Third, the expansion of the low-wage job supply is taking place in locations which are strategic nodal and productive points for the management and control of the global economic system. Furthermore, it is happening at a time, the 1970s, when central components of the native supply of low-wage labor are characterized by political alienation, increasingly weak labor-market attachments, rising expectations, and so on. In this context, availability of immigrant labor that is low-wage and considered to be highly disciplined acquires added significance: it offers a solution to the cheap-labor question in strategic locations of the economy at a time when important processes of economic restructuring and reorganization are taking place.

This chapter examines two sets of issues. First I will discuss how the geographic dispersion of manufacturing, clerical and certain types of service activities has contributed to the growth of the headquarters and producers services complex in major cities. The developments discussed in the preceding chapter are one component of this geographic dispersion. The technical transformation of the work process is a key variable facilitating this territorial reorganization consisting of new forms of dispersion and new forms of centralization. I will also discuss how this restructuring contains inducements for the informalization of a growing range of economic activities located in major cities. Finally, I will examine the growth of foreign investment in the U.S., a subject I return to in chapter 6; this is a development that has played an important role in the consolidation of key components in the new economic core of major cities.

Second, I will analyze how this economic restructuring has wrought major changes in the job supply. I will be particularly interested in examining the generation of low-wage jobs in major growth sectors, notably in the producer services, in high-technology industries and in other components of the downgraded manufacturing sector. The most extreme case is that of the producer services sector, a generator of very high-income professional and technical jobs which also generates a considerable supply of low-wage jobs with few skill or language proficiency requirements and no history of unionization. That is to say, even the most dynamic and technologically developed sectors in the economy generate jobs that can conceivably be held by unskilled foreign-language workers.

Two analytical distinctions basic to my argument are the distinction between job characteristics and sector characteristics and the distinction between sector characteristics and components of economic growth. Backward jobs can be part of the most modern sector of the economy and backward sectors can be part of major growth trends in the economy. Use of these two sets of distinctions also leads me to a partial reconceptualization of what has been called the informal sector, another source of low-wage jobs. I will argue that the emergence of an informal sector in major American cities is largely a function of the kinds of growth trends presently concentrated in such cities, rather than – as is often argued – a function of rising unemployment *per se* or an import from the less-developed world brought in by the massive immigrant influx.

The timing, magnitude and destination of the new immigration become particularly noteworthy when juxtaposed with the pronounced changes in the job supply in major urban centers. In the empirical elaboration of the argument I will focus particularly, though not exclusively, on the cases of New York City and Los Angeles. These are the two major producers of financial and other advanced services in the U.S. They also contain two of the largest downgraded manufacturing sectors of any city. And they are major recipients of the new immigration. Yet in the middle of the 1970s each of these cities was a consummate instance of what are usually seen as two very different configurations: the declining Frostbelt and the ascendant Sunbelt. Within the national economy they each do indeed contain distinct trends of decline and growth associated with each of these regions. However, in the context of the major developments in the world economy discussed in the preceding chapter, what comes to the fore is their role as centers for the servicing and management of the vastly decentralized manufacturing sector and for the globalization of economic activity generally. This role would also explain why both have been major recipients of direct foreign investment in banking and other advanced services over the last few years, particularly from Western Europe and Japan. Western European and Japanese manufacturing is becoming decentralized in ways akin to those of the

U.S., including redeployment of plants to select less developed countries *and to the U.S.* This generates a similar need for centralized management and servicing. New York City and Los Angeles also seem to fill part of these functions for Western European economies alongside major cities in their home countries.

CENTRALIZING GLOBAL MANAGEMENT AND SERVICING

The decentralization of the manufacturing sector, together with the transnationalization of capital generally, have contributed to a sharp rise in the domestic and international demand for advanced services. Many factories left major urban centers. But the services, particularly management and control operations largely remained there and expanded. Furthermore, the transnationalization of capital generally has induced a sharp expansion in the financial system. The production of highly specialized services, including the vastly expanded financial system, tends to be concentrated in major world centers. New York City remains the leading such center in the U.S. and the world; Los Angeles is, today, the second in the U.S.

Several trends have fed the need for an expanded production of the organizational commodities that make possible centralized control, management and specialized servicing. They are (1) the geographic dispersion of manufacturing and office work; (2) the move of large corporations into the consumer services sector; and (3) the increasing size and product diversification of large corporations. These trends have intensified the importance of planning, marketing, internal administration and distribution, control over a wide variety of types of information, and other activities that entail centralization of management, control and specialized servicing.[1] While large corporations are a key agent for this intensified role of centralizing activities, it is important to note that governments too face an increasingly complex situation and can make use of some of these organizational commodities.[2] The actual production of a wide range of these inputs takes place in a market of free standing specialized service firms. The smaller share of production occurs within the large corporation. Thus eventually foreign governments and small firms here and abroad have also emerged as buyers of these organizational inputs.

Of all these trends the decentralization of manufacturing has received most attention and become almost synonymous with the notion of capital mobility. There is a vast and excellent literature ranging from studies on deindustrialization at the core to studies on direct foreign investment and the new international division of labor. The spatial reorganization of production has become the pivot around which these analyses move, it being one of the more distinct traits in the current phase and one that has brought the issue of capital mobility to the fore.

Besides consisting of a spatial reorganization of production, the decentralization of manufacturing is also constituted in technical and social terms. Different kinds of processes have fed this decentralization. On the one hand, the dismantling of the old industrial complex with its strong organized labor component was an attempt to dismantle the capital-labor relation around which production had been organized. On the other hand, the decentralization of production in high-tech industries was a result of the introduction of new technologies where design separated low-wage, routine tasks from highly skilled tasks, therewith maximizing locational options. Relocating and setting up rubber tire production to open shops in the Sunbelt or automobile assembly plants to Mexico involves the recomposition of old industries, while setting up low-wage semiconductor assembly plants in South-East Asia involves the organization of a new industry. Both, however, entail an organization of the capital–labor relation that tends to maximize the use of low-wage labor and to minimize the effectiveness of mechanisms that empower labor vis-à-vis capital. Thus the term decentralization, while suggestive of a spatial aspect, clearly involves a complex political, social, and technical reorganization of production as well.

There are several indicators of the magnitude of this transformation in the organization of production. Plant closings in old industrial centers and reopenings in open-shop regions, notably in the Sunbelt, are probably the most dramatic instance.[3] Disinvestment, shrinking, attrition, lack of maintenance, all these represent mechanisms for deindustrialization which, while not as direct as plant closings, entail a severe erosion of the old industrial complex. From 1969 to 1976, shutdowns are estimated to have eliminated 22 million jobs in the U.S. (Bluestone and Harrison, 1982: 29), and this trend continues. Plant shutdowns in 1982 alone resulted in 1.2 million jobs lost (Bureau of National Affairs, Inc., 1982). During this same period, U.S. direct foreign investment in low-wage countries more than quadrupled, from $8.8 billion in 1966 to $42.4 billion in 1980 (Whichard, 1981a; see Table 4.3), most of it for manufacturing and associated services. A growing share of this investment is for production or assembly of components imported from the core and exported back after processing or assembly. A partial indicator of this is the value of goods entering the U.S. under Tariff Items 806.30 and 807, which increased threefold from 1966 to 1978. The value of such products coming from less developed countries represented only 6.3 percent of the total in 1966 but increased to 44 percent in 1978. These production units are distributed among 80 Export Processing Zones and a large number of world market factories. (See table 4.12 in chapter 4.)

The concrete territorial and social organization of production underlying these figures is characterized by, first, a vast expansion in the spatial organization of production to incorporate, via relocation or first-time location, domestic and foreign areas with low-wage labor. Low-wage labor here may mean skilled and unskilled workers in the American Sunbelt, unskilled workers in South-East Asia, skilled workers in Ireland, or highly trained engineers in Israel. Second, there is a reorganization of the work process resulting from the new spatial organization of production as well as the expanded use of certain types of organization of production and the work process, such as small plants, sweatshops, industrial homework and generally the fragmentation of production into multiple separate assembly and processing operations.

A major new pattern in the organization of work is the decentraliz-ation of office jobs. It involves the shipping or transmission of routine tasks to various foreign or domestic "off-shore" locations, whether low-wage countries or suburban homes at the core.

Mechanical decentralization – shipping out data processing work to be key-punched or put on discs and returned via air transport began fifteen years ago. In many ways this form of decentralization limited the possibility of using off-shore locations to very large data entry jobs with no immediate deadlines. Today, the use of satellite transmission broadens the range of jobs that can be shipped abroad and minimizes the weight of distance both in terms of time and cost. The work is typed into a computer in one location and transmitted via satellite to another. For example, Pacific Data Services, a Dallas company, recently opened a data-entry business in China which will have 96 computer terminals operating during three shifts a day. A crucial cost factor was that of earth stations and equipment. Once installed and given the growing market, the costs of transmission have declined.[4] New developments such as the word processor are replacing traditional data-entry work as documents are being prepared directly in electronic form. In conjunction with the development of satellite transmission, this will broaden the range of possibilities.

The cost of labor is clearly a key factor in this decentralization. Currently Barbados and Jamaica are two desirable locations for overseas office work because of overall high literacy and English-speaking populations. In the early 1980s employees earned about $1.50 an hour for work which in the States pays from $4 to $12 an hour. Within the U.S., the suburban labor market may also assume increasing importance for less routine tasks because of the large number of highly educated women who, due to child-care responsibilities, may be unwilling or unable to hold a full-time job outside the home. The push to get individuals to buy computers for personal use acquires added meaning: garment homeworkers provide their own sewing machines and the clerical homeworkers their own computers.

Another factor that needs to be considered is that the international flow of these types of items fits into the expanding trade in services generally. No tariffs are levied against international flows of computer data. The U.S. government has for years tried to prevent other countries from levying such tariffs. There is great resistance to such tariffs at various levels, from U.S. Congress formulations regulating international trade in services to GATT negotiations aimed at ensuring and maximizing the free flow of services (U.S. Senate, 1982). In this context it is interesting to note that services are the most rapidly growing American export (DiLullo, 1981).[5]

As happened with manufacturing plants, governments from various countries are trying to draw firms to locate offshore service facilities. These governments are providing subsidies to draw investors, including the training of workers for the facilities. For example, the government in Barbados has subsidized the training of employees for a U.S. data firm. The facility is located in a factory building, it is referred to as a factory and it is run as a factory.

A third area that has contributed to the expansion of centralized management and control operations is the move by large corporations into the retailing of consumer services. The globalization of markets and production together with product diversification demand the investment of greater resources in planning and marketing to reach the consumer. Advertising and consumer finance have become increasingly important components in the final product or service. The possibility of economies of scale in the delivery of such services and the expanding market for such services have led large corporations to produce for the open market consumer services that were usually produced only by small entrepreneurs. This has brought about what Levitt (1976) has called the "industrialization of service."

Standardization and economies of scale in production and delivery of services are predicated upon shifting certain components away from the actual service delivery establishments and to headquarters. These come to centralize planning, development, franchising, purchasing and other such functions. The result has been a growth of large new firms or divisions within firms engaged in service delivery via multiple retail outlets and centralization of specialized functions. This fragmentation of the work process, parallel to that in manufacturing, is evident in hotels, restaurants, various kinds of repair services, movie theaters, car rental, and photo development agencies, retail outlets for a broad range of consumer goods, from food to flowers, and a vast array of other service activities which used to be largely the domain of small, local entrepreneurs.

A fourth factor that has contributed to the expansion of centralized management and control operations and the advanced services sector is the very size of corporations. The large national or transnational corporations have been key agents in the restructuring of economic activity. The increasing size and product diversification of the large corporation in turn have intensified the importance of planning, marketing, internal administration and distribution, and other such activities. The organization of production on a global scale with a large number of plants or service outlets requires a vast expansion of the control and management apparatus. This has generated a large demand for highly specialized services produced both within the corporation's headquarters and bought from outside firms.

The decentralization of manufacturing and of office work, the move of large corporations into the retailing of consumer services, and the growing size and product diversification of large corporations have all intensified the role of management and control operations and of the advanced services in economic activity generally. The technological transformation of the work process has made possible and in turn been further induced by these developments.

In theory, the decentralization of production units can represent more than one type of ownership organization. Indeed, subcontracting has expanded greatly, both domestically and internationally. And there has been a significant growth of small, highly specialized firms in services and manufacturing associated with new production technologies and new products. There even were predictions that the shift to a service economy would reduce the average size of firms and the influence of large firms over the economy (Fuchs, 1968). But ultimately it is a limited number of corporations which control a large share of production and increasingly of service delivery as well. The decentralization of economic activity and the associated global labor force create new requirements in terms of planning, organization, distribution, marketing, and finance. The result is an expanding central apparatus needed for the control, management, and servicing of the decentralized production process and the global labor force. This operates both at the micro level of individual corporations and at the macro level of the system, that is, in the realm where the state intervenes to regulate and organize the increasingly complex system that has a local, national, and international arena of operation. All of these feed into the importance and expansion of centralized management and control operations.

Correspondingly, there has been a growing demand on the part of the various agents, from governments to corporations, for highly specialized services which have become a key input.[6] The development of the advanced services has further reinforced these various trends which in turn have generated a growing need for this input. The changing structure of production affects the demand and supply of various services (Caves, 1980), a fact that has not received sufficient attention in statements on the shift to a service economy. In the current phase, the need for a vast apparatus for control and management of the global political-economic system has transformed the shape of the service sector. Once only a support structure, today the producer services have become a sort of new basic industry.[7]

The evidence, though inadequate, is quite useful in documenting some of the issues of concern here. The evidence points to the growth and locational concentration of economic activities that generate key inputs for firms, particularly large corporations (U.S. Bureau of the Census, 1976a; 1981a; Singelmann, 1978; Stanback and Noyelle, 1982). The evidence also shows the pronounced growth in the export of such inputs and how these exports are associated with the growth of an off-shore manufacturing sector (U.S. Department of Commerce,

1980a; Economic Consulting Services, 1981; DiLullo, 1981). There is also evidence showing that a few core cities produce such inputs for export to other domestic areas (Conservation of Human Resources, 1977; Drennan, 1983; Cohen, 1981; Stanback *et al.*, 1981).

The concentration of these activities in major cities and the corresponding internationalization in the economic base of such cities has brought about a pronounced reorganization in the capital–labor relation. The manufacturing sector, once the economic base and key export sector in major cities, no longer shapes the organization of this relation. One indication of this reorganization is the increasing polarization in the occupational and income distribution of the labor force. The evidence shows a sharp expansion in a stratum of very high-income workers, including as a key component what I call the new cadres in control, management and servicing operations. Secondly, it shows a shrinking of middle-income workers, a function of the expulsion from the production process of a wide range of white and blue-collar middle-income jobs. And thirdly, the evidence points to a vast expansion in the supply of low-wage jobs, a function not only of declining sectors – as is often believed – but primarily of growth sectors.

First I will discuss the evidence pointing to the emergence of major cities as sites for the production and export of producer services and management and control operations. Next, I will discuss the evidence on the restructuring of the job supply and work process as an indicator of the reorganization of the capital–labor relation.

## CAPITAL: THE PRODUCTION OF GLOBAL CONTROL CAPABILITY

The industrial recomposition in the economic base of major cities is not simply a function of the general shift from a manufacturing to a service economy. Thus, while all cities contain a core of service industries, location quotients for different size Standard Metropolitan Statistical Areas (henceforth SMSAs) clearly show the largest to have a disproportionate concentration of certain types of service industries, such as producer and distributive services.[8] These two account for a third of the GNP and are, together with nonprofit services, the fastest growing sector in the economy (Stanback *et al.*, 1981; Conservation of Human Resources, 1977). Secondly, the production of services for export to the world market is disproportionately concentrated in a few major cities (Drennan, 1983; Cohen, 1981; Sassen-Koob, 1984b), at a time when services are the fastest growing and largest U.S. export (DiLullo, 1981).

Though inadequate, there are various types of information that can be used to document the new economic base in major core cities and the fact that it is distinguishable from that of other core cities. I will use evidence on the characteristics of production and locational patterns of various industries, particularly the producer services, a key input for the global control and management capability of capital. Secondly, I will discuss the evidence on the internationalization of the economic base in these cities, particularly in the service sector. This can be done using data on the export of services, the locational concentration of large corporations with high export activity, and the levels and locational concentration of foreign investment.

In a classification of the 140 largest SMSAs for 1976, Stanback and Noyelle (1982: 20–26) found a distinct relation between size and functional specialization. Of the 16 largest SMSAs (population over 2 million), 12 were centers for the production and export of producer and distributive services and the other 4 were government and educational centers. Of those 12, 4 were global centers and the remaining 8 were regional. Furthermore, controlling for type of service export, the authors found a direct relation between size and type of service export. The larger the SMSA, the greater the weight of producer services compared with distributive services. It should be noted that the larger SMSAs were once predominantly centers for the production and export of manufactures.

On the other hand, the group of smaller SMSAs (population under one million) had the highest single concentration of "production centers," mostly in manufacturing. Indeed, the authors found that comparing the location quotient of manufacturing in the smaller SMSAs for 1976 with 1959, the importance of manufacturing had increased. This was sharpest in SMSAs with populations under 250,000 where the manufacturing quotient went from 92.8 in 1959 to 113.0 in 1976. In contrast, in the largest SMSAs this quotient went from 99.0 in 1959 to 90.5 in 1976. In terms of employment shares, the share of manufacturing rises as the size of the SMSA declines. However, the share of the "corporate headquarters complex" declines with size, ranging from 20 percent in the largest SMSAs to 8.7 percent in the smallest.

The ascendance of the producer services in economic activity generally and the development of the modern corporation make a distinction between local, regional and global service firms increasingly important. Thus, the 8.7 percent employment share in the "corporate headquarters complex" in the smallest SMSAs most probably describes regional or local market firms. I find the term "corporate headquarters complex" (cf. Conservation of Human Resources, 1977) inadequate when dealing with such a wide range of sizes in the SMSAs. Any city has legal, accounting and banking services. But only a few major service firms are global in their operation and derive a significant share of their earnings from the export of their services. These firms also handle the business for most of the large corporations and they are concentrated in major cities.

The locational concentration of these growth sectors is particularly significant if we consider that the overall share of services in GNP has hardly grown, rising by only 12 percent from 1948 to 1977, from 54 to 66 percent. Indeed, except for producer, nonprofit and distributive services, the GNP shares of all other service categories had declined (Singelmann, 1978; Stanback et al., 1981). In terms of employment shares, producer and nonprofit services doubled their shares of employment while that of consumer services had declined. The outcome of this is that the production of services as final outputs, notably consumer services, is actually declining. Consequently the production of services as intermediate outputs, i.e., producer and distributive services is increasing (Denison, 1979; Stanback et al., 1981; Singelmann, 1978; Myers, 1980). This shift from final consumer to intermediate services is another indicator of the restructuring.

The locational concentration of producer services is in part explained by the characteristics of production of these services. These characteristics, in conjunction with the ascendance of such services in economic activity generally, both domestically and worldwide, are helpful in explaining the centralization of management and servicing functions that have fed the economic boom in global cities like New York and Los Angeles. Producer services, unlike other types of services, are mostly not dependent on vicinity to the buyers. Hence concentration of production in suitable locations and export, both domestically and abroad, are feasible. Agglomeration economies induce locational concentration in producer services. Production of these services benefits from proximity to other services, particularly when there is a wide array of specialized firms. Agglomeration economies occur to such firms when they locate close to others which may be sellers of key inputs or necessary for joint production of certain service offerings (Stanback and Noyelle, 1982: 17–18). This would contribute to explain why, while New York City continued to lose corporate headquarters throughout the decade, the number and employment of firms servicing such headquarters kept growing rapidly (Conservation of Human Resources, 1977; Cohen, 1981). Another kind of agglomeration economy consists in the amenities and lifestyles that large urban centers can offer the high-income personnel employed in the producer services. In brief, independence of proximity to buyers in combination with the existence of agglomeration economies makes feasible concentration of production in suitable locations and export to other areas domestically and abroad. As a result we see the development of global centers, e.g., New York and Los Angeles, and of regional centers, e.g., Denver and Houston, for the production of such services.

Whether the production of these services is internalized by a firm or bought on the market depends on a number of factors. The available evidence shows that the freestanding producer services industry is growing fast and accounts for a significant share of GNP. Thus we know that a large share of these inputs are bought. In what has become a classic on the services industry, Stigler (1951) posited that the growing size of markets would increase both specialization and the realization of economies of scale on the production of such services. Stanback *et al.* (1981) note that Stigler failed to see that specialization preceded the possibility of realizing economies of scale. The increasing specialization of service functions which arose first within the large firm indicated to entrepreneurs that there was a market for these services, whence we see the development of a specialized producer services industry. Greenfield (1966) argues that specialization, rather than economies of scale, is the key factor pushing towards externalization. Eventually, a large demand reduces the price of such producer services and extends the market of such services also to small firms which otherwise would have been unable to buy them. This in turn further expands the specialized services industry largely concentrated in major cities. The development of such a market entails a specialization of inputs in the production of services and a standardization of outputs – that is, these services can be sold to a large number of firms. The specialization of inputs explains why there is a freestanding market of such services with a large number of small firms. The standardization of outputs with its corresponding expansion of the market points to the possibility of large corporations also moving into this market, as they did with consumer services. This would entail a shift of highly specialized functions to headquarters and the downgrading of what are now producer services firms to outlets for the sale of such services. But at the current stage, it is the high specialization of the inputs which explains the externalization of these types of production on the part of large corporations, a trend that is currently still in a growth phase.

The same characteristics in the production of advanced services that facilitate locational concentration also make possible their production for export. There has been a massive increase in the international trade of such services and in direct foreign investment in services – another form of the export of such services. The data illustrate major patterns. At the national level, the 1980 U.S. international trade balance recorded a $21 billion surplus in the service account. From 1970 to 1980, service exports increased at an average annual rate of 19 percent to $121 billion in 1980, making it "a decade of unprecedented expansion in these transactions" (DiLullo, 1981: 29; U.S. Senate, 1982; see note 5). Direct foreign investment in services also has increased significantly, reaching 28.4 percent of all such investment by 1981 (Whichard, 1981b). For example, the top 14 American accounting firms had 746 affiliates in developing countries by 1978 compared with 895 domestic offices (Economic Consulting Services, Inc., 1981). It is important to distinguish among the various categories included in the account. For example, receipts of income on American investment abroad increased at a faster rate than receipts for other services: they grew from $8.2 billion in 1970 to $36.8 billion in 1980 (DiLullo, 1981: 42). Though more slowly, many of these other services, such as technical and consulting services have also grown as a result of the increase in American direct foreign investment abroad (U.S. Department of Commerce, 1980a). Such investments are one component in the decentralization of manufacturing and ancillary services. The appropriation of the returns on these investments, on the other hand, contributes to activities feeding the centralization of global management and advanced servicing.

Data on individual service industries provide another indicator of the sale of services abroad. The earnings from such sales were found to be rather high for ten major industries in a U.S. Department of

Commerce study (1980a). For example, for the top 83 advertising firms in the U.S., gross income from sales abroad represented 37.6 percent of their total income in 1980; for the top ten this share was 51.7 percent (Economic Consulting Services, Inc., 1981: 85). The top eight American accounting firms earned 40 percent of their income from sales abroad in 1977, and in 1978 the two largest derived over half their revenues from such sales (U.S. Department of Commerce, 1980a: 13–15).

Banking, a key service industry, has expanded its international operations at an accelerated pace over the last few years. From 1971 to 1981 foreign branch assets of U.S. banks increased sixfold, from $55.1 billion to $320 billion. A United Nations Centre on Transnational Corporations Study (1981) found that transnational banks of six countries accounted for 76 percent of the assets of all such banks in 1978. U.S. banks held the leading position. And within the U.S., New York City and Los Angeles are the two major financial centers.

The functional specialization within the early factories finds a contemporary counterpart in the pronounced spatial and organizational fragmentation of the work process with its corresponding need for increased centralization and complexity of management, control and planning. The development of the modern corporation and its massive participation in world markets and foreign countries has made planning, internal administration, product development and research increasingly complex and important. Diversification of product lines, mergers, transnationalization of economic activities, all require highly specialized skills and have increased the importance of elaborate organizational structures (Chandler, 1977). What were once support resources for major corporations have today become key inputs in corporate decision making (Cohen, 1981). The decentralization of manufacturing and of office work has brought about the need for new types of planning in production and distribution, new types of control over financial and international information as well as the need to regulate and control a highly diversified and geographically dispersed workforce.

## LABOR: ECONOMIC RESTRUCTURING AS CLASS POLARIZATION

This structure of economic activity has brought about changes in the organization of work and in labor demand. These are reflected in a

Table 5.1 *Distribution of employment among earnings classes for each industry and for total United States, 1975 (percentages)*

| | Earnings classes[a] | | | | |
|---|---|---|---|---|---|
| | 1.60 and above | 1.60 to 1.20 | 1.20 to 0.80 | 0.80 to 0.40 | 0.40 and below |
| All industry (total U.S.)[b] | 12.0 | 22.2 | 27.8 | 28.4 | 9.6 |
| Construction | 2.5 | 17.2 | 61.1 | 18.8 | 0.3 |
| Manufacturing | 20.4 | 17.4 | 45.0 | 17.2 | — |
| Distributive services | 32.2 | 27.8 | 30.3 | 9.3 | 0.4 |
| TCU | 20.9 | 41.0 | 36.1 | 2.0 | — |
| Wholesale | 48.5 | 8.8 | 21.9 | 19.8 | 1.0 |
| Retail | — | 7.1 | 32.9 | 57.1 | 2.9 |
| Producer services | 13.5 | 38.0 | 2.8 | 45.7 | — |
| Fire | 5.2 | 46.0 | 2.3 | 46.5 | — |
| Corporate services | 24.6 | 27.3 | 3.4 | 44.7 | — |
| Consumer services | — | 4.1 | 13.7 | 16.8 | 65.4 |
| Nonprofit services | 6.8 | 34.1 | 10.7 | 48.4 | — |
| Health | 17.3 | 2.3 | 24.2 | 56.3 | — |
| Education | — | 54.6 | 2.1 | 43.3 | — |
| Public administration | 22.1 | 50.6 | 20.9 | 6.4 | — |

[a]Earnings class intervals make use of earning indexes in which the index of the 1975 average earnings for all industry is equal to 1.0
[b]Each line adds up to 100 percent
Source: Thomas M. Stanback, Jr. and Thierry Noyelle, *Cities in Transition.* Totowa, N.J.: Allanheld, Osmun Publishers, 1982; Based on U.S. Bureau of Labor Statistics, *Survey of Income and Education,* 1976

pronounced change in the job supply with a strong polarization in the income and occupational distribution. Decentralization has reduced the supply of middle-income jobs in major cities while centralization activities have generated expansion of very high income and low-wage jobs (see Table 5.1).

There are significant differences in the occupational and earnings distributions of industries. Some, like the distributive services, have a preponderance of medium- and high-income jobs while others, like retailing, are heavily weighted towards low-income jobs.

Three trends come to the fore in examining the available evidence on occupational and earnings characteristics by industry. First, in view of the major shift to services, it is important to note the differences among individual service industries. For example, while professional workers account for 36 percent of jobs in nonprofit services, they account for only 3.3 percent in distributive services and

1 percent in retailing. And while service workers account for only 1 percent of jobs in wholesale trade, they account for 12 percent in corporate services and 44 percent in consumer services.

Secondly, earnings vary not only according to occupation but also according to industry for a given occupation (U.S. Bureau of the Census, 1976c). The differences in average earnings among industries can only be partly explained by differences in the occupational mix of each of these industries. A ranking of average earnings in each of the occupations for the major industrial groups shows considerable variation. In professional occupations the index varied from 2.02 in manufacturing and 2.11 in producer services to 1.28 in education. The national average for professional occupations was 1.62 in 1975. Among service workers, for example, the index varied from 0.33 in manufacturing, 0.59 in producer services and 0.90 in Transport, Communications and Utilities.

Thirdly, the overall result of a different occupational mix and different average earnings for occupations in different industries provides an earnings profile for each industry. Some industries, notably consumer services and retailing, are low-paying industries: they have low average pay across occupations and a high incidence of low-paid occupations. Distributive services and public administration, on the other hand, have few poorly paid jobs. Among producer and nonprofit services there is a polarization with concentrations in both well and poorly paid jobs and occupations. Stanback and Noyelle (1982) ranked the average annual earnings for each industry and occupational subgroup and found distributive services, manufacturing and public administration to have the highest average rank. The producer services ranked somewhere in the middle while consumer services and retailing were the lowest. The data on earnings classes show a very high incidence of the next to lowest earnings class in all services, except distributive services and public administration. Almost half of all workers in the producer services were in this earnings class, compared with 17 percent of manufacturing and 18.8 percent of construction workers. The other half of workers in producer services are in the two highest earnings classes. On the other hand, half of all construction and manufacturing workers are in the middle earnings class compared with 2.8 percent of workers in the producer services. The highest single concentrations in the top earnings class are in wholesale and in corporate services. Stanback and Noyelle (1982: 33) find that "for the services as a

Table 5.2 *Distribution of total U.S. labor force among earnings classes, 1970 and 1980*[a]

| Earnings classes[b] | Distribution of total U.S. labor force (%) | | | | | |
| | 1970 | | | 1980 | | |
| | Total | Female | Male | Total | Female | Male |
|---|---|---|---|---|---|---|
| 1.60 and above | 11.3 ⎫ 32.2 | 7.5 | 9.4 | 12.9 ⎫ 37.1 | 4.8 | 11.0 |
| 1.59 to 1.30 | 20.9 ⎭ | 18.6 | 18.9 | 24.2 ⎭ | 14.5 | 20.7 |
| 1.29 to 1.00 | 18.9 ⎫ 35.8 | 21.5 | 23.1 | 12.8 ⎫ 24.5 | 12.8 | 15.6 |
| 0.99 to 0.70 | 16.9 ⎭ | 10.5 | 14.3 | 11.7 ⎭ | 15.8 | 17.0 |
| 0.69 to 0.40 | 22.8 ⎫ 32.0 | 13.5 | 15.4 | 25.2 ⎫ 38.5 | 16.7 | 11.8 |
| 0.39 and below | 9.2 ⎭ | 28.4 | 19.0 | 13.3 ⎭ | 35.4 | 23.9 |

[a] Civilian workers 14 years and over by total money earnings
[b] Earnings classes are derived from the application of 1975 average earnings for each major occupation within each industry group. A basic assumption is that the relative income at 1975 levels for each occupational-industrial subgroup is constant – in this case from 1970 to 1980. I followed the method used by Stanback and Noyelle (1982) in their comparison of 1960 and 1975 earnings for industry-occupational cells. The total earnings distribution obtained is then divided into sixtiles. The major industry groups are Manufacturing, Construction, Distributive Services, Retail, Producer Services, Consumer Services, Nonprofit Services (Health and Education), Public Administration. Not included are Agriculture, Fisheries and Mining. The major occupational groups are Professional, Technical, Manager, Office Clerical, Nonoffice Clerical, Sales, Craft Workers, Operatives, Service Workers, Laborers.
Source: Based on U.S. Bureau of the Census, 1982. *Money Income of Households, Families and Persons in the United States: 1980.* (Current Population Reports: Series P-60, No. 132); and U.S. Bureau of the Census, 1972, *Money Income of Households, Families and Persons in the United States: 1970*

whole, the important observation is that there tend to be heavy concentrations of employment in better-than-average and in poorer-than-average jobs. In contrast, in manufacturing and construction the distributions are more heavily weighted toward medium and above-average income jobs."

The different occupational and earnings distributions of industries in conjunction with the changes in the industrial mix of the economy express themselves in a growing income polarization among workers over the last decade. Comparing the distribution of earnings for 1970 and 1980 on the basis of Census data, I found a significant reduction in the two middle earnings classes (see Table 5.2). The share of national income of the two highest earnings classes increased from 32 percent to 37 percent, that of the two middle classes was reduced from 35.8 to 24.5 percent and that of the two lowest earnings classes increased from 32 to 38.5 percent.

Several trends that contribute to an additional expansion in the supply of low-wage jobs particularly in global cities, bring about greater income polarization. First, the existence of a critical mass of very high-income workers provides the conditions for a rapidly expanding process of high-income residential and commercial "gentrification." This entails not only a physical upgrading, but also a reorganization of the consumption structure, both of which generate a demand for low-wage workers. Many components of high-income gentrification are labor intensive: residential building attendants, workers producing services or goods for specialty and gourmet food shops, dog walkers, errand runners, cleaners of all sorts, and so on. The demand for low-wage workers to service the high-income lifestyles of the rapidly expanding top-level workforce is one key factor in the expansion of an informal sector in cities like New York and Los Angeles. Part of the goods and services produced in the informal sector circulate through the modern sector of the economy that caters to these high-income lifestyles. It would explain why the expansion of an informal sector is most developed in major urban centers experiencing very dynamic growth and not in cities like Detroit.

Second, there has been an expansion of low-wage jobs in the manufacturing sector as a result of (a) the social reorganization of the work process, notably the expansion of sweatshops and industrial homework; (b) the technological transformation of the work process that has downgraded a variety of jobs; and (c) the rapid growth of high-technology industries which are characterized by a large share of low-wage production jobs. These three trends have resulted in what I call a downgraded manufacturing sector. It is important to note that the *downgrading* of the manufacturing sector is part of major *growth* trends: the development of high-tech industries, the technological transformation of the work process (which has also upgraded a large array of jobs), and the growth of an informal sector that contains a large number of sweatshops. Sweatshop work and electronics production are often considered to be two very different if not opposing developments, one representing backwardness and the other modernity. Yet both have a similar outcome: an expansion in the supply of dead-end low-wage jobs. Furthermore, they entail a "disenfranchisement" of workers, notably the drop in levels of unionization most visible in areas with rapid growth in high-tech industries such as Los Angeles and Orange counties. Finally, the expansion of sweatshops and industrial homework is not only associated with the garment industry (Waldinger, 1983). It is occurring in electronics as well (New York State Department of

Labor, 1982a, 1982b; Sassen-Koob and Benamou, 1985; Solorzano, 1983).

The politicization of the traditional low-wage labor supplies during the 1960s and early 1970s and the above-average wage levels typical of major urban centers such as New York and Los Angeles acquire added significance in the context of (a) their expanded role as centers for the management and servicing of the global economy, and (b) the increase in the supply of low-wage jobs resulting from major growth trends. This was not simply class struggle as usual. It was class struggle in a moment of major restructuring and concentration of key economic sectors.

The large influx of immigrants from low-wage countries over the last fifteen years which reached massive levels in the second half of the 1970s cannot be understood apart from this restructuring. It is a mistake to view this new immigration phase as a result mostly of the new legislation and as being absorbed primarily in declining sectors of the economy. The expansion in the supply of low-wage jobs generated by major growth sectors is one of the key factors in the *continuation* at ever higher levels of the current immigration. It reinforces the emigration impact of economic restructuring occurring in sending countries (see Chapter 4).

New York and Los Angeles, two major arenas for the consolidation of these trends, contain a disproportionate share of the new immigrants compared with their share of the native population. They have the largest Hispanic population, including Mexicans and Puerto Ricans, of all SMSAs. The latter are, furthermore, much larger than the Hispanic populations that follow in size. Chicago and Miami each have about 580,000 Hispanics compared with 2 million in Los Angeles and 1.4 million in New York. These two cities, together with San Francisco contain the vast majority of Asians. And New York City is the leading recipient of West Indians.

The next two sections focus on these two cities for the empirical elaboration of the various trends described.

NEW YORK CITY AND LOS ANGELES: RESTRUCTURED
ECONOMY AND NEW LABOR DEMAND

The configuration of decentralized manufacturing, technological transformation of the work process and centralization of global servicing and management contains major growth trends that have fed the economic boom in New York City and Los Angeles, as well as a number of other major urban centers. These growth trends have given that boom a distinct content that makes these urban centers increasingly similar: the vast expansion of their role as centers for the production of advanced services and management control, with a growing presence of foreign investors in both of these activities.

Yet, according to other criteria, these were two very different cities in the 1970s, one representing the declining Frostbelt and the other the rising Sunbelt; one characterized by high-technology industries and the other by a backward and rapidly declining garment industry; one known for its modernity and newness and the other for its obsolete and decaying infrastructure; one with declining overall employment levels throughout the 1970s and the other with an explosion in overall employment.

I will argue that the sharp differences characterizing these two cities have a similar outcome in terms of the socioeconomic structure of the job supply, notably an expansion in the supply of very high-income jobs, a shrinking of traditional middle-income, blue- and white-collar jobs and an expansion of low-wage jobs. I will argue that this outcome is not accidental, but is, on the contrary, an expression of systematic patterns that transcend certain domestic configurations, such as Frostbelt and Sunbelt, and that have to do with a basic restructuring at the national and global levels. That is to say, the same basic processes that feed major growth trends in the U.S. economy, also feed decline trends. The massive expansion in the supply of low-wage jobs is as much a function of growth trends as is the large expansion in the supply of very high-income professional and technical jobs.

It becomes important, then, to elaborate on the pronounced differences between New York City and Los Angeles before examining the similarity in the restructuring of the job supply.

There is a vast amount of evidence that shows a relentless decline in old world centers in the 1970s: reduction in absolute employment levels and in population size, growth of inner-city poverty, an old and inefficient building stock and a severely decaying infrastructure. In this context, major growth trends in such cities pose problems analytically because we have inherited a conceptual framework for the evaluation of these data that is rooted in a past phase of the development of major centers. The fact that New York City clearly had a boom of some sort as suggested by massive high-income gentrification and large-scale construction in the 1980s emerges as a paradox.

Table 5.3 *New York City wage and salary employment by major industry, 1960–1984 (in thousands)*

|  | 1960 | 1970 | 1977 | 1980 | 1984 |
|---|---|---|---|---|---|
| Manufacturing | 946.8 | 766.2 | 538.6 | 498.7 | 429.6 |
| Construction | 126.9 | 110.1 | 64.2 | 74.7 | 94.5 |
| Transportation, communications and public utilities | 318.1 | 323.3 | 258.2 | 257.2 | 237.0 |
| Wholesale and retail trade | 744.8 | 735.4 | 620.1 | 614.9 | 630.5 |
| Finance, insurance and real estate | 384.4 | 458.2 | 414.4 | 445.8 | 500.5 |
| Services and miscellaneous | 609.2 | 787.3 | 784.6 | 890.4 | 1,005.8 |
| Government | 408.2 | 562.8 | 507.8 | 516.6 | 535.6 |
| Total | 3538.4 | 3743.3 | 3187.9 | 3298.3 | 3,434.9 |

*Source:* The Port Authority of New York and New Jersey, *Regional Perspectives: The Regional Economy 1981 Review, 1982 Outlook,* 1982, p. 18 and the City of New York, Office of Management and Budget and Office of Economic Development, *Report on Economic Conditions in New York City, July–December, 1984,* 1985.

The massive expansion of Caribbean Basin and Asian immigration to New York City occurred in a context of large losses of factory and office jobs in the entire Northern and Northeastern region. New York City was disproportionately affected by the exodus of jobs abroad and to the Sunbelt. The aggregate data for New York City from 1970 to 1980 show major decline trends: a decline in the absolute level of employment from 3.7 to 3.3 million, a 35 percent loss in manufacturing jobs, a 41 percent loss of headquarters' office jobs, a 15 percent overall decline in office jobs, and the departure of a significant share of corporate headquarters. We can include in this list the decay in the infrastructure and the fiscal crisis. Furthermore, there were particularly large job losses in sectors of the economy likely to employ immigrants. Netzer (1974) estimated that between 1968 and 1972, New York City lost 334,000 goods handling jobs and 99,000 retail and consumer services jobs. Between 1969 and 1977, Manhattan's central business district alone had a 30 percent decline in factory employment, down from 570,000 to 400,000 (Tobier, 1979: 15–16). Table 5.3 provides general information on New York City's employment distribution over the last two decades.

Los Angeles presents at first glance a strikingly different situation. It had one of the nation's highest growth rates in manufacturing employment during the 1970s to the point that the greater Los Angeles area, including Los Angeles, Orange, San Bernardino, Riverside and Ventura Counties, has become one of the largest metropolitan industrial regions in the world (Soja, Morales, Wolff, 1983). Between 1970 and 1980 when New York City lost over a third of a million manufacturing jobs, the Los Angeles region added 225,000. This represents, furthermore, a significant share of the total net national increase of one million manufacturing jobs from 1970 to 1980. Orange County alone, one of the highest growth poles in the Los Angeles region, had reached a total manufacturing employment of 255,000 by 1980, a figure higher than Houston's 251,600 for that same year (*California Business*, September 1982). Again, unlike New York City, where total population and total employment declined in the decade from 1970 to 1980, in Los Angeles population grew by 1.3 million and employment by 1.3 million as well.

Furthermore, the particular content of the major growth sectors in manufacturing in Los Angeles – high-technology industries – could hardly contrast more with New York City's manufacturing base, the relentlessly backward garment industry. The aerospace and electronics industries, the high-tech core in the region, represent the largest such concentration in the country and perhaps in the world. In the decade of the seventies this cluster grew by 50 percent. Employment growth in high-tech industries has been larger than total growth of manufacturing employment in other major Sunbelt cities. Total employment in electronics in the Los Angeles region is higher than in the leading high-tech center in the country, Silicon Valley in Santa Clara County. The Los Angeles region has increased its share of total U.S. employment in all these industries except for aircraft and parts where it declined from 22 to 19 percent.

Finally, the infrastructure of both these cities contrasts sharply, perhaps epitomized by Los Angeles' post-World War II highway system and New York City's pre-World War II subway system. The typical New York City industrial structure – the loft building – is generally considered obsolete and one of the reasons that New York City's industrial base will not recover from its collapse. Los Angeles has a sprawling modern factory complex that extends into the whole region and is spatially organized into different industrial centers. The possibilities of expansion are such that the Los Angeles region is fast becoming the largest industrial center in the world. To this should be added nearby San Diego County with its 62 percent growth in manufacturing over the last few years and massive projects of industrial parks under construction for both American and foreign companies.[9]

When we disaggregate some of the economic data for these two cities, we find major growth sectors amidst New York City's massive decline trends and major declines amidst Los Angeles massive growth trends.[10] While overall employment and population in New York City declined in absolute terms, there was a 17 percent increase in employment in the nine major white collar industries. Similarly, while overall figures in manufacturing generally and garments particularly declined, there has in fact been a major expansion in manufacturing jobs but mostly in forms of organization of work that are not easily recorded in official figures, notably sweatshops and industrial homework, including homework in electronics.

On the other hand, Los Angeles has experienced a massive decline in its older, established industries, notable the automobile industry, once second only to Detroit, rubber tires and a cluster of industries associated with the automobile industry (California, 1981b, c; n.d.; 1983). But it also has had decline in aircraft and parts. There has been an associated rapid decline in the share of unionized workers which had fallen to 19 percent by 1980. Interestingly, the sharpest decline, down to 13 percent, occurred in Orange County which also had the sharpest increase in high-tech industries (Soja, Morales, Wolff, 1983). An examination of the job supply in high-tech industries shows a massive expansion in low-wage assembly line jobs, mostly not unionized and held by immigrant or native minority women. Finally, well over a third of the net addition of jobs from 1970 to 1980 was in garments. Both in garments and electronics, sweatshop and industrial homework have expanded massively. I will return to all these issues in detail.

When we examine the effects on the job supply of these very different configurations represented by New York City and Los Angeles, what emerges most strongly are two trends that point to fundamental similarities in the restructuring of labor demand, the issue of primary importance to my analysis. First, there has been a pronounced expansion in the supply of high-income professional and technical jobs associated with the growth of the advanced services and headquarters complex in both cities, further fed, in the case of Los Angeles, by research staff in high-tech industries.[11] Besides the increase of such jobs associated with the growth of these sectors, the technological transformation of the work process has upgraded a vast array of what used to be middle or lower-middle income jobs. Second, there has been a pronounced expansion of low-wage jobs associated with the recomposition of industry, an outcome of (a) the technological transformation of the work process which has, besides upgrading, also downgraded a vast array of jobs through the transfer of skills into machines (b) changes in the industrial mix, notably the decline of older established manufacturing industries in Los Angeles and the rise of high-tech industries, and (c) the transformation of the organization of the labor process, notably the shift of certain jobs from unionized shops to sweatshops or industrial homeworkers.[12]

The next section provides detailed information on economic restructuring in New York City and Los Angeles. The discussion is organized into two parts. The first part focuses on the expansion of the advanced services and headquarters complex; the second on the recomposition of the manufacturing sector.

ADVANCED SERVICES, DOWNGRADED MANUFACTURING, AND INFORMALIZATION

Disaggregated data on employment in New York City and Los Angeles reveal four kinds of trends which point to an economic base capable of generating a demand for an expanded immigrant work force. First, there has been a major expansion in the advanced services, particularly after 1976 (U.S. Bureau of Labor Statistics, 1981b). The functioning of this sector requires an infrastructure of low-wage jobs which often involve night and weekend shifts and are generally undesirable. Second, foreign investment in New York City and Los Angeles increased significantly after 1976 and played a central role in the growth and recovery of certain sectors of the New York City economy (Port Authority New York and New Jersey, 1981) and the major expansion of the Los Angeles economy. Third, the flight of manufacturing capital from New York City and the Northeast generally has not affected all components of labor-intensive industries equally. In fact, there has been an expansion of a downgraded manufacturing sector – that is, one where sweatshops and industrial homework are key forms of production. The increase in sweatshops and industrial homework has affected not only the garment industry, but also the toy, footwear and electronics industries (New York State Department of Labor, 1982a; 1982b; Sassen-Koob, 1984b). Fourth, the massive growth of high-tech industries in the Los Angeles region has generated a vast supply of low-wage assembly work and has spawned the growth of sweatshops and industrial homework even in the most advanced industries such as microprocessors. I will discuss these various trends in the next two sections, one dealing with the advanced services complex and the other with the downgraded manufacturing sector.

## The advanced services and headquarters complex

Less well known than the scale of New York City declines and losses is the scale of the growth trends. As was pointed out earlier, along with the major losses there were significant growth trends, notably an overall 17 percent increase in white-collar employment from 1977 to 1980. Within these industries, some had employment growth rates of over 50 percent (computer services) and others hovered around 20 to 30 percent (management consulting and public relations, engineering and architecture, accounting, protective services, securities, etc.) (U.S. Bureau of Labor Statistics 1982a).[13]

Two-fifths of the jobs in these industries are in the higher-pay, higher-status professional, technical, managerial, and administrative occupations (U.S. Bureau of Labor Statistics, 1980; 1981b). Between 1977 and 1980, employment increased by 7.7 percent in finance, insurance and real estate, by 9.4 percent in communications and media, and by 24.7 percent in business services. Also, employment expanded by 8.9 percent in educational services and research institutions, by 7.4 percent in entertainment, culture, and tourism, and by 3.9 percent in social services (U.S. Bureau of Labor Statistics, 1982a).

Data on employment growth in various service industries shed some light on the different economic evolution of a manufacturing center like Detroit and the "new" global centers like New York City and Los Angeles whose economies were once based on manufacturing. These data are inadequate as an index for industrial growth insofar as employment is an imprecise measure particularly when dealing with highly capital-intensive industries like some of the advanced services. The ratio between employment share and GNP share varies considerably from one service industry to another. Based on the analysis of Stanback *et al.* (1981), it would seem that the ratio of employment share to GNP share is 1:2 in the case of producer services, and almost the opposite in the case of consumer services. Secondly, some of these industries produce both final and intermediate outputs, e.g., banking. Contextual characteristics will make for significant differences in the weight of each. Thus, while New York

City and Los Angeles both have a large consumer banking sector by the mere fact of the size of the population, the greater weight in economic terms comes from the banking industry as a producer of intermediate outputs. This is less the case in Detroit. But these differences notwithstanding, the data show that employment growth in mostly producer services industries between 1977 and 1981 was 11.8 percent in Detroit, 20.1 percent in New York City and 30.4 percent in Los Angeles. The percentage of total workers employed in producer services industries in these cities in 1981 was 12.6 percent, 30.7 percent and 24.9 percent respectively (see tables 5.4 and 5.5).

These growth rates, together with the decline in office and manufacturing jobs, point to a recomposition of New York City's economy. In 1950, manufacturing supplied almost one job in three while services supplied one in seven. By 1980, these figures were reversed. There was a parallel loss of office jobs, particularly headquarters' *office* jobs which declined by 41 percent between 1969 (highest employment) and 1980 (Ehrenhalt, 1981: 46).

The banking and financial system, including foreign branches and companies located in the city, expanded massively (see Table 5.6). Foreign investments in banking increased, and in December 1981 International Banking Facilities were established. Of the 140 IBFs announced that month, 100 were in New York City. IBFs facilitate international transactions of domestic banks and branches of foreign banks by removing Federal Reserve regulations or reserve requirements and interest rate ceilings. IBFs which locate in New York City are also exempt from state and city taxes (City of New York, 1982: 18). We can expect a continuing growth in domestic and foreign banking operations in the city.

Another fact that underlines the coexistence of decline and growth trends in New York City is that while a large number of Fortune 500 firms moved their headquarters out of the city, those which remained showed higher growth, especially in international activity, than those which left. Profits of the 81 city-based firms on the list rose from 19 percent in 1978 of all Fortune 500 firms to 25 percent in 1980; in 1980, inflation adjusted profits of city-based firms rose 12.6 percent compared with a 4.6 percent decline for the Fortune 500 list as a whole (City of New York, 1982: 29). The absence of steel and automobile company headquarters in the city can account for only part of this difference.

Similar developments have taken place in Los Angeles. Once a

Table 5.4 *Employment growth rates in mostly producer service industries, New York City, Los Angeles, and Detroit, 1977–1981*

| SIC[a] | Industry | New York City | Los Angeles | Detroit |
|---|---|---|---|---|
| 60 | Banking | 20.9 | 44.6 | 4.1 |
| 61 | Credit agencies | 29.1 | 16.0 | 13.3 |
| 62 | Commodity brokers | 34.1 | 14.5 | −1.4 |
| 63 | Insurance carriers | 8.4 | 5.7 | −7.3 |
| 64 | Insurance agents | 21.8 | 24.7 | 13.7 |
| 65 | Real estate | 1.1 | 43.9 | −3.6 |
| 66 | Combined R.E. and insurance | 98.2 | −30.0 | −0.2 |
| 67 | Holding, investment office | 7.1 | 33.8 | — |
| 73 | Business services | 24.7 | 33.2 | −1.1 |
| 731 | Advertising | 17.3 | 12.6 | −17.8 |
| 737 | Computer and data processing | 65.4 | 41.2 | 88.2 |
| 81 | Legal services | 28.3 | 48.7 | 31.3 |
| 86 | Membership organizations | −0.1 | 13.8 | 4.7 |
| 89 | Miscellaneous business services | 38.0 | 64.7 | 20.2 |
| 891 | Engineering services | 65.0 | 75.5 | — |
| 892 | Research organizations | 13.2 | 29.8 | — |
| 893 | Accounting, auditing | 17.8 | 51.3 | — |
| *Average growth rates* | | *20.1* | *30.4* | *11.8* |

[a]Standard Industrial Classification
*Source:* **Based on U.S. Bureau of the Census,** *County Business Patterns, New York, 1977* (CBP-77-34); *County Business Patterns, New York, 1980* (CBP-80-34); *County Business Patterns, New York, 1981* (CBP-81-34); *County Business Patterns, California, 1977* (CBP-77-6); *County Business Patterns, California, 1980* (CBP-80-6); *County Business Patterns, California, 1981* (CBP-81-6); *County Business Patterns, Michigan, 1977* (CBP-77-24); *County Business Patterns, Michigan, 1980* (CBP-80-24); *County Business Patterns, Michigan, 1981* (CBP-81-24)

Table 5.5 *Employment share of producer services in all industries, New York City, Los Angeles, and Detroit, 1977 and 1981*

| | New York City | Los Angeles | Detroit |
|---|---|---|---|
| *1977* | | | |
| Employment share | 28.1% | 22.7% | 11.3% |
| Employment in all industries (n. in thousands) | (3,188) | (1,367) | (490) |
| *1981* | | | |
| Employment share | 30.7% | 24.9% | 12.6% |
| Employment in all industries (n. in thousands) | (3,340) | (1,398) | (395) |

*Note:* producer services include SIC 60–67, 73, 81, 86 and 89.
*Source:* **Based on U.S. Bureau of the Census,** *County Business Patterns* (Various Issues); *Advance Estimates of Social, Economic and Housing Characteristics, California* (1983); *Advance Estimates of Social, Economic and Housing Characteristics, New York* (1983); *Advance Estimates of Social, Economic and Housing Characteristics – Michigan* (1983); City of Detroit, Planning Department, *Annual Overall Economic Development Program Report and Program Projection* (1983)

Table 5.6 *Foreign-owned banks and other financial institutions, New York City, 1978–1980*

|  | Cumulative inventory | | | Change from 1978 to 1980 | |
|---|---|---|---|---|---|
|  | 1978 | 1979 | 1980 |  |  |
| Foreign banks | 68 | 77 | 81 | +13 | 20% |
| Foreign bank agencies | 54 | 61 | 62 | + 8 | 14% |
| Subtotal: combined foreign bank branches and agencies | 122 | 138 | 143 | +21 | 17% |
| Foreign-owned trust companies | 19 | 20 | 23 | + 4 | 19% |
| Total: bank branches, agencies and trust companies | 141 | 158 | 166 | +25 | 18% |
| Foreign-owned investment companies | 6 | 6 | 6 | — | — |

*Source:* New York State Department of Banking, Foreign Banks Division; The Port Authority of New York and New Jersey Planning and Development: Department of Regional Research Section

collection of suburbs, today it contains the second largest advanced services and headquarters complex in the country. As in New York City, foreign investment in key sectors of the city's economy as well as the internationalization of domestic firms have been important elements in this expansion. Foreign banks have expanded their operations sharply. Of the 78 foreign agents of international banks in California – second only to New York as an international banking center in the U.S. – 57 are based in Los Angeles. The largest presence is Asian, particularly Japanese. Four of the leading eight inter-national accounting firms (all British owned) are located in down-town Los Angeles. It is estimated that at least 21 of the 75 most valuable real estate properties are owned by foreign-based companies (*The Los Angeles Times*, April 25, 1982). Japanese and Canadian capital have interests in major hotels, insurance companies and other service-sector industries.

By 1980, the Los Angeles region was second only to the Greater New York Area in total deposits and savings in financial institutions. And although the difference is still significant, $294 versus $104 billion, the trend is toward a narrowing. Eleven of the twelve largest U.S. banks headquartered outside California have their sole Cal-ifornia office in Los Angeles.

Finally, by 1980 Los Angeles had increased its number of Fortune 500 firms to 21, still far behind New York City's 81 but a signifi-cant concentration nonetheless (*California Business*, 1982). The Los

Angeles region contains, furthermore, 60 percent of California's largest industrial firms (*The Los Angeles Times* Roster of leading California firms, May 18, 1982).

As in New York City, the major components of this growth are highly specialized professional firms such as law, engineering, and accounting concerns, as well as research, development, and services firms associated with high technology industries. Employment in finance, insurance and real estate grew by 47 percent in the decade, which is significantly higher than the 32 percent increase nationally. Even larger increases in employment were registered in various business services, especially in management, consulting, and public relations.

These major growth trends also were reflected in a sharp increase in construction activity. In the last two years there has been a massive expansion in construction, mostly of office buildings. Total construction activity in New York City was up 7.1 percent between 1980 and 1981, compared with 1.2 percent nationally (Port Authority, 1982: 14). In 1981, contracts awarded for office construction in Manhattan amounted to over $600 million in addition to $700 million in 1980. The demand for office space has been very strong in Manhattan: in 1981, for a third consecutive year, the amount of space that was pre-leased exceeded the current inventory of available space, a fact reflected in the 14 percent increase in the average rental price from 1981 to 1982 (Port Authority, 1982: 15–16).

In Los Angeles there was a 50 percent increase from 1972 to 1982 in high-rise office space, amounting to an addition of 30 million square feet. A similar boom has occurred in smaller scale office building space. An additional 20 million square feet of office space were under construction in 1982. There has been an associated jump in rental values, and though these are still well below those prevalent in Manhattan, they are among the highest in the country.

In both New York City and Los Angeles, foreign capital has played a central role in the office, hotel, and high-rise residential construction boom of the late 1970s. In Manhattan "much of the construction of the first hotels to be built in fifteen years . . . can be traced to the influence, direct and indirect, of investors, visitors, and new residents from abroad" (Goldmark, 1979). Furthermore, there has been a rapid increase in the number of foreign banks and in foreign purchases of major retail establishments, such as Saks Fifth Avenue in Manhattan. From 1978 to 1980, twenty-one new foreign bank branches and agencies were added in New York City. This represents an increase of 17 percent and brought the total number to 143 (see Table 5.6). Assets of all foreign banks and branches increased by 42.6 percent over that same period, going from $79.1 billion in 1978 to $112.8 billion by June 1980 (Drennan, 1983).

A central element of my argument is that major growth sectors in these cities' economies generate low-wage jobs that can conceivably employ immigrants because these jobs typically require low skill levels, minimal language proficiency, and often include undesirable night or weekend shifts. In other words, contrary to prevailing opinions it is not merely the declining sectors that are likely to generate types of jobs for which immigrants are a highly desirable labor force.

While it is easy to show that the growth of sweatshops results in an expansion of low-wage jobs, this is not the case with the advanced services and headquarters complex. To argue that the expansion of this sector, one of the most technologically advanced and requiring large shares of very highly trained personnel, has also generated a supply of semi- or unskilled, low-wage jobs goes against much accepted lore.

And yet, a detailed empirical examination of the major service industries shows a significant generation of low-wage jobs, with few if any skill and language requirements and no history of unionization – in brief, jobs that both demand the existence of and contribute to the expansion of an underclass.

Using the data from a New York State Department of Labor (1979; 1980) occupational survey of major service industries, I identified the full array of such jobs.[14] These data have many limitations. First, only establishments covered by New York State Unemployment Insurance are represented in the sample. Secondly, the sample was drawn in 1978, a time when the high growth trends in the advanced services had only begun after the financial crisis of the middle 1970s. Thirdly, the sample excludes restaurants, hospitals, and private households, all of which furnish low-wage jobs likely to attract immigrants. Fourthly, the subsample underestimates the availability of low-wage jobs because some jobs identified were too broad in terms of income range for inclusion in our low-wage subsample. Many of these jobs, such as cook or waiter/waitress, are held by immigrants. Finally, the sample's universe covered only one-third of all of New York City's officially counted jobs.

These data limitations notwithstanding, the results are suggestive (see Table 5.7). First, there is an abundance of low-wage unskilled or semiskilled service jobs lacking language proficiency requirements and mostly offering few if any advancement possibilities. Of all occupations in all the service industries covered by the sample, 16.7 percent were identified as low-wage jobs: of these, 10.8 percent were in finance, insurance and real estate; 23.9 percent were in business services, and 18.9 percent were in the remaining service industries. Secondly, the highest incidence of such jobs is found in one of the fastest-growing employment sectors in the city (and in the nation as a whole) – that is, business services.[15] General studies on the structure of the service sector show that, contrary to much that has been said, "the services are characterized by a larger proportion of workers at the lower end of the earnings scale . . ." than non-service employment (Stanback, 1979: 4).

The expansion of the advanced service sector also generates an increase in the category of very high-income workers whose life styles, in turn, generate a demand for low-wage workers. Many of these jobs fall outside any of the major industry counts, not so much because they may involve illegal immigrants, but because they are part of that expanding category usually referred to as "off-the-books jobs". The expansion of low-wage jobs that service the high-income lifestyles of the rapidly expanding top level workforce in the advanced services and other high-income occupations is a key factor in the expansion of an informal sector in cities like New York (Sassen-Koob, 1984b). Part of the goods and services produced in the underground economy circulate through the modern sector of the economy that caters to these high-income lifestyles: the preparation of specialty and gourmet foods, the production of decorative items and luxury clothing and other personal goods, various kinds of services for cleaning, repair, errand-running, etc. The demand generated in the modern sector of the economy, together with the downgrading of manufacturing, stimulate the expansion of an informal sector. This also explains why this type of configuration is most developed in major urban centers experiencing very dynamic growth and not in cities such as Detroit.

In sum, the existence of a major growth sector as is the advanced service sector generates low-wage jobs directly, through the structure of the work process, and indirectly, through the structure of the high-income lifestyles of those therein employed.

Table 5.7 *Low-wage, unskilled jobs likely to employ immigrants: select service industries, New York City, 1978*[a]

| | Select service industries | | | |
| | Finance, insurance real estate[b] | Business services[c] | Other service industries[d] | Total |
|---|---|---|---|---|
| Managers, professionals and technical | 104,460 | 65,800 | 140,600 | 310,860 |
| *Services* | | | | |
| Low-wage jobs | 30,520 | 52,430 | 40,900 | 123,850 |
| Total | 36,980 | 54,950 | 83,520 | 175,450 |
| *Maintenance* | | | | |
| Low-wage jobs | 9,150 | 1,980 | 19,590 | 30,720 |
| Total | 12,700 | 15,880 | 45,510 | 74,090 |
| *Clerical* | | | | |
| Low-wage jobs | 1,420 | 5,020 | 3,450 | 9,890 |
| Total | 201,630 | 102,140 | 80,710 | 384,480 |
| Sales | 23,890 | 10,180 | 4,490 | 38,560 |
| Total low-wage jobs[e] (n) | 41,090 | 59,430 | 63,940 | 164,460 |
| % of total | 10.8% | 23.9% | 18.9% | 16.7% |
| Total all occupations | 379,660 | 248,950 | 354,830 | 983,440 |

[a] This is derived from a survey by the New York State Department of Labor (1980, 1979). The sample was drawn from establishments (only those covered by New York State Unemployment Law) in select service industries. Excluded from the sample were the following service industries: educational services (SIC 82), private households (SIC 88), and the hospitals industry sub-group (SCI 806). Private households and hospitals contain significant numbers of low-wage jobs known to be held by immigrants. Excluded from the sample were establishments and activities which include significant numbers of low-wage jobs known to employ immigrants, notably, restaurants.
[b] SIC codes 61–65
[c] SIC codes 73, 81
[d] SIC codes 70, 72, 75–80, 83, 84, 86, 89
[e] The jobs identified as low-wage are only a segment of all low-wage jobs. They are those that lack language proficiency requirements, are not part of a well-defined advancement ladder and are not usually part of a highly unionized occupation.
Source: Based on New York State Department of Labor, Division of Research and Statistics, *Occupational Employment Statistics, New York State, April–June, 1978,* 1980, and New York State Department of Labor, Division of Research and Statistics *Occupational Employment Statistics: Finance, Insurance, and Real Estate, New York State, May–June, 1978,* 1979

*The downgraded manufacturing sector: reorganizing the labor process*

When we disaggregate the data for the manufacturing sector we find, behind the remarkably different industrial profiles of these two cities, a parallel restructuring of the job supply. Notwithstanding the distinct industrial mix characterizing each of these cities, both have had a major expansion in the supply of low-wage jobs. This expansion is a function of several developments that increasingly present themselves as integral to advanced industrial economies. Technology has made possible the downgrading of a vast array of jobs, transferring the skills from the worker to the machine. Thus high-tech industries require a large number of workers for routine assembly line operations, many of which have in fact been redeployed to less-developed countries (as discussed in the preceding chapter). Furthermore, the transformation of the industrial mix has entailed a decline of older, established manufacturing industries with higher rates of unionization and higher shares of well-paid, skilled jobs. Finally, the transformation of the organization of the labor process associated with these two developments has facilitated the expansion of forms of production that rely on cheap, powerless labor, notably sweatshops and industrial homework.

The concrete expression of these developments in the cases of New York City and Los Angeles amounts to a consolidation and expansion of a downgraded manufacturing sector. First, in the case of New York City, not all components of labor-intensive industries were affected equally by capital flight from the city. In the garment industry, the city's largest employer, the bigger shops with mechanized production were the ones to move (NACLA, 1978). The less mechanized branches and small shops as well as the industry's marketing and design operations have remained in the city. Secondly, in the case of Los Angeles, the two major components in the net growth of manufacturing jobs, high-tech industries and garments, contain a vast array of low-wage, unskilled or semi-skilled jobs. Thirdly, the expansion and consolidation of a downgraded manufacturing sector partly involves the same industries which had employed mostly unionized workers but now use different forms of production and organization of the work process. Though inadequate, the evidence points to a massive growth of sweatshops and industrial homework in garments, toys, footwear and, increasingly, electronics in both cities (New York State Department of Labor, 1982a, b; Sassen-Koob, 1987). Fourthly, small-scale immigrant-owned operations have grown in number rapidly in view of easy access to cheap labor and, more importantly, a growing demand for their products in these cities. Finally, foreign investors have shown considerable interest in both areas. Thus, of all the new factories acquired or started by foreign investors from 1976 to 1980, New York State had the single largest increase, 196, followed by 161 in California, the second largest (Port Authority, 1981; Conference Board, 1981; Sassen-Koob, 1981b). The following discussion treats these various issues in greater detail.

Both New York City and Los Angeles experienced a severe loss in their older, traditional manufacturing industries during the decade of the seventies. New York City lost 160,000 garment jobs, the city's largest single manufacturing employer. Since 1973, the printing industry, another key industry in the city's economy, has shrunk by over a third. Los Angeles has had an accelerated decline in its older industries, particularly automobile production, rubber tires, and the auto-related glass, steel and steel products sector. Since 1978, 75 percent of the workers in these industries have lost their jobs. These were also the most unionized industries and those containing a high share of well-paid manufacturing jobs. Even the aircraft and parts industry declined slightly in the decade. On the other hand, the garment industry in Los Angeles had a net gain of 80,000 jobs – probably an underestimate since it excludes sweatshops and homework.

Two pronounced trends are thus evident in these cities' manufacturing bases over the last decade. One is the large loss in manufacturing jobs associated with the closure or shift of plants in traditional manufacturing industries. The other is the pronounced expansion of a downgraded manufacturing sector, either involving the same branches, but using different forms of production and organization of the work process, or involving new, often high-tech, industries. These developments were accompanied by a considerable decline in average wage levels for factory production workers as a share of the national average (U.S. Bureau of Labor Statistics, 1979; 1985). From 1961 onwards it held at about 94 percent of the national average in New York City, reaching an all-time high of 101 percent in 1970. By 1982 it was down to 87.6 percent, probably a significant overestimate since it excludes sweatshops and industrial homeworkers. In Los Angeles, it declined from 109 percent to 101 percent of the national average (see Table 5.8).

The garment and electronics industries, two extremes in the technological spectrum, are both key components in the expansion of a downgraded manufacturing sector. The same characteristics of production that explain this expansion have also made possible their large-scale redeployment to South-East Asia, the Caribbean Basin,

Table 5.8 *Hourly wages of production workers in manufacturing industries, New York City, Los Angeles, and U.S., 1970 and 1982 (in \$U.S.)*

|  | 1970 | 1982 |
|---|---|---|
| *U.S. Average (A)* | *3.31* | *8.50* |
| New York City (B) | 3.35 | 7.45 |
| B/A (%) | (101.2%) | (87.6%) |
| Los Angeles (C) | 3.60 | 8.56 |
| C/A (%) | (108.8%) | (100.7%) |

*Source:* U.S. Department of Labor, Bureau of Labor Statistics, *Employment and Earnings* (various issues)

and Mexico. They were the first two industries to undergo major internationalization in their production and are today the most internationalized. Up to 80 percent of workers employed in Export Processing Zones around the world are employed in these two industries. Los Angeles, with its major growth in electronics and garments, is a microcosm for these various trends and production characteristics.

Since the electronics industry was discussed in the preceding chapter to explain how its production characteristics made possible the employment of workers in less developed countries, here I will focus principally on the garment industry. Like the footwear industry (also briefly discussed), the garment industry contains a number of trends that are quite illuminating in terms of the facility for and the constraints to relocation as well as of the restructuring of the job supply that emerges from such relocations and the ensuing increase in import-trade jobs.

The garment industry, one of the first to undergo internationalization, shows a variety of patterns: (1) the development of large, rather automated operations, mostly in the Southwest, that have come to incorporate the jobs once existing in New York City; (2) the loss of medium-sized operations, typically unionized, that constituted the core of the city's industry; and (3) the growth of sweatshops and industrial homework. I will also briefly discuss the case of the footwear industry, one important to the Northeast as a whole and one where a polarized mode of recomposition has been developing, entailing large, mostly mechanized factories that monopolize domestic production, coupled with an expansion of sweatshops and industrial homework. The medium-sized plants, mostly unionized, are the ones that have disproportionately experienced closings. Of added significance to New York City and Los Angeles is the fact that the replacement of a large share of domestic production by imports has generated service jobs associated with import and distribution activities, many of which are located in these two cities.

Capital emigration did not affect all components of labor-intensive industries equally. In the case of the garment industry, the production of shirts, undergarments, and work clothing moved to the Sunbelt, but branches more tied to fashion, with higher seasonal requirements, demanding more tailoring skill, remained in the North. These often very small shops employ between 5 and 30 workers, are subject to intense competition, and specialize in highly fashionable or very cheap, fast-selling garments. Highly specialized finishing work also remains in New York City. (For more detailed data see Council on Wage and Price Stability, 1978; NACLA, 1978; Sassen-Koob and Benamou, 1985.) The experience of the garment industry over the last twenty years shows that components of labor-intensive industries with high overall rates of emigration tend, nonetheless, to remain in the old manufacturing centers, as indicated in Table 5.9.

A key variable explaining both the emigration of garment industry jobs and their continued presence in old centers is the nature of the production process. The possibility of deskilling a share of the jobs, lowering ratios of fixed assets per worker, and limited economies of scale can dramatically alter the nature of the production process. In other words, it is easy to move an apparel factory because the necessary investment is relatively small; it does not require a highly skilled labor force; and those components of the production process that demand high skills can be separated from the rest.

One requisite for internationalization is the possibility of breaking down production tasks to isolate low-skill operations for export to cheap labor areas. First, the very simple, basically unchanging technology of the industry has two important consequences. The basic fixed asset is the sewing machine, which makes possible a pronounced fragmentation of the production process (unitized production) without sacrificing economies of scale. It makes economic sense to open up a plant with 5 or 30 sewing machines, an impossibility in many types of industry where scale determines

Table 5.9 *Employment in the apparel industry, United States and selected states, 1958–1980 (in thousands)*

| Year | United States | New York | New Jersey | Pennsylvania | North Carolina | Georgia | Alabama | Florida | Texas | California | All other states |
|------|------|------|------|------|------|------|------|------|------|------|------|
| 1958 | 1,171.8 | 329.0 | 76.7 | 157.8 | 27.1 | 41.8 | 21.5 | 7.3 | 32.5 | 54.5 | 423.6 |
| 1960 | 2,233.2 | 318.9 | 77.7 | 168.1 | 35.3 | 47.6 | 25.8 | 8.7 | 35.7 | 59.5 | 455.9 |
| 1965 | 1,354.2 | 291.4 | 77.3 | 180.1 | 57.1 | 63.4 | 37.4 | 13.2 | 47.1 | 65.6 | 521.6 |
| 1970 | 1,364.6 | 249.2 | 72.3 | 171.2 | 75.1 | 70.0 | 44.9 | 23.7 | 61.3 | 72.7 | 524.2 |
| 1975 | 1,243.3 | 180.8 | 57.9 | 132.7 | 75.4 | 66.7 | 48.4 | 27.5 | 69.8 | 91.6 | 492.5 |
| 1980 | 1,265.8 | 170.0 | 55.3 | 124.2 | 87.9 | 72.4 | 53.9 | 34.1 | 75.0 | 107.0 | 486.0 |

*Source:* U.S. Department of Labor, Bureau of Labor Statistics, Current Employment Statistics

economic feasibility. Furthermore, the practice of subcontracting and section work, which started in the late 1800s, created a type of organization of work that later facilitated the export of certain jobs. Subcontracting and section work entailed the replacement of highly skilled workers who prepared a whole garment by semi- or unskilled workers who massproduced one piece. This practice permits taking advantage of dispersed production sites.

From this derives the second consequence: the possibility of starting an apparel factory with a small amount of initial capital. The typical garment shop has 50 production workers with about $6,000 in fixed assets per worker – figures proposed by the government as those needed to establish an efficient operation. But a NACLA study (1978) found that apparel factories can start on as little as $10,000. In the late 1970s a large apparel factory, which is rare, could have as much as $15,000 worth of fixed assets per worker; this contrasts markedly with the situation in advanced industries, where fixed assets per production worker range between $40,000 and $70,000.

In addition to unitized production and skill standardization – two conditions which facilitate plant relocation – the weight of labor costs is important in explaining internationalization. Though in recent years a few large United States apparel companies have become more automated, for most of the 15,000 apparel companies labor accounts for about 27 percent of production costs. Thus, this factor is of major significance for profit levels, and partly explains the continued decline in wages over the last thirty years as a means of maintaining profit levels. In 1947, the average wage of apparel workers was 95 percent of average manufacturing wages; by 1977 it had declined to 64 percent (Council on Wage and Price Stability, 1978: 27). It is the nature of the production process (one in which labor costs play such a significant role) that explains this decline in wages, not simply the availability of cheap immigrant labor *per se*.

The same characteristics of the production process which explain the facility and desirability of plant relocation in the garment industry also explain why certain branches of this industry can continue to operate in New York City. Highly skilled or fashion-linked components of the production process can be isolated and carried out on a small scale and with minimal initial investment. This also makes possible production of cheap garments for a mass market given the availability of an abundant low-wage labor supply that can be drawn into industrial homework and sweatshops. The same

Table 5.10 *Domestic shoe industry and imports, 1966 and 1976*[a]

|  | 1966 | 1976 | 1976 as a percentage of 1966 |
|---|---|---|---|
| Total employees | 241,500 | 169,000 | 70 |
| Number of companies | 675 | 376 | 56 |
| Effective capacity (000 pairs) | 782,952 | 568,404 | 73 |
| Census production (000 pairs) | 641,696 | 413,087 | 69 |
| Imports (000 pairs) | 96,135 | 369,814 | 384 |
| Value of shipments (millions of $) | 2,474 | 3,482 | 141 |
| Value of imports (millions of $) | 158 | 1,448 | 916 |
| Average weekly earnings | $71.81 | $70.22 | 98 |

[a] The figure for 1966 is gross average weekly earnings in current dollars. The figure for 1976 is gross earnings deflated by the change in the consumer price index from 1966 and 1976.
*Source:* Evans (1979): 319. Based on American Footwear Industries Association. *Footwear Manual,* 1977, tables 10, 11, 37, 38; AFIA Statistical Reporter, Quarterly Report, 4th Quarter, 1977.

characteristics also explain how during the last few years the garment industry could begin to expand again in a place like New York City, with its outmoded physical plants, its fiscal precariousness, its scarce and high-cost commercial space, and so forth.

Another form of this differential impact of capital migration in labor-intensive industries is illustrated by the footwear industry, until recently a significant component of the Northeast's economy. The replacement of U.S.-manufactured shoes by imports, in part the result of American investment abroad, has had a devastating impact on the domestic footwear industry. Between 1966 and 1976, shoe imports increased by 916 percent in terms of dollar value, and by 384 percent in terms of units (pairs of shoes). During that same period, domestic employment in the shoe industry declined by 30 percent, average weekly earnings declined slightly (even controlling for inflation), production of units dropped by 30 percent, and production capacity fell by 27 percent (Evans, 1979: 318–320). As Evans points out, the U.S. shoe industry was not becoming more modern and less labor intensive, it was simply losing its production base (see Table 5.10).

A more detailed examination reveals selected processes of industry recomposition that make for a more complex pattern than that represented by a generally declining industry (Evans, 1979). First, the largest firms in the U.S. shoe industry had higher profit levels between 1970 and 1973 than between 1963 and 1966. Secondly, a high degree of concentration characterizes the footwear industry: a few companies account for a large share of total output, and over half of all small companies have disappeared (300 out of 517). By 1976, 21 large companies produced half of the country's total output. Thirdly, some of the larger companies have invested heavily in plants abroad (in Taiwan and South Korea) and have become importers as well as U.S. producers, thereby exercising control over both a large share of domestic output and imports. Fourthly, other large domestic producers have become heavily involved in import trade. Finally, in certain styles, such as heavy leather footwear and casual shoes, American producers dominate. This is also the case in higher-priced, fashion-linked lines. The enterprises that have suffered most from high imports and relocation of plants abroad are the small manufacturers producing large volumes of low-priced footwear. Larger producers are becoming more competitive in this line through their involvement in the import trade.

In sum, the overall picture that emerges in the case of the footwear industry is one of a growing concentration where a few large companies control the market through domestic production, production abroad, and control over imports. Some domestic footwear industry firms are thriving; others are declining severely. Insofar as domestic producers are heavily involved in the import trade, certain components of the industry are expanding.

The overall relevance of this discussion to my central argument is that disaggregated data on capital emigration from the Northeast, especially from New York, show that (1) certain branches within labor-intensive industries such as apparel and footwear continue to operate in the Northeast and are actually expanding; (2) types of production that make relocation easy and desirable are also conducive to continued operation in places like New York City which have highly skilled and cheap unskilled labor pools available; and (3) the severe shrinking of the production base of an industry such as footwear due to expanding imports may generate a whole range of jobs associated with the import trade. This development may be particularly significant to New York City as a commercial center because the transfer of production jobs from an area outside New

York City to foreign countries has generated a new set of jobs within the city. These three trends do not by any means overcome the devastating impact of capital emigration from New York City during the last two decades, but they are elements of an explanation that seeks to resolve the apparent contradiction of the coexistence in one place of a massive job loss and a massive influx of immigrants.

CONCLUSIONS

These two very different areas, New York City and Los Angeles, contain a number of major growth trends that result in similar socio-economic conditions: an increased skill and income polarization in the workforce, the expansion of a downgraded manufacturing sector, and the growth of an informal economy. These two cities, which are the major producers of financial and other advanced services, are also major generators of low-wage jobs and major receivers of the new immigration. They represent two major instances of economic restructuring both in terms of economic activity and the organization of the work process. The massive immigrant influx and the cor-responding transformation in the social and political composition of the labor supply needs to be understood in this broader context. Major world centers have become the loci for new forms of the concentration of economic growth and the associated new forms of economic inequality.

The contrast is made more remarkable by the fact that in the 1970s each of these two cities constituted a consummate instance of what were usually seen as two very different configurations: the declining Frostbelt and the ascending Sunbelt. There was a tendency to associate the first with irreversible decline and the second with high-technology growth.

The notion of economic decline adequately describes what is happening in several industries that were central components of the Northeast economy. However, it fails to capture the emergence of novel kinds of manufacturing, the expansion of sweatshops, and, more fundamentally, the expansion of highly specialized services. The notion of capital flight adequately describes what is happening with many of the manufacturing firms and corporate headquarters that had traditionally operated from New York City, but it disregards the new trends in capital investment for which New York City is a suitable and desirable location: professional services; banking; hotels and restaurants; the construction of offices and luxury high-income residental building, with all of their associated services; specialized manufacturing firms directed toward a small, identifiable clientele; the buying and selling of art and antiques; and so forth.

On the other hand, what dominates in the case of Los Angeles is modernity, newness, and high technology. Yet underneath these we find a massive expansion of sweatshops in garments and electronics, and an increase of low-wage assembly jobs in high-technology industries. We observe the large-scale employment of non-unionized, often immigrant and female workers in the new industries and the decimation of the old, established and highly unionized industries. Areas with the highest growth in manufacturing have experienced the sharpest decline in levels of unionization. Finally, we also see a large section of the city in total decay and one of the most ghettoized cities in the country, while at the same time there is the beginning of high-income gentrification in areas once occupied by middle- and lower-middle income people.

This pattern of internal differentiation of the growth and decline trends in Los Angeles and New York City can also be applied to the composition of immigration. To say that immigration provides cheap labor is correct, but this oversimplifies the supply and demand relationship. Low-wage jobs are common in declining sectors of the economy. As the migration literature has shown, firms in this sector often depend on low-wage immigrants for sheer survival. Higher-wage workers would contribute to the closing of such firms. *But low-wage jobs are also numerous in highly dynamic growth sectors of the economy*. It is this fact which partly resolves the lack of correspondence between the size of immigration and that of the job loss. If we juxtapose the large immigrant influx during the last fifteen years in New York City and the large job loss over that same period, then it would seem that low-wage jobs in the declining sector of the economy would not suffice to absorb the immigrant influx. Yet, the available evidence for New York City shows that a majority of immigrants find employment in rather low-wage jobs. The mistake lies in assuming that low-wage jobs are predominantly a function of decline and backwardness.

The expansion of the low-wage job supply as a function of major growth sectors, notably the advanced services and headquarters complex and the downgraded manufacturing sector, contributes to explain two characteristics of the new immigration: (1) its *continued* concentration in New York City and Los Angeles, and (2) the *continued* increase in entry levels, much higher in the late seventies than in the late sixties. As I discussed earlier, important elements of an explanation can be found in the change of legislation after 1965 and the prior existence of immigrant communities in both cities. However, they are not sufficient to explain the continuity of the flow and its increasing magnitude in view of rising inflation and unemployment prevalent in the U.S. throughout the 1970s. Nor are they sufficient to explain the persistently disproportionate concentration in major cities now that these are no longer the centers of light-manufacturing they once were.

# 6

# The reconcentration of capital in the United States: a new investment zone?

There is today a global marketplace of production sites. The decade of the 1970s saw the massive and rapid development of such production sites in select areas of South-East Asia and the Caribbean Basin. And towards the late 1970s cities such as New York and Los Angeles emerge as major locations for the placement of international financial investments and for the production of specialized services for the world market. To these two developments I would add a third pattern, becoming evident in the 1980s: the possibility that several regions in highly industrialized countries are becoming competitive with industrial zones in the Third World as locations for direct investment, both foreign and national. Reasons for this can be found in new locational constraints due to technological requirements, protectionist policies, notably in the United States, and rising political and economic costs of production in Third World export manufacturing zones. These changes involve mostly the United States. Technical, economic, and political constraints along with changes in the territorial organization of production and the availability of a low-wage immigrant work force make certain regions in the U.S. internationally competitive and thus part of the global marketplace of production sites. Some of the less industrialized countries in the developed world, such as Spain and Ireland, are also emerging as investment zones for world capital.

One indication of this new pattern can be derived from the pronounced changes in overall flows of direct foreign investment since the early 1980s. From being the leading exporter of direct foreign investment throughout the post-war period and peaking in 1979, the U.S. had become the leading recipient of such investment by 1981. In addition to the rapidity of the reversal, its magnitude is also worth noting. In 1970 direct foreign investment into the U.S. represented under 9 percent of global flows; in 1981 it reached 48 percent (UN Centre on Transnational Corporations, 1985; U.S. Department of

Commerce, 1984; OECD, 1981). Alongside the U.S. the fastest growing recipient areas are the South-East Asian nations discussed in Chapter 4. The main losing areas are the large Latin American and major Western European countries which received most of the direct foreign investment taking place in the 1950s and 1960s. In all these areas, direct foreign investment tends to be concentrated in certain regions and sectors. This is a trend that has increased in the case of less developed countries. In 1970 the twenty leading recipients accounted for two-thirds of all direct foreign investment; by 1981 this share had increased to 90 percent (U.S. Department of Commerce, 1984; UN Centre on Transnational Corporations, 1985). Investment goes to three sets of activities: development of oil resources and other minerals; production geared to domestic markets in the receiving country; and assembly and production of manufactures for export. Most countries in the Third World have not received much if any direct foreign investment even when governments offered significant incentives. This regional and sectoral concentration is also evident in the less industrialized European countries that have experienced rapid growth in direct foreign investment inflows, particularly Spain and Ireland. And it is evident in the United States, as will be discussed below in detail.

The notion of a global marketplace of production sites is further suggested by three trends. One is the massive increase in global direct foreign investment flows, from $60 billion in 1960, $213 billion in 1973, to almost $600 billion in 1983 (U.S. Department of Commerce, 1984; OECD, 1981). Europe, Japan and the U.S. all had rapid increases in their absolute levels of investment abroad. Secondly, since the 1960s direct foreign investment has increasingly been concentrated in manufacturing and services, activities that tend to be exempt from the type of locational constraints typical of raw materials production. And thirdly, transnational corporations of the developed countries accounted for over 90 percent of all flows throughout much of the post-World War II era and continuing today. The combination of these three trends indicates that much of the global flow in direct foreign investment represents the internationalization of production on the part of transnational corporations. In this context it is worth noting that before World War II portfolio investment was far more important than direct foreign investment in overall foreign investment flows. It is this internationalization of financial investments, under the umbrella of transnational corporations that contributes to the expansion of centralized management and servicing operations discussed in Chapter 5. The internationalization of production continues, especially in South-East Asia, the Caribbean Basin, and some of the less industrialized European countries. And the U.S. continues to export capital but has now itself become a site for internationalized production.

This is the general argument underlining the more detailed discussion on foreign investment in the U.S. I will first briefly examine some of the technical, political, and economic constraints that may be contributing to a reconcentration of capital in the highly industrialized countries, mostly the United States. This discussion will focus on industrial capital, the subject of financial capital having been discussed in the preceding chapter.

ELEMENTS FOR CHANGE IN THE SPATIAL DISTRIBUTION OF
INVESTMENT

Over the last few years a number of regions in highly industrialized countries have emerged as attractive locations for foreign investors. In the United States, Southern California, Texas and the New York–New Jersey Metropolitan Area have become key recipients of foreign investment in manufacturing. Furthermore, one of the central factors in the rapid growth trends of the late 1970s in New York City and Los Angeles was a pronounced increase in foreign investment in several important industries: banking, real estate, hotels and restaurants, and manufacturing. The importance of this for New York at a time of massive departures by domestic capital and an all-time low in employment levels, has increasingly been recognized by government officials and the private sector (Port Authority, 1981; 1982; City of New York, 1982; The Conference Board, 1981; Goldmark, 1979).

There are good economic reasons for foreign investment in the United States generally. Firms with sizeable exports to the United States may benefit from direct production here to consolidate and expand their markets and to avoid import restrictions, especially in view of continuing U.S. merchandise trade deficits. The declining value of the dollar during the 1970s made U.S. investments, acquisitions, and construction of the plants in the U.S. relatively more profitable to outsiders. Finally, one factor that cannot be disregarded is the intense competition and active lobbying on the part of local governments to draw investors, both domestic and foreign.

But the magnitude of the increase in foreign investment is sufficient to raise the possibility of some more basic trend at work in these shifts. There is some evidence pointing to technically and economically induced locational constraints in the more advanced sectors of manufacturing. On the other hand, the consolidation of a large supply of immigrant workers in combination with the severe losses by organized labor, lowers the cost of labor-intensive activities in both advanced and "backward" sectors of the economy. We may be seeing the operation of a threshold effect whereby the conjunction of new or increased locational constraints and the availability of a large supply of low-wage workers have made investment in several economic sectors competitive with what were once preferred locations in the Third World and Western Europe.

In the particular case of manufacturing, the argument is that several regions in the United States contain a combination of resources that makes them competitive with Third World areas producing for export, notably Export Processing Zones. This would mean that behind the massive increase in direct foreign investment in the U.S. beginning in the late 1970s, lies a shift in global investment patterns. This shift has also involved U.S. investment patterns. The particular combination of resources that makes such regions in the U.S. competitive is not necessarily the same as that which makes Third World countries competitive. Rather it is the emergence of various technical, economic, and political constraints that are inducing a transformation in the territorial organization of production in several industries. On the other hand, rising demands by workers and host governments in Third World countries that received most of the foreign investment for export production have reduced their competitive edge.

Among the key developments that have contributed to this competitiveness are the following. First, there are new technical and economic constraints that promote agglomeration economies and disincentives towards vertical integration. Notable among these are the requirements of production in (a) the most advanced sectors of high-technology industries, and (b) the expansion of commercial applications of microelectronics. Both, even if involving at times very different kinds of production, require vicinity to centers of research, control and design, as well as to intermediate buyers. The overall result is a tendency towards a clustering arrangement of a broad range of firms, some specializing in similar and others in complementary lines of production.

There are two consequences of interest to this study. One is that insofar as the centers for technical control and design tend to be located in the highly industrialized countries, and especially in the United States, the latter emerge as desirable sites for production facilities. In this context, the availability of an abundant supply of Third World labor inside the United States acquires added significance. A second consequence one might infer from these tendencies towards clustering, is that certain regions in the United States will be more adequate than others. Besides access to technical resources and suitable labor supplies, this clustering arrangement presupposes access to a rather large, somewhat contiguous territory. Space becomes a resource only on the collective level: the category "adequate space" cannot be reduced to the land needs of a single establishment. While localization economies have probably been a factor in many different economic periods and sectors, such economies are not the same for establishments with high levels of vertical integration as for clusterings of small firms with high levels of vertical disintegration. If we introduce such an elaboration of the category space, then one can argue that certain regions with the appropriate combination of resources can be conceived of as investment "zones," for foreign and U.S. capital (Sassen-Koob, 1987).

Secondly, the large availability of an immigrant workforce in combination with changes in the consumption structure are inducing a reconcentration of small-scale, labor-intensive manufacturing in large cities. As was discussed in Chapter 5, the tendency towards income polarization in large cities has brought about a parallel segmentation in the consumption structure. There has been an expansion in the demand for customized, highly priced goods and services. And there has been an increase in the demand for extremely cheap goods and services. The first has brought about an increase in small manufacturing shops catering to specific clienteles; standardization and mechanization of production are not feasible or profitable under these conditions and neither is vertical integration. These small shops need to be located in large cities, since this is where their clients are located and access to suppliers is adequate. In the case of the growing demand for extremely cheap items, what we are seeing is that the existence of a critical mass of workers willing to work at home or in

sweatshops has made cities like New York and Los Angeles competitive with Hong Kong or Taiwan as locations for the production of
extremely cheap garments, footwear, bedding, toys, and a range of
household items. The central issue here is not so much the fact that
foreign investment, including small-scale investments by immigrants
who arrive with some capital, has been a significant factor in the
constitution and viability of this type of manufacturing. More
important is the fact that such a sector is developing and expanding in
the midst of what are often thought of as "post-industrial" cities. An
integral part of this development is the formation of an informal
sector, encompassing the production of both highly priced customized goods and services and very cheap ones. The expansion of
small, labor-intensive shops relying heavily on immigrant workers
and including a growing informal sector, makes large cities in a highly
industrialized country like the U.S. a competitive location for certain
types of labor-intensive manufacturing. If this hypothesis is correct, it
represents a development that analyses of advanced industrialization
have typically not foreseen.

   Thirdly, the emergence of a number of constraints in the industrial
zones (Export Processing Zones, or Free Trade Zones) in the Third
World may make investment in these relatively less attractive than it
was in the 1970s. These constraints involve, among others: (a)
pressures by the governments on foreign companies operating in their
territories to transfer more advanced technologies and more capital-
intensive production, while it is precisely the more labor-intensive
and simpler segments of production that have typically been located
in these zones; (b) labor shortages in some of the better established
zones, largely due to the marked preference for employing young
women and the high turnover rates; (c) growing militancy among
workers employed in these zones and export industries generally,
notwithstanding the government's ruthless disciplining of workers
and various repressive measures; (d) a consistent trend towards rising
wages which may be reducing the relative desirability of locating
plants off-shore, especially given a growing supply of immigrant
workers in the U.S. and the severe defeats suffered by organized labor.

   A fourth factor of considerable weight to foreign investors is access
to the U.S. market and, in the case of certain industries, access to
high-level technologies through the acquisition of U.S. firms. The
U.S. is still the largest single market in the world and one which a
range of foreign firms want to secure in the face of rising pressures

towards protection against imports. Acquisition by foreign investors of U.S. manufacturing firms as a way of gaining access to the U.S. market and to advanced technology has accelerated since the late 1970s if we use the figures on acquisitions as an indicator (Sassen-Koob, 1987). There may of course be a number of other reasons inducing such acquisitions, including the relative decline in the attractiveness of investing in the Third World.

## DIRECT FOREIGN INVESTMENT IN THE UNITED STATES

Total foreign investment in the U.S. stood at $874 billion in 1984. This represented a doubling from the $416 billion in 1979. The 1984 figure is not insignificant considering a GNP of $3.6 trillion in 1984 and a national budget of about $800 billion. Indeed some analysts maintain that foreign investment financed part of the economic recovery in the early 1980s. Data Resources, Inc. for example, estimates that foreign investment financed 26 percent of U.S. corporate capital spending in 1984, which would represent a doubling from the 1980 level and an unprecedentedly high share.

Besides direct foreign investment, major categories of foreign investment are private portfolio holdings of U.S. stocks, bonds, loans and government securities, private deposits in U.S. banks, and foreign government holdings. The fastest-growing category and the largest in volume by 1984 was private portfolio holdings and private deposits. It more than doubled since 1979 and reached almost $500 billion in 1984. Private government holdings, which as recently as 1978 were the largest single category, grew little over the last five years, reaching $196 billion in 1984 (see Table 6.1).

It is almost impossible to obtain precise measures of the national origin of this investment. Approximately $400 billion came from Western Europe, a doubling of the 1979 figure. Canada and Japan each provided about $180 billion, also a doubling of their 1979 levels. Finally, Latin America and other countries also doubled their 1979 levels, reaching over $50 billion each.

Until the middle of the 1970s, U.S. direct investment abroad grew more rapidly than direct foreign investment in the U.S. From 1954 through 1966, such investment in the U.S. grew from $4.6 billion to $11.8 billion, or by 257 percent, while U.S. DFI abroad grew from $17.7 billion to $67 billion, or by 379 percent. This trend began to reverse in the 1970s. U.S. DFI grew from $67 billion in 1969 to $148.8

Table 6.1 *Net international investment position of the United States 1978–1984 (in billions of $ U.S.)*[a]

| | 1978 | 1979 | 1980 | 1981 | 1982 | 1983 | 1984 |
|---|---|---|---|---|---|---|---|
| Net international investment position | 76.2 | 94.6 | 120.6 | 156.5 | 149.6 | 105.7 | 35.2 |
| *Assets* | 447.9 | 510.6 | 606.7 | 716.9 | 838.2 | 887.4 | 908.7 |
| Official assets | 72.9 | 77.4 | 90.3 | 98.5 | 108.4 | 113.0 | 121.7 |
| Foreign direct investment | 162.7 | 187.9 | 215.4 | 226.4 | 221.5 | 226.1 | 232.1 |
| Other private assets | 212.3 | 245.3 | 301.0 | 392.0 | 508.3 | 548.3 | 554.9 |
| *Liabilities* | 371.7 | 416.0 | 486.1 | 560.4 | 688.6 | 781.7 | 873.5 |
| Official liabilities | 173.0 | 159.7 | 176.0 | 180.9 | 189.0 | 193.1 | 196.1 |
| Foreign direct investment | 42.5 | 54.5 | 68.4 | 90.4 | 121.9 | 133.5 | 154.7 |
| Other liabilities | 156.2 | 201.8 | 241.7 | 289.1 | 377.7 | 454.1 | 522.7 |

[a] Including petroleum industry
*Source:* UN Centre on Transnational Corporations, 1985: 21; based on United States Department of Commerce, *Survey of Current Business* (various issues)

billion in 1977, or by 222 percent, while DFI in the U.S. grew from $11.8 billion to $34.1 billion, or by 285 percent. After 1977 there is a rapid acceleration in the rate of growth of DFI in the U.S., quadrupling from 1977 to 1984. DFI in the U.S. for the first time exceeds U.S. outflows in 1981 after 30-plus years of net outflows. In the early 1980s the rate of growth of U.S. DFI declines considerably – to 5 percent in 1981, the lowest in the post World War II period (Whichard, 1982: 11). In contrast, the rate of growth of DFI in the U.S. reaches 31 percent annually, a level at which it remains (Howenstine and Fouch, 1982: 32).

Throughout most of the decade of the 1970s, European and Japanese direct foreign investment increased rapidly and was mostly directed to the Third World. Towards the late 1970s and early 1980s most of this investment is directed to the U.S. These shifts are reflected in the changing distribution of outflows among the developed countries. In 1970–71, the U.S. accounted for almost 61 percent of all outflows, Europe's most developed countries for 35 percent. By 1981, the U.S. share had declined to 15 percent, Europe's had risen to over 57 percent, and the share of the developed non-European countries (Japan, New Zealand, Canada, Australia, and South Africa) had increased to 28 percent. The distribution of inflows among the developed countries also underwent a parallel transformation, with the world share of the most developed European countries declining from 45 percent in 1970–71 to 27 percent in 1981. The U.S.

Table 6.2 *Inward direct investment flows (percentage distribution among eight countries)*

|              | 1961–67 | 1968–73 | 1974–78 |
|--------------|---------|---------|---------|
| W. Germany   | 24.0    | 19.3    | 17.0    |
| Canada       | 18.0    | 14.2    | 3.7     |
| Australia    | 17.4    | 15.1    | 11.0    |
| Italy        | 12.7    | 9.7     | 5.8     |
| U.K.         | 10.8    | 19.3    | 17.0    |
| France       | 9.1     | 9.6     | 17.6    |
| Netherlands  | 5.2     | 10.0    | 6.9     |
| U.S.         | 2.8     | 13.4    | 30.9    |

*Source:* OECD, *Recent International Direct Investment Trends* (Paris: OECD, 1981)

share went from 9 percent to 47.5 percent. And that of the third group of countries declined from 24 percent to 0.2 percent (UN Centre on Transnational Corporations, 1985: 18). This transformation is evident in the distribution of direct foreign investment inflows among the developed European countries and the U.S. (see Table 6.2). The largest recipients in the early 1960s (West Germany, Canada, Australia, and Italy) all had experienced pronounced declines in their shares by the late 1970s. West Germany, the largest recipient, accounted for a fourth of all such flows in the developed world during the 1960s, a share that had declined to 17 percent by the middle of the 1970s. On the other hand, France, the United Kingdom, and the United States all increased their shares (OECD, 1981). Spain, Ireland, and Greece also experienced large increases in their direct foreign investment inflows.

The national distribution of the direct foreign investment position in the U.S. shows that Europe accounted for 66 percent, a share it held with fluctuations over the last two decades (see Table 6.3). The significant changes were the increases in the shares of Japan and other countries, mostly accounted for by Latin America. Behind the decline in Canada's share and Europe's unchanging share from 1962 to 1980 lie absolute increases.

By 1980, the stock of direct foreign investment in manufacturing stood at $25.1 billion, or almost 40 percent of all such investment (Howenstine and Fouch, 1982). The value of direct foreign investments in plants and equipment has more than doubled since 1973. In 1979 alone, about 400 foreign firms built or bought manufacturing

Table 6.3 *Direct foreign investment position in the U.S. by source, 1962–1980*
*(in millions of $ U.S.)*

|  | 1962 | 1966 | 1970 | 1974 | 1980 |
|---|---|---|---|---|---|
| *Total* | 7,612 | 9,054 | 13,270 | 25,144 | 65,413 |
| Canada | 2,064 | 2,439 | 3,117 | 5,136 | 9,810 |
|  | (27.1%) | (26.9%) | (23.5%) | (20.4%) | (15.0%) |
| *Europe* | 5,247 | 6,274 | 9,554 | 16,756 | 43,467 |
| of which | (68.9%) | (69.3%) | (72.0%) | (66.6%) | (66.5%) |
| U.K. | 2,474 | 2,864 | 4,127 | 5,744 | 11,342 |
| Netherlands | 1,082 | 1,402 | 2,151 | 4,698 | 16,159 |
| Switzerland | 836 | 949 | 1,545 | 1,949 | 3,682 |
| France | 183 | 215 | 286 | 1,139 | 2,672 |
| Germany | 152 | 247 | 680 | 1,535 | 5,290 |
| Japan | 112 | 103 | 229 | 345 | 4,219 |
|  | (1.5%) | (1.1%) | (1.7%) | (1.4%) | (6.5%) |
| OPEC | * | * | * | 201 | 576 |
| Other | 189 | 238 | 370 | 2,706 | 7,341 |
|  | (2.5%) | (2.6%) | (2.8%) | (10.8%) | (11.2%) |

*Source: Survey of Current Business* (various issues)
* Specific amount not published

facilities in the U.S. (Port Authority, 1981; 1982). In 1981, foreign-owned firms accounted for about 4.5 percent of manufacturing employment in the U.S. (Little, 1983). The actual employment impact is considerably higher given the tendency towards concentration in certain regions and in certain industries. The stock of total direct foreign investment in manufacturing is largely concentrated in the Mideast, New England, and Great Lakes regions; foreign investments for new facilities, however, are occurring primarily in the Southeast and Far West regions (Little, 1983).

Foreign investors have shown a strong inclination for buying plants or building new ones in the old manufacturing centers that are in severe decline. A 1976 study by the Conference Board found that over one-quarter of all investments by foreign firms between 1968 and 1975 were in New England and mid-Atlantic states (New York, New Jersey, and Pennsylvania), a region with a high incidence of domestic capital emigration and with more than 5,000 factory closures over that period (Bauer, 1980). A 1978 study for the Federal Reserve Bank of Boston found that, adjusting for differences in population and land area of individual states, the Northeastern industrial areas had received the largest share of foreign investments. Furthermore, foreign acquisitions of U.S. plants in operation, though typically with the threat of closing down, tended to be concentrated in areas with high unemployment rates that are losing industry. German, English, and Swiss firms were the ones most likely to locate facilities in such areas, while Japanese firms were less likely to do so (cited in Bauer, 1980). Furthermore, rather than leveling off in response to the worsening situation in the Northern manufacturing centers, foreign investments actually increased throughout the decade of the seventies.

New York and California have been, and continue to be, the major recipients of foreign investment (in actual numbers of investment) since the early 1980s (Conference Board, various issues). New York and New Jersey had 18.6 percent of all foreign-owned manufacturing plants in 1980. This is not an insignificant share given the severe economic decline of this region in the 1970s, and considering that booming states such as Texas and Georgia have 4.6 and 3.9 percent, respectively (see Table 6.4). Furthermore, New York had the largest net increase, between 1976 and 1980, of all states – 196 plants added, compared to 161 in California, 87 in Texas, 94 in North Carolina, and so forth. These figures are undercounts because they cover only plants employing 50 or more workers. In urban locations, small size is probably an important variable, and only firms in activities where small size does not affect profitability will be likely to locate in cities. We know, for example, that many plants in New York City have fewer than 50 workers on the payroll; we also know that there are several plants owned by investors from Hong Kong, not only one, as shown in Table 6.5.

Little (1983) estimates the relative dependence of different regions on foreign investments by industry. The Far West region, which includes Southern California, evidences a very high dependence on foreign investment in electric and electronic equipment, as well as instruments and related products. The Southwest, in contrast, shows little foreign investment in these industries. In fact, the Far West region evidences one of the highest levels of dependence on any single country, in this case Japan. The Southwest shows high levels of dependence on the Netherlands and France and very low on Japan.

Non-electrical and electrical machinery have received a substantial amount of foreign investment in recent years; they accounted for 9 percent of all foreign owned manufacturing firms in 1975 and 17 percent in 1981 (Conference Board, various issues; Department of

Table 6.4 *Foreign-owned manufacturing firms, selected states and U.S. total, 1980*

| | Cumulative total through 1975 | 1976 | 1977 | 1978 | 1979 | 1980 | Cumulative total through 1980 | % U.S. | Net increase 1976–80 |
|---|---|---|---|---|---|---|---|---|---|
| New York State | 222 | 42 | 45 | 36 | 50 | 23 | 418 | 11.4 | 196 |
| New Jersey | 178 | 13 | 21 | 16 | 17 | 18 | 263 | 7.2 | 85 |
| NY–NJ Metropolitan Region | (234) | (9) | (17) | (18) | (28) | (16) | (322) | — | (88) |
| California | 103 | 16 | 22 | 43 | 50 | 30 | 264 | 7.2 | 161 |
| Texas | 82 | 6 | 14 | 16 | 31 | 20 | 169 | 5.8 | 87 |
| North Carolina | 90 | 6 | 11 | 16 | 25 | 36 | 184 | 5.0 | 94 |
| Pennsylvania | 125 | 10 | 16 | 14 | 19 | 30 | 214 | 4.6 | 89 |
| Georgia | 68 | 5 | 5 | 20 | 22 | 23 | 143 | 3.9 | 75 |
| Illinois | 92 | 10 | 5 | 6 | 10 | 13 | 136 | 3.7 | 44 |
| All other | 1006 | 137 | 135 | 191 | 210 | 194 | 1873 | 51.2 | 867 |
| U.S. total | 1966 | 245 | 274 | 358 | 434 | 387 | 3664 | 100.0 | 1698 |

*Source:* The Conference Board, Inc.; The Port Authority of NY and NJ Planning and Development Department, Regional Research Section

Table 6.5 *Foreign-owned manufacturing plants by country of ownership in the New York–New Jersey Metropolitan Area, 1980*

| Foreign owner | Plants (n) | Distribution |
|---|---|---|
| Germany | 81 | 25.2 |
| United Kingdom | 67 | 20.8 |
| France | 35 | 10.9 |
| Netherlands | 29 | 9.0 |
| Japan | 23 | 7.2 |
| Canada | 22 | 6.8 |
| Switzerland | 22 | 6.8 |
| Sweden | 8 | 2.4 |
| Denmark | 7 | 2.2 |
| South Africa | 7 | 2.2 |
| Belgium | 6 | 1.9 |
| Italy | 5 | 1.6 |
| Austria | 3 | 0.9 |
| Australia | 3 | 0.9 |
| Norway | 1 | 0.3 |
| Saudi Arabia | 1 | 0.3 |
| Pakistan | 1 | 0.3 |
| Hong Kong | 1 | 0.3 |
| Total | 322 | 100.0 |

*Source:* The Conference Board, Inc.; The Port Authority of New York and New Jersey Planning and Development Department, Regional Research Section

Commerce, 1982). Primary metals and instruments also showed marked growth in their shares, while fabricated metals, foods and chemicals declined significantly. Even those industries whose share of total foreign investment in manufacturing declined, however, increased their absolute levels of foreign investment. In sum, direct foreign investment in U.S. manufacturing is increasing and it evidences a pattern of sectoral and regional differentiation.

Using IMF and OECD data, the UN Centre on Transnational Corporations (1985) estimated that the share of foreign direct investment in gross fixed capital formation in the U.S. has gone from 0.5 percent in 1970–71 to 4.1 percent in 1980–81. While this may seem very small, it is worth noting that in a country such as South Africa, considered to be rather dependent on foreign investment, this share stood at 6.1 percent in 1970–71, before massive disinvestment reduced this share to 1 percent. The 1980–81 figure for the U.S. is similar to that of Spain and Ireland, two countries that are becoming increasingly competitive as locations for foreign investment in manufacturing. In those countries closest to the U.S. in level of industrialization and overall development, notably West Germany and Japan, foreign direct investment amounts to one percent of gross fixed capital formation. One might hypothesize for the case of Germany that it may eventually experience an increase in this share for reasons similar to those of the U.S. including a large immigrant workforce. There are some indications that this may be happening, especially in areas of Southern Germany (Sassen-Koob, 1987). Ireland and Spain represent a combination of resources somewhat similar to that posited here for Southern California: a combination of highly skilled and of low wage labor in the same location, vicinity to centers of technical research, control and design, and availability of industrial land in order to accommodate a territorial organization of production characterized by clustering of a number of firms rather than one single plant with high levels of vertical integration.

Foreign investment in U.S. manufacturing occurs for any number of reasons, including a desire to gain access to U.S. technology and management expertise, import substitution to avoid tariff restrictions, and problems with domestic market regulation; nonetheless, lower production costs may provide a significant inducement. Labor costs in the United States grew more slowly than in most other major industrialized countries during the 1970s. Whereas the average compensation of U.S. manufacturing workers increased by 80 percent between 1965 and 1975, it increased by 109 percent, 307 percent, 150 percent, 213 percent, 162 percent and 207 percent in, respectively, Canada, Japan, Germany, the Netherlands, Sweden, and the United Kingdom. Furthermore, hourly compensation in Belgium (6.60), the Netherlands (6.53) and Sweden (7.18) was higher than in the United States (6.35) in 1975 (U.S. Bureau of Labor Statistics, 1982a).

CONCLUSION

The processes of capital relocation discussed in the preceding chapters contribute to the emergence of conditions which may eventually engender a new or altered logic of investment. There is a trend towards the concentration of foreign investment flows in the United States. This process can be conceived of as the development of investment zones for world capital, including both United States and foreign capital. The evidence on direct foreign investment patterns provides an indicator for this trend. After growing rapidly in the 1970s, overall direct foreign investment fell by one quarter in the developed and by a third in the less developed countries. The United States was the exception in this pattern. Direct foreign investment and foreign investment generally reached historic highs. From being the lead exporter of direct foreign investment in 1979, the United States became the leading importer in 1981.

It is probably useful to distinguish among the different components of foreign investment in the U.S. One could posit that what we are seeing is the development of two types of investment zones: financial and industrial. The combination of resources represented by New York City and Los Angeles makes these cities desirable locations for the placement of financial investments. On the other hand, the combination of inputs and markets has made certain regions in the U.S. competitive with Third World areas providing low production costs and a disciplined low-wage workforce. Southern California and the New York Metropolitan area are examples of such industrial zones.

My argument is that technical, political and economic constraints in combination with a new territorial organization of production contribute to make certain regions in the U.S. internationally competitive and therewith part of a global marketplace of production sites. This manner of conceptualizing I think of as an analytical device, not strict empirical description. It aids in understanding changes in international investment flows as these affect conceptualizations of the world economy that rest on the dichotomy core–periphery or highly developed–less developed.

# Conclusion

Organizing this book is the attempt to capture analytically and empirically the articulation of the process of labor migration with fundamental processes in the contemporary phase of the world economy. One such process is the internationalization of production. Commonly this is understood to describe the development of an off-shore manufacturing and clerical sector. I expand this notion to include two additional processes I consider central. One is the development of major cities into centers for global management and servicing. The other is the recent growth of direct foreign investment in manufacturing, finance, and related services in the U.S. Major locations for these three processes are the newly industrializing countries in South East Asia and several Caribbean Basin countries, major cities such as New York and Los Angeles, and regions in the U.S. such as Southern California and the New York Metropolitan Area. All these locations are also significant for the process of labor migration. Production for export in South-East Asia and the Caribbean Basin has generated large internal migrations; most of the new immigrants to the U.S. originate in these countries; New York City and Los Angeles are key recipient areas; and the general region around these cities accounts for a large share of all immigrants. The preceding chapters document the specific forms of the articulation between both processes.

These developments can be seen as representing a rather rapid reorganization of the spatial distribution of growth. The industrial zones in the Third World, the economic boom in New York City and Los Angeles, the massive redirection of direct foreign investment to the U.S., can be counterposed to the loss of jobs in old manufacturing centers of the developed countries and the loss of foreign investment in Third World countries that were until recently leading recipients. Less tentatively one could conceive of these developments as contributing to the formation of a global marketplace of sites for the production of manufactures, clerical tasks, and specialized services.

It is the concentration and sudden implantation of conditions creating an equally sudden demand for a large supply of labor which gives migration its specificity as a process crucial to the formation of the needed labor supply. A less sudden and concentrated demand for labor conceivably can correspond to a whole range of processes inducing the formation of the needed labor supply. The complexity of migration, which is always the migration of *people*, cannot be reduced to this specific aspect. But it is this specific aspect which contains the articulation of the new labor migrations with the recomposition of capital as it takes place in the new industrial zones in Third World countries.

This new territorial organization characterized by the internationalization of finance, manufacturing, and clerical activities entails, in turn, new forms of concentration for the control and servicing of the global production apparatus. The strong tendency for such activities to be located in major cities makes these into strategic nodes in the organization of the world economy. The direct and indirect generation of low-wage jobs induced by the new core economic sector gives the demand for low-wage workers in these sectors its specific character, one that distinguishes it from the demand for low-wage workers in declining or non-strategic sectors. The context within which this demand for low-wage workers occurs, however, is one of political disaffection and remnants of the militance of the 1960s in the minority populations which constitute the mass of low-wage workers in major cities. The specificity of labor migration in this instance is derived from its capacity to meet the demand for low-wage, politically disciplined workers in what are strategic sectors in strategic locations of the world economy. Again, the process of migration cannot be reduced to this specific capacity. It is always the migration of people. Furthermore, migration also provides workers for declining and marginal sectors. But it is the specific capacity to meet the demand in strategic sectors which provides the central articulation with the process of capital recomposition as it takes place in these locations.

These processes of relocation and consolidation of new core economic sectors, together with other major components of the recomposition of capital, contribute to the emergence of new conditions. These new conditions are not necessarily conducive to the reproduction of the arrangements that engender them. For example, growing political pressures and declining economic returns in the Third World make the continuing relocation of capital to these areas somewhat less attractive today than ten years ago. At the same time, there has been a consolidation of a large supply of immigrant workers in the U.S., along with a weakening of the politico-economic position of native workers and a general context more favorable to capital than was the case in the 1960s.

Alongside more purely technical constraints, these political and economic trends have begun to induce a reconcentration of industrial capital in the U.S. This process can be conceived of as the development of new investment zones for world capital. The specificity of immigration in this case is the capacity to provide a large supply of low-wage, disciplined manual workers in a social context characterized by middle-class aspirations or a degree of political disaffection that becomes problematic in the eyes of employers searching for low-wage workers.

One question emerging from this reasoning concerns the political implications of incorporating immigrant workers in growth sectors. History suggests that workers in growth sectors – and in the U.S. these have been immigrants in several crucial periods – have possibilities for organizing which those in declining or marginal sectors lack. The possibility of raising the economic and political situation of immigrant workers would then put in motion conditions that would, again, not be conducive to reproducing this new arrangement over time. It would create new diseconomies from the perspective of capital in a way similar to the growing militance of workers in the new industrial zones of the periphery after a decade of disciplined hard work – a militance that is one of the conditions contributing to the reconcentration of industrial capital in core areas.

# Notes

## 2 *The use of foreign workers*

1 Rapid industrialization has made possible a very high level of expenditure of oil revenues, much of it for imports from the core. Luxury consumption by the elites of these countries could not have generated such a large-scale re-injection of oil revenues into the world accumulation process. On the other hand, the higher price of oil was financed to a large extent by a higher cost of living and a decline in real wages in the core countries. Inflation, another name for this process, can then be seen as a mechanism for the transfer of these savings to the oil-exporting countries and to transnational capital. This suggests that the interests of the states at the core and transnational capital no longer coincide to the extent they did at the turn of the century and up to the immediate post-World War II period. (I have fully developed this argument in Sassen-Koob, 1981a.) It is in this sense that the labor migrations into the oil-exporting countries are to be distinguished from the classical pattern of immigration into high growth areas.

2 Today's large-scale labor imports in Western Europe are typically seen as a reversal of the pre-World War II period and the nineteenth century. But immigration started long before. Already in 1916 Lenin noted that one of the "special features of imperialism . . . is the decline in emigration from the imperialist countries and the increase in immigration into these countries from the more backward countries where lower wages are paid" (1939: 127). He went on to note that this decline had already started in the 1880s and that Germany, for example, had 1.3 million foreign workers by 1907. These facts have been overshadowed in our reading of history by the migrations into the New World, especially the U.S.

3 For example, of the 15 million Italians who emigrated between 1876 and 1920, almost half are estimated to have gone to other European countries, especially Germany, Switzerland, and France (Cinanni, 1968: 29).

4 Employment of a significant level of immigrant workers in these countries has an anti-cyclical effect because the possibility of exporting unemployment by repatriating immigrants in addition to their typically below average demand for goods and services exempts the economy from the need to build the kinds of infrastructure and service organizations that would be required by an equal number of national workers. This will tend to decrease the differences in levels of consumption, employment and utilization of the economy between cycles of expansion and contraction.

5 The use of immigrants to depress wages and weaken unions can already be found earlier in the United States. More generally, the emphasis on technological development as a variable explaining the organization of the labor process has obscured the importance of the struggle between workers and managers for control at the workplace in shaping that organization (Montgomery, 1979; Edwards, 1979). For an analysis of the role of immigrant and minority workers in this process, see Sassen-Koob, 1980.

6 *Encomienda* was a system by which Indians under Spanish colonial rule in Latin America were forced to provide labor or tribute. *Mita* was a similar system but without the option to provide tribute.

7 I am here referring to a specific historical phenomenon. There were, for example, massive migrations in what is today China, involving many different ethnic nations and having a strong colonizing orientation dating from the early second millennium B.C. (Lee, 1978: 20). Furthermore, there are important differences among colonizing migrations (Omvedt, 1973).

8 At the same time, a new politically motivated type of *involuntary* migration emerged in the nineteenth century on a large scale. With fluctuations, it has continued since then. After World War II, some of the largest displacements of people were the result of political and not narrowly economic factors. For an analysis of the relationship between these movements and the consolidation of the world economy, see Zolberg (1978).

9 This consolidation does not follow a fixed, lineal pattern. Rather, it is a historical process in which changing conditions generate new forms of incorporation. Thus, migrants in the more industrialized, developing countries today face new circumstances because the traditional modes of using the rural labor supply in Western Europe – factories in cities – have been exhausted. McGee (1978) points out that the countryside, rather than the cities, has absorbed most of the population increase in highly populated countries in South-East Asia. The historical nature of this process is further brought out by the technological transformation of the secondary sector (Singelmann, 1978). Export industrialization represents yet another phase in this process, a new form of incorporation (see Chapter 4).

10 The most extreme form of the large-scale transfer of manufacturing plants to the developing countries is the development of export-processing zones and world market factories. In both of these, production is mostly for export to the developed countries where the capital originated. This phenomenon began on a large scale in the late 1960s. By 1975, there were 79 export-processing zones, most of them concentrated in South-East Asia and the Caribbean.

11 After World War II, with industrialization fully under way, France was one of the most liberal immigration countries in Western Europe.

12 The growth of the "dangerous poor" expelled from the land and concentrated in urban centers was an important factor in making emigration acceptable. Besides providing a means of creating new markets, emigration came to be seen as a way of applying redundant capital and redundant people to the colonies.

13 For example, the United States saved an estimated $850 million in investment costs in both 1971 and 1972 by admitting technical and professional immigrants from low-wage countries (Committee on Foreign Affairs, 1974). The United

Nations Conference on Trade and Development (UNCTAD) estimated that the United States gained a net income of $3.7 billion in 1970 from such immigration.

14 The size of remittances is a function of this low consumption-to-production ratio. For example, recorded remittances in 1978 amounted to almost one million dollars each in Greece, Spain, and Turkey. This excludes money not transferred through formal channels. A considerable share of these remittances is re-injected into Western Europe through the import of consumption goods (SOPEMI, 1979).

15 Immigrants are commonly thought to retard technological development. But a 1973 survey of 719 firms in southwestern Germany, where the use of foreign labor has been most marked, showed: (1) a greater proportion of firms employing immigrants (54 percent) had introduced technological innovations than firms not employing immigrants (40 percent); (2) the higher the share of immigrants in the workforce, the more innovative the firms were; and (3) capital widening took place more often in firms without immigrants but investments aimed at reducing labor were more frequent in firms with immigrants, such that the degree of foreign employment correlated negatively with capital widening and positively with innovations aimed at reducing labor (Büllinger and Huber, 1974). Furthermore, in research on 26 branches of manufacturing in West Germany, no systematic relationship was found between capital or labor intensity and the level of employment of immigrants in a firm's workforce (Böhning, 1975). I return to this issue in Chapter 5.

16 The cost-lowering effects associated with the institutional differentiation of reproduction and maintenance structures are further accentuated by the system of class relations within which they take place, insofar as employment of immigrants weakens the position of a country's working class as a whole and reduces the average wage level (Castells, 1975; Castles and Kosack, 1973; Oppenheimer, 1974).

17 A 1965 amendment to the Immigration and Naturalization Act turned U.S. immigration policy away from the ethnic preference system and towards family reunion. Recently proposed changes in immigration law would not alter this shift. They aim at implementing programs for (a) the legalization of undocumented aliens who can prove continuous residency as of a given date (typically 1982); (b) sanctions against employers who knowingly hire undocumented workers; and (c) expanded use of contract-labor.

18 There has always been a considerable flow of Mexican immigrants to urban areas (Cardenas, 1978). Recent data also indicate that agricultural employment is less central to undocumented workers, especially Mexicans (Jenkins, 1978). This supports the view that undocumented immigrants are increasingly going to the large cities (Chaney and Sutton, 1979).

19 For a detailed analysis of these issues, and job exports and immigration in New York City in particular, see Sassen-Koob (1981b).

20 Other oil-exporting countries also rely heavily on foreign workers. Iraq lifted all requirements, except a valid passport, for the entry of Arab workers; in the late 1970s it became the largest importer of Egyptian labor. The government also contracted for more selective kinds of labor, such as the import of 200 Moroccan families as farm settlers. These families were given free land, tools, and other

benefits. The war with Iran brought about restrictions in various programs. In Venuezuela, foreigners are estimated to make up about 20 percent of the population. The government has arranged for labor imports with several countries and incorporated such imports into its Fifth Development Plan (1976–80). In addition, Venezuela's government openly recognizes the need for a large, undocumented labor force, especially in agriculture (Venezuela, 1977; Kritz and Gurak, 1979).

21 All these countries have launched drives against illegals. Saudi Arabia, for example, deported more than 56,000 illegals in 1978, and in Jidda, a city on the Red Sea, there were about 300 arrests daily in early 1979. There are, in addition, various ways in which foreign populations are controlled. Kuwait prohibits foreigners from owning property and recently passed a regulation restricting the entry *and exit* of foreigners. In all the Arab oil-exporting countries, the Palestinian population has become a source of concern. In this context it in interesting to note that, in the last decade, a majority of new immigrant workers comes from South and South-East Asia – a reversal of the pre-1970 situation.

22 Employers in Jordan now have to pay wages nearly equal to those of the Arab labor-importing countries. The government has tried to stop the outflow of workers through a number of measures, including a ban on advertisements for jobs abroad.

23 In 1979, remittances supplied 30 percent of Egypt's foreign exchange. It is estimated that two million Egyptian workers were abroad in 1980, mostly in the Arab countries. This would represent about 15 percent of Egypt's labor force. Given the importance of labor exports for the Egyptian economy, the growing presence of South-East Asian workers in the labor-importing countries has created concern. One specific issue is the greater competitiveness of Korean firms which bring in their own labor force rather than recruiting in the host country (Birks and Sinclair, 1979). In general, remittances are an important source of foreign exchange for all the labor-exporting countries. In 1978, estimated remittances from the Middle East to South Korea were over two billion dollars; to India and Pakistan each, 1.6 billion dollars (Keely, 1980).

24 In this context, the price of oil can be seen as a means of extracting savings from people in developed countries – under the guise of an increased cost of living – and injecting them into the world accumulation process (Sassen-Koob, 1981a).

25 There are differences in policy among these countries. While South Korea exports whole projects in which labor is but one component, countries such as Bangladesh export labor by itself. South Korea sees its workers' productivity – from management through to unskilled workers – as a central factor in its competitiveness. It is willing to suffer labor shortages at home for the sake of building up the export sector. Thus, the government has prohibited the recruitment of Korean construction workers by foreign firms. Bangladesh, on the other hand, has included minimum five-year targets for labor exports to the Middle East in its 20-year plan for 1980–2000. The government has training programs geared to the labor export market (Keely, 1980).

26 Here I am clearly taking some liberties with Emmanuel's theory. This theory posits the transfer of value from low-wage to high-wage countries through international trade, even under conditions of free and competitive trade and

equalization of profit rates worldwide. Under these conditions, a value transfer can only occur in the case of specific commodities, that is, commodities produced by only one of the trading partners (Janvry and Kramer, 1979). An argument can be made that labor exports represent a specific commodity.

27 The permanent resident foreign population has increased in these countries, however, due to family reunion and natural increase. Thus, in West Germany, the resident foreign population rose from about four million throughout most of the 1970s to 4.1 million in 1979 and 4.4 million in 1980. After years of stability, we may be seeing a new trend.

28 The second generation is important here. Migrants under 25 years of age represent 40 percent of the total foreign resident population in the main labor-receiving countries. The impact of the second generation on the labor force will be considerable and, to some extent, makes possible a restrictive immigration policy, insofar as it constitutes an internal labor reserve for the less desirable jobs. Political factors may of course intervene in this development, as was the case with the second generation of black migrants in the northern cities of the United States and with the second generation of Puerto Ricans in New York City.

## 3 The new immigration

1 Northern employers advertised in newspapers with a Black readership and used the Federal Department of Labor to recruit and transport workers from the South; there were special trains running between Mississippi and Northern industrial cities (Rossiter, 1922: 56; Chicago Commission on Race Relations, 1968: 86–87). Some local governments in the South reacted by requiring labor recruiters to buy licenses; others imposed fines or jail sentences on any person or organization "enticing, persuading or influencing" labor to leave (Forman, 1971: 16–17).

2 Though legislation was passed in 1921 ending the era of open immigration, this was probably less important in reducing the inflow of foreigners in the subsequent decades than the emergence of alternative sources of low-wage labor. Although fears about the introduction of bolshevism and anarchism in addition to growing prejudice against the new ethnic groups were factors pushing for the passing of this legislation, they were not sufficient to support its restrictions for the next four decades.

3 A 1950 census special study on rural migrants found them to be disproportionately concentrated in lower level occupations, such as laboring and operative jobs and under-represented in white collar and service jobs. However, they were only slightly under-represented in professional and technical jobs, pointing to the high mobility of rural college graduates (Bureau of the Census, 1957: Table 3). Blau and Duncan also found that rural migrants held significantly lower status occupations than those born in cities (1967: 270). However, once settled in cities, White rural migrants, unlike Blacks, tend to have upward occupational mobility and at a faster rate than urban residents with similar qualifications.

4 For example, in 1910, immigrants made up 37 percent of all non-farm laborers and non-Whites, 17.2; in 1950, the corresponding shares were 9.6 and 25.8

percent (for all occupations see Wool and Phillips, 1976: 46, Table 2.3 adapted from: Edwards, 1943; Bureau of the Census, 1953a; Hutchinson, 1956; Kaplan and Casey, 1958).

5  The share of non-Whites in higher level occupations rose from 15.7 percent in 1960 to 27.3 percent in 1970 while that in the lower level occupations declined from 44.3 to 29.4 percent (Wool and Phillips, 1976: 106).

6  General patterns mask differences in labor force participation rates of immigrant women according to national origin, marital status, household strategies to meet income and childcare needs, and place of residence (Pessar, 1982; Castro, 1982; Kuo, 1981; Kritz and Gurak, 1985). While the presence of children is generally associated with lower labor force participation rates for women, such rates tend to be higher for women who head households than for those with a spouse as primary earner. These participation rates in turn have been found to be affected by place of residence and associated differences in access to public assistance. For example, the labor force participation rates of Puerto Rican women who head households are lower than those with a spouse; this may be explained partly by their concentration in New York City and access to a public assistance program such as Aid to Dependent Children by women heads of household. Kritz and Gurak (1985) found a similar pattern in their study of Colombian and Dominican women in New York City. The authors reason that the high level of public assistance among heads of household in all three groups suggests that location may have something to do with it, that is to say, public assistance is a more feasible alternative to low-wage employment in New York City than in many other areas of the country.

7  This over-representation of immigrants in certain areas is further underlined by facts such as the location of the major voluntary resettlement agencies in New York City. One result is that New York ranks third among states in recent Indochinese placements from overseas and continues to receive over 100 Indochinese migrants from other regions every month. The New York Metropolitan area also has two-thirds of the nation's Haitian immigrants and the largest Cuban community outside of Florida. In many ways this concentration of Haitians, Cubans and Indochinese in New York is worth examining since other geographic locations would seem to make more sense.

8  The return rates are, however, rather different for each of the major nationality groups, a fact to be considered in evaluating the growth rates of the respective immigrant populations. Jasso and Rosenzweig (1982) examined the 1971 cohort of legal immigrants and estimated their cumulative emigration rates as of 1979. Using administrative and survey data, they found that emigration rates for Caribbean Basin and South American immigrants in the U.S. were at least 50 percent and could have been as high as 70 percent. Emigration rates for Korean and Chinese immigrants in the U.S. could not have exceeded 22 percent over that same eight-year period.

9  Furthermore, these Census-data-based categories include natives (though they are largely part of immigrant communities), and, in the case of Hispanics, non-Western Hemisphere Spanish-language people.

10  The stereotype in popular imagery, that urban areas taken over by immigrant colonies tend to become slum-like, is in many cases incorrect. For example, in New York City's Borough of Queens, which has one of the largest concentrations

of Hispanic immigrants, there has been a visible and rapid upgrading in the Hispanic neighborhoods. Areas which used to be boarded up, poorly kept, are now thriving commercial districts with nicely kept family homes, a growing rate of home ownership, streets that are safe at night, and so on (Sassen-Koob, 1981b 1979; Chaney, 1976).

11  An important factor here is the closing of the temporary contract labor program with Mexico (generally referred to as the "bracero" program) in 1964, which as late as 1960 provided almost half a million farm workers annually. As the number of temporary workers fell, the number of those apprehended rose, pointing to an increase in undocumented entries which came to replace the "braceros." However, long before the "bracero" program was ended, there were very high levels of undocumented Mexicans reaching well over half a million in the early 1950s (Samora *et al.*, 1971: 43–47). It is quite possible that the initiation of the contract labor program created the conditions for undocumented immigration as well. This is the pattern we find in New York City today, where the mostly legal immigration of South Americans and Caribbeans in the early 1960s was followed by large-scale undocumented immigration in the 1970s.

12  In 1976, for example, of the 875,915 deportable aliens located by the INS, 781,474 were Mexicans and almost all of these were EWIs (INS, 1978: 136).

13  INS apprehensions of Mexicans outside the Southwest increased nineteen-fold between 1964 and 1974, and the share of these apprehensions in the total for Mexicans increased as well (National Commission, 1978: 129).

14  South American and Caribbean undocumented aliens have a far more elaborate set of barriers to cross than Mexicans insofar as they have to deal with consular authorities and formal documentation requirements. This ability typically requires a certain level of literacy. For a description of how Colombians and Dominicans manage to reach New York City, see Sassen-Koob (1979: 316–321).

15  At the time of the survey, 1975, there were three minimum wage levels in effect: $1.80 for farm workers, $2.10 for most non-farm workers, and $2.00 for persons in industries that were being transferred to full minimum wage coverage. Using these wage levels and industry identification, North and Houstoun (1976: 119ff.) found that 76 percent of undocumented workers in their sample of INS apprehensions were paid above the corresponding minimum wage. Their sample was weighted so as to eliminate the over-representation of EWIs and Mexicans typical of INS data.

## 4 The globalization of production

1  Besides providing various kinds of concessions and subsidies, these zones respond to structural and organizational needs of foreign companies. In fact, in some cases the foreign companies help plan and organize the management of such zones. Finally, in some cases, the foreign companies control the zones, notably La Romana Zone in the Dominican Republic whose government has given control over the zone to foreign capital for 30 years. One corporation's interest in having a zone in Indonesia led to its involvement in promoting and developing the zone and subsequently to a management and technical assistance contract to assist in the running of the Pulo Gadung Industrial Estate. Examples like these are not uncommon (UNIDO, 1980: 19).

2 This is a development that may well continue. Thus while some analysts identify absorptive capacity for imports in developed countries with current levels of imports and hence argue that future expansion of such imports from less developed countries is unlikely, precisely because the share of imports is small in total consumption one might argue that there still is considerable room for expansion. This is particularly so if the comparative advantage of the less developed countries cannot be easily overcome by technological developments (e.g., in garments) or is precisely a function of very modern labor-intensive techniques (e.g., semi-conductor assembly plants). Secondly, diversification is another way in which exports can be expanded, one that we see already happening. The range of goods that are being incorporated in off-shore processing and assembly operations continues to increase. Thirdly, the expansion of exports for some countries may be at the cost of others. We are beginning to see a shift of plants from some of the older newly industrializing countries to other less developed countries: Malaysia and the Philippines are more recent locations than Singapore and Hong Kong, but they in turn are beginning to experience competition from Sri Lanka and African countries. Finally, while the developed countries are still the major market, the centrally planned and other less developed countries may eventually come to represent significant markets. It is worth noting in this regard that imports by developing countries grew at a faster rate from 1970 to 1976 than imports for the world as a whole, 3.3 percent and 2.6 percent respectively (UNIDO, 1980: 157).

3 Less developed countries accounted for 7 percent of manufactured imports in developed countries and for 1 percent of domestic sales of manufactures. In the U.S., textiles and clothing imports were 1.7 percent and 3.3 percent of total supply in the domestic market. Less developed countries accounted for 32 percent of all textile imports to the U.S. and 60 percent of all clothing imports. However it should be noted that the percentage supplied by the less developed countries to the U.S., Japan and Western Europe in each of several key products rose from 1970 to 1976. The percentage going to the developed countries was always higher than that going to other less developed countries. The export of clothing reached a value in 1975–76 that was almost three times its value in 1970–1971; similar increases took place in chemicals and machinery. Correspondingly, the imports – though a small share of all consumption – by developed countries also increased over the same period, e.g., Japan's imports of clothing increased five-fold from 1970–71 to 1975–76. If we put these trends in the context of the high levels of concentration of export manufacturing in a few less developed countries, then we can see that these trends carry a distinct weight in these countries.

4 At one time, the bulk of exports by less developed countries was semi-processed products (foodstuffs and raw materials) to be processed in developed countries. Towards the end of the 1960s, the bulk of exports was consumer goods. It is important to control for rapid increase of price of oil and rapid increase in world trade to specify the correct weight of consumer goods exports. Thus while both in 1968 and 1974 such exports accounted for 17 percent of all exports, this constant share actually represents a sharp value increase given the rise in value of oil exports and the overall rise in world trade. There also was a very high growth rate in the export of capital goods by less developed countries, averaging about 45

percent a year from 1970 to 1976. The top ten exporters provided 86 percent of all such exports from the less developed world. (Information based on Commodity Trade Statistics, various issues.)

5 Furthermore, given the fact that the bulk of export production from the less developed countries is imported by the developed countries, the legal arrangements on imports become a crucial variable: only when there are powerful interests in the developed countries involved in this export production is there likely to be a favorable tariff structure (Helleiner, 1973: 28). This is particularly so given the protectionist position assumed by several powerful labor unions in the developed countries.

6 The growth in manufacturing employment in less developed countries was high compared not only with developed countries but also with centrally planned economies and with historical levels. And the growth in output was higher even than that of employment which points to gains in productivity. However, the gap in productivity between the less developed and the developed countries continues to grow. Thus it is interesting to note that the rate of employment growth in the less developed countries contributes more to output growth than gains in productivity, something which is not the case in the developed countries where capital deepening rather than widening is the rule.

7 Until 1968, the developed countries accounted for 50 percent of world manufacturing employment while the less developed countries accounted for 26.7 percent. By 1975, the share of the latter had risen to 33.1 percent and that of the developed countries had dropped by over 6 percent. During this period, the share of the centrally planned economies remained at 23.5 percent (UNIDO, 1980: 224–227). Furthermore, the growth rate in manufacturing employment in the less developed countries was higher than that of all sectors together in these countries. Growth in manufacturing employment was thus higher than that in other non-agricultural sectors, something that goes counter to a common view regarding less developed countries. This higher growth in manufacturing for the less developed countries as a whole underestimates the magnitude of such growth due to the high concentration of manufacturing production in only a few countries.

8 This strategy is quite significant if we consider, for example, that the share of North America in world exports fell from 37 percent in 1960 to 27 percent in 1975, that of Japan rose from 3 to 7 percent and that of the less developed countries went from 6.9 to 9 percent and most of it is accounted for by a few countries (UNIDO, 1980: 37).

9 There are advantages in such zones for less developed countries seeking to draw foreign investment. The zones are a device for concentrating a variety of benefits and subsidies and in this sense are more cost-effective for the governments of the host countries. Such concentration facilitates planning and installation of external infrastructure, particularly power, water, telephones, sewers, roads, airport facilities.

10 Beneria (1984) shows extensive use of women as homeworkers or in sweatshops by multinational firms selling to the domestic market in Mexico. Industries covered in her study were garments, electronics, toys, plastics, and other branches commonly found in the new industrial zones producing for export.

## 5 The rise of global cities

1  Rapid new product development, product diversification and expansion into new markets generate a vast array of costs usually referred to as transaction and adjustment costs. (For a detailed classification of these costs see Williamson, 1980). Transaction costs are those involved in bringing together the supply and demand side of a market; adjustment costs are those involved in increasing the supply of resources whose production demands time, notably highly skilled labor, organization structures, technologically advanced machinery, etc. These costs, particularly transaction costs, involve a variety of services such as advertising, strategic planning, financial services, public relations and other liaison activities, lobbying, research and forecasting, etc. These are specialized services produced for firms either in-house or on the market which have become basic inputs in a firm's operation. Case studies of particular corporations have found that these kind of costs have become increasingly important with the growing size of firms and greater product diversification.

2  Chandler (1977: 6) notes that the organizational characteristics of today's large corporations "appeared for the first time in history when the volume of economic activities reached a level that made administrative coordination more efficient and more profitable than market coordination." There is a noteworthy dynamic here. Given the large size of firms it becomes more profitable for a firm to internalize transaction and circulation costs. At the same time this new expanded organization structure generates a rapidly growing need for highly specialized services which given their degree of specialization are most profitably produced on an open market rather than internalized. This has given rise to a free-standing market of producer services.

3  The actual closing and moving of factories is only one component of the relocation of manufacturing, probably a relatively small one. More significant in terms of actual job losses are various kinds of disinvestment that amount to a gradual contraction of the manufacturing base: (a) the shift of profits and savings of a given plant to plants in other locations, or their investment in other types of activities; (b) gradual moving of equipment and jobs, without necessarily closing the plant; (c) no new investments for plant maintenance or new equipment acquisitions.

4  A development that may further speed the decentralization of office work is deregulation of the telecommunications industry. Until 1982 companies that needed satellite data-transmission facilities had to purchase these services from one of the international carriers, such as ITT or AT&T. These are basically re-sellers of these services because the only one that can sell international satellite services in the case of the U.S. is Comstat, the U.S. representative in the Intersat system. Comsat has a monopoly on international satellite services and until 1982 could sell those services only to the international communications companies. Since 1982, the FCC has ruled that companies can now purchase these services directly from Comsat, a fact that lowers the costs of acquisition and facilitates access. Now companies can develop their own transmission system.

5  The data on the international trade balance are inadequate. There have been growing surpluses in "invisibles." But these cannot be fully attributed to the sales

of services. On the other hand, some of the receipts of service industries are reported under the merchandise account. A full analysis on sources of information on service exports can be found in Economic Consulting Services (1981) and the U.S. Department of Commerce (1980a).

6 The technological transformation in manufacturing and the possibility of centralizing the management of a dispersed manufacturing base also means that the development of manufacturing in Third World countries can rely on the import of advanced services from the highly developed countries. The case of OPEC members is of interest here. After the 1973 increase in the international price of oil and the decision to transform the large influx of oil revenues into vast accelerated development programs, there was an immense rise in the import of services by these countries. From 1973 to 1978, overall oil revenues for OPEC members were $700 billion. During that same period the value of imports reached $530 billion, of which well over a third was for services.

7 Producer services do not fit neatly into standard classifications. Viewed as intermediate outputs, they include finance, insurance and real estate, wholesaling and a wide range of business services. These three account for a large share of the intermediate outputs sold by all service firms (Greenfield, 1966; Stanback, 1979).

8 Standard classifications of economic activities have become increasingly problematic with the technological transformation of the work process. Here I use the classification first developed by Browning and Singelmann (1978), further elaborated by Singelmann (1978: 28–36) and Stanback, Jr, *et al.* (1981). In this classification, producer services refer to industries that provide services mostly to producers of goods or property related operations. They are then a type of intermediate output (Greenfield, 1966: 11; Machlup, 1962: 39–40). They include banking, credit and other financial services; insurance; real estate; engineering and architectural services; accounting and bookkeeping; miscellaneous business services; legal services (Singelmann, 1978: 31). Producer services represent the following SIC branches: 60 to 67, 73, 81, 83 (after 1974), 86 and 89.

9 The magnitude of the increases in foreign and domestic investment and in the construction of industrial parks in adjacent San Diego county is clearly beginning to outpace growth in the Los Angeles area. The available evidence suggests that this represents in good part an expansion of the Los Angeles industrial complex. Of significance here is the nearby 38,600 acre Mesa de Otay, half each on either side of the Mexico–U.S. border, which it is expected will be developed as a twin-plant zone. To this should be added a novel kind of development, the relocation of plants away from areas that have been major recipients of such plants, notably Taiwan, Hong Kong and Mexico, and into San Diego County. It seems that these relocations respond to two kinds of constraints: the fact that Southern California has a plentiful supply of immigrant labor, and second, problems of quality control which require vicinity to technical centers. The combination of resources in an area like Southern California – a large supply of cheap and docile labor *and* of highly trained technical personnel and researchers – points to the development of regions like these as industrial zones for world investment that are an alternative, under certain conditions, to zones in the Caribbean Basin or South-East Asia (Sassen-Koob, 1987; San Diego, 1981; 1983).

10  It should be noted, however, that this brought the actual number of manufacturing jobs in the Greater New York Area to 1.3 million, that is, the same as in the Los Angeles Area. The similarity in this level reflects a 19 percent decline from 1970 to 1980 for New York City and a 23 percent increase for Los Angeles over that same period. The increase for the U.S. as a whole was 5 percent. The high absolute number of jobs in manufacturing in these two areas and the characteristics of these jobs are of significance in explaining the absorption of a good share of the large immigrant influx. Marshall (1983) notes the increasing relative and absolute participation of immigrants in manufacturing in New York City during the 1970s.

11  There are different locations for various segments of the highly paid new professional stratum. Engineers and technical personnel linked directly with high-tech industry and the associated research operations are clustered in various key high-tech or research locations: Silicon Valley, Orange County, Austin, the Route 128 area around Boston. These are, in some ways, to be distinguished from those employed in the advanced services. The first are ultimately the new cadres of what is today's basic industry, the development and production of microprocessors. The second are involved in control, management and servicing functions. The locations of these two sets of activities frequently are distinct, but at times they overlap, e.g., in Los Angeles, a site for both the production of control, management and servicing functions and a site for the production of engineering and technical operations. These distinctions bring to mind some of the work done on the manufacturing sector that views the geographic distribution of industry as a spatial division of labor (Storper and Walker 1983).

12  In a study on the auto industry in Los Angeles, Morales (1983) found considerable restructuring in the auto-parts branches: a shift from native to immigrant, including undocumented, workers and a shift from less to more automated forms of production which allowed for the incorporation of cheaper, often immigrant workers and expulsion of more highly paid workers. Similarly, see Balmori (1983) on the construction industry in New York City. See also Christopherson (1983) on the regional specificity of segmentation in different immigrant labor markets.

13  A more detailed analysis of the service sector shows that the highest growth rates were in computer services (51.8 percent), personnel agencies and temporary employment agencies (65.6 percent), management consulting and public relations (31.1 percent), engineering and architecture (24.2 percent), accounting (18.8 percent), protective services (19.9 percent), securities dealers (19.5 percent), theaters (excluding movie theaters) (21.0 percent), and in out-patient care facilities (48.4 percent) (U.S. Bureau of Labor Statistics, 1982).

14  Among the low-wage jobs included in the subsample are the following (as listed in the study): maid, cleaner (light and heavy), janitor, porter, baggage porter, bellhop, kitchen helper, pantry, sandwich/coffee maker, food service worker, room service attendant, ticket taker, stock clerk (stock room, warehouse, storage yard), washer, machine washer, dry cleaner (hand), spotter (dry cleaning, washable materials), laundry presser, laundry folder, rug cleaner (hand and machine), shoe repairer, delivery and route worker, parking lot attendant, exterminator, packager, etc.

15 The biggest components of New York City business services are advertising, legal, building maintenance, research and development, and management and consulting services. The above cited survey on major service industries lists advertising and legal as two separate industries.

# References

Ahmad, M. and A. Jenkins, 1980. "Traditional paddy husking – an appropriate technology under pressure," *Appropriate Technology* (London). 7 (2): 28–30

Amin, 1974a. *Accumulation on a World Scale: A Critique of the Theory of Underdevelopment*, vols. 1 and 2. New York: Monthly Review Press

1974b. *Modern Migrations in West Africa*. New York: Oxford University Press

1976. *Unequal Development: An Essay on the Social Formations of Peripheral Capitalism*. New York: Monthly Review Press

Arrighi, G. and J. Saul (eds.), 1973. *Essays on the Political Economy of Africa*. New York: Monthly Review Press

Arrigo, Linda G., 1980. "The industrial work force of young women in Taiwan," *Bulletin of Concerned Asia Scholars* 12 (2): 25–37

Bach, Robert L., 1978. "Mexican immigration and the American state," *International Migration Review* 12 (Winter): 536–558

Bach, Robert L. and M. Tienda, 1984. "Contemporary immigration and refugee movements and employment adjustment policies," pp. 37–82 in V.M. Briggs, Jr, and M. Tienda (eds.), *Immigration Issues and Policies*. Salt Lake City: Olympus Publishing Co.

Bailey, Tom and Marcia Freedman, 1981. "The restaurant industry in New York City." New York: Conservation of Human Resources, Columbia University. Project on Newcomers to New York City (Conservation of Human Resources). Working Paper No. 2

Balke, S. 1966. "Die Ausländerbeschäftigung aus der Sicht der Wirtschaft," *Magnet Bundesrepublik* (Bundesvereinigung der Deutschen Arbeitgeberverbande) 42: 168–172

Balmori, D., 1983. "Hispanic immigrants in the construction industry: New York City, 1960–1982," Center for Latin American and Caribbean Studies, New York University, *Occasional Papers*, No. 38

Banco de la República (Colombia), 1982. *Revista del Banco de la República*. Bogotá: Banco de la República

The Bank of Korea, 1982. *Economic Statistics Yearbook 1981*. Seoul: The Bank of Korea

Bauer, David, 1980. "The question of foreign investment," *New York Affairs* 6(2): 52–58

Baxandall, Rosalyn, Linda Gordon, and Susan Reverby, 1976. *America's Working Women, A Documentary History – 1600 to the Present*. New York: Vintage Books

Beckford, George, 1972. *Persistent Poverty*. London: Oxford University Press

Beneria, Lourdes, 1984. "Industrial Homework and the Decentralization of Modern Production." *The Urban Informal Sector: Recent Trends in Research and Theory*

(Proceedings of the Seminar on the Informal Sector in Center and Periphery). Baltimore: The Johns Hopkins University

Birks, Stace and Clive Sinclair, 1979. "Contractors: current trends offer little to Arab contractors," *Construction*, Special Reports, April

Blair, John, 1982. *Economic Concentration*. New York: Holt, Rinehart

Blau, Peter M. and Otis Dudley Duncan, 1967. *The American Occupational Structure*. New York: John Wiley and Sons

Bluestone, Barry and Bennett Harrison, 1982. The *Deindustrialization of America*. New York: Basic Books

Bluestone, Barry, Bennett Harrison, and Lucy Gorham, 1984. "Storm clouds on the horizon: labor market crisis and industrial policy." Brookline, MA: Economic Education Project (May 1984)

Böhning, W. R., 1975a. *Mediterranean Workers in Western Europe: Effects on Home Countries and Countries of Employment*. Geneva: International Labor Office, World Employment Programme, Working Paper

  1975b. "Some thoughts on emigration from the Mediterranean basin," *International Labor Review* 3 (March): 251–77

  1976. "Migration from developing to high-income countries," pp. 119–138, in International Labor Office Tripartite World Conference on Employment, Income Distribution and Social Progress and the International Division of Labor, Background Papers, I

Böhning, W. R. and Denis Maillat, 1974. *The Effects of the Employment of Foreign Workers*. Paris: Organization of Economic Cooperation and Development, Division of Manpower and Social Affairs

Bonilla, Frank and Ricardo Campos, 1982. "Boot straps and Enterprise Zones: the underside of late capitalism in Puerto Rico and the United States," *Review* 4 (Spring): 556–590

Boserup, E., 1970. *Woman's Role in Economic Development*. New York: St Martin's Press

Boulding, E., 1980. *Women: The Fifth World*. Washington, D.C.: Foreign Policy Association, Headline Series 248 (Feb.)

Braverman, Harry, 1974. *Labor and Monopoly Capital: The Degradation of Labor in the Twentieth Century*. New York: Monthly Review Press

Briggs, V. M., W. F. Schmidt and F. M. Schmidt, 1977. *The Chicano Worker*. Austin: University of Texas Press

Browning, Harley L. and Joachim Singelmann, 1978. "The transformation of the U.S. labor force: the interaction of industry and occupation," *Politics and Society* 8 (3 and 4)

Bryce-Laporte, Roy S. and Delores M. Mortimer (eds.), 1981. *Female Immigrants to the United States: Caribbean, Latin American and African Experiences*. RIIES Occasional Papers No. 2. Washington, D.C.: Smithsonian Institution, Research Institute on Immigration and Ethnic Studies

Büllinger, S. and P. Huber, 1974. "Ausländerbeschäftigung aus Unternehmersicht: Quantitative und Qualitative Ergebnisse einer Unternehmerbefrägung in Baden-Wurtenberg." Tubingen: Institut für Angewandte Wirtschaftsforschung

Burawoy, Michael, 1976. "The functions and reproduction of migrant labor: comparative material from Southern Africa and the United States," *American Journal of Sociology* 81 (March): 1050–1087

1981. "Terrains of contest: factory and state under capitalism and socialism," *Socialist Review* (July–August 1981)

Burbach, G. and S. Flynn, 1980. *Agribusiness in the Americas*. New York: Monthly Review Press and NACLA

Bureau of National Affairs, 1982. *Layoffs, Plant Closings, and Concession Bargaining*. Washington, D.C.: Bureau of National Affairs (April)

Bustamante, Jorge A., 1972. "The historical context of the undocumented immigration from Mexico to the United States," *Aztlan* 3 (Fall): 257–282

1976. "More on the impact of the undocumented immigration from Mexico on the U.S.–Mexican economies." Unpublished paper

Byerlee, D., 1972. "Research on migration in Africa: past, present, and future," Department of Agricultural Economics, African Rural Employment Paper No. 2 Michigan State University (Sept.)

California, Department of Economic and Business Development, 1981a. *California Labor Market Bulletin – Statistical Supplement* (December)

1981b. "Employment growth in the California electronics industry" (Mimeo) DEBD, Office of Economic Policy, Planning and Research (June)

1981c. "The aerospace industry in California" (Mimeo; April)

1981d. "Investments in economic strength" (Mimeo; April)

1982. "California's technological future: emerging economic opportunities in the 1980s" (March)

n.d. "A preliminary shift-share analysis of employment in California, 1960–1980" (Mimeo)

California, Employment Development Department, 1983. "Closed businesses in California: Feb. 1980 to Apr. 1983" (Mimeo; June)

*California Business*, 1982. "A California business magazine economic report: Orange County, 1982" September

Cardenas, Gilberto, 1976. "United States immigration policy toward Mexico: a historical perspective." Unpublished paper. Department of Sociology, University of Texas, Austin

1978. "Chicanos in the Midwest," *Aztlan*, Special Issue, 7 (Fall)

Carey, Max L., 1976. "Revised occupational projections to 1985," *Monthly Labor Review* 99 (11; November): 10–22, U.S. Department of Labor, Bureau of Labor Statistics

Castells, Manuel, 1975. "Immigrants, workers and class struggles in advanced capitalism: the Western European experience," *Politics and Society* 5 (1): 33–66

Castles, Stephen and Godula Kosack, 1973. *Immigrant Workers and Class Structure in Western Europe*. London: Oxford University Press, Institute of Race Relations

Castro, Garcia M., 1982. "'Mary's and 'Eve's' social reproduction in the 'Big Apple': Colombian voices." New York Research Program in Inter-American Affairs, New York University, *Occasional Papers*, no. 35

Caughman, S. and M. N'diaye Thiam, 1980. "Soap-making: the experiences of a women's co-operative in Mali," *Appropriate Technology* (London) 7 (3; December): 4–6

Caves, R. E., 1976. "International corporations: the industrial economics of foreign investment," *Economica*, n.s., 38 (149; February): 1–27

Caves, R. E., 1980. "Industrial organization, corporate strategy, and structure," *Journal of Economic Literature* 28 (1): 64–92

CCA–URM, 1981. *Struggling to Survive: Women' Workers in Asia.* Hong Kong: CCA–URM

Centro de Estudios Puertorriqueños, 1979. *Labor Migration Under Capitalism: The Puerto Rican Experience.* History Task Force. New York: Monthly Review Press

Cetin, I., 1974. "Migrant workers, wages, and labor markets." USAID Staff Papers, no. 18, Ankara

Chandler, Alfred, 1977. *The Visible Hand: The Managerial Revolution in American Business.* Cambridge, Mass.: Harvard University Press

Chaney, Elsa, 1976. *Colombian Migration to the United States* (Part 2). Occasional Monograph Series, Smithsonian Institution, Interdisciplinary Communications Program, vol. 2, no. 5

    1980. *Women in International Migration: Issues in Development Planning.* Washington, D.C.: Office for Women in Development, U.S. Agency for International Development

    1984. *Women of the World: Latin America and the Caribbean.* Washington D.C.: Office for Women in Development, U.S. Agency for International Development (May)

Chaney, Elsa and Constance Sutton (eds.), 1979. "Caribbean migration to New York," *International Migration Review,* Special Issue, 13 (Summer)

Chicago Commission on Race Relations, 1968. *The Negro in Chicago.* (Originally published by University of Chicago Press, 1922.) Reprinted, Arno

Cho, S. K., 1984. "The feminization of the labor movement in South Korea." Unpublished paper, Department of Sociology, University of California, Berkeley

Christopherson, S., 1983. "Segmentation in Sunbelt labor markets." Research Report Series. Center for U.S.–Mexican Studies, University of California, San Diego

Cinanni, Paolo, 1968. *Emigrazione e imperialismo.* Rome: Editori Riuniti

City of New York, 1982. *Report on Economic Conditions in New York City: July–December 1981.* New York: Office of Management and Budget and Office of Economic Development

    1985. *Report on Economic Conditions in New York City: July–December 1984.* New York: Office of Management and Budget and Office of Economic Development

Cohen, Robert, 1979. *The Impact of Foreign Direct Investment on U.S. Cities and Regions.* Washington, D.C.: U.S. Department of Housing and Urban Development

    1981. "The new international division of labor, multinational corporations and urban hierarchy," in Michael Dear and Allen Scott (eds.), *Urbanization and Urban Planning in Capitalist Society.* New York: Methuen

Cohen, S. and Saskia Sassen-Koob, 1982. "Survey of six immigrant groups in Queens." Department of Sociology, Queens College, City University of New York

Colombia Information Service, 1979. "Foreign investment trends in Colombia." Colombia Center, New York

Commission des Communautés Européennes, 1977. *Statistiques sur l'emploi des étrangers: 1976.* Brussels

Committee on Foreign Affairs, U.S. House of Representatives, 1974. *Brain Drain: A Study of the Present Issue of International Scientific Mobility.* Washington D.C.: U.S. Government Printing Office

Commodity Trade Statistics [various issues]. *Statistical Papers, Series D, Commodity Trade Statistics.* ST/ESA/STAT/SER. D. New York: United Nations Department of International Economic and Social Affairs, Statistical Office of the United Nations

Conference Board, Inc., 1981. *Announcements of Foreign Investment in U.S. Manufacturing Industries.* 1st, 2nd, 3rd, and 4th Quarter. New York: The Conference Board, Inc
    1983. "International trade in services: a growing force in the world economy," *World Business Perspectives* no. 75 (October)

Conservation of Human Resources, 1977. *The Corporate Headquarters Complex in New York City.* Columbia University: Conservation of Human Resources Project

Cornelius, Wayne A., 1977. "Illegal Mexican migration to the United States: recent research findings and policy implications," pp. 7062–7068 in *Congressional Record-House* (July 13)
    1981. *Mexican Migration to the U.S.: The Limits of Government Intervention. Working Papers,* No. 5. Center for U.S.–Mexican Studies, University of California, San Diego

Council on Wage and Price Stability, 1978. "A study of textile and apparel industries." Washington, D.C.: The Council on Wage and Price Stability (July), 27

County of San Diego, 1982a. *Otay Special Project Final Economic and Fiscal Impact Report.* County of San Diego Otay Special Project Office (July 13)
    1982b. *1981–1982 San Diego County Border Task Force; Findings and Recommendations Concerning Otay Mesa.* County of San Diego (June 1)
    1982c. *Annual Planning Information: San Diego Standard Metropolitan Statistical Area, 1982–1983.* State of California: Health and Welfare Agency (Prepared by John C. Nevell, III)

Curtin, Phillip D., 1969. *The Atlantic Slave Trade: A Census.* Madison: University of Wisconsin Press

Dauber, R. and M. L. Cain (eds.), 1981. *Women and Technological Change in Developing Countries.* Boulder, CO: Westview Press

DAWN [Development Alternatives with Women for a New Era] 1985. *Development, Crises, and Alternative Visions: Third World Women's Perspectives.* New Delhi: DAWN

Deere, C. D., 1976. "Rural women's subsistence production in the capitalist periphery," *Review of Radical Political Economy* 8(1): 9–17

Delatour, Leslie, 1979. "The evolution of international subcontracting industries in Haiti." Presented at UNCTAD Seminar, July 16–20, Mexico [mimeo]

Delaunoy, I.V., 1975. "Formación, Empleo y Seguridad Social de la Mujer en America Latina y el Caribe," pp. 59–114 in Henriques de Paredes, P. Izaguirre and I. V. Delaunoy (eds.), *Participación de la Mujer en el Desarrollo de America Latina y el Caribe.* Santiago, Chile: UNICEF Regional Office

Denison, Edward, 1979. *Accounting for Slower Economic Growth: The U.S. in the 1970s.* Washington, D.C.: Brookings Institution

Deyo, Frederic, 1981. *Dependent Development and Industrial Order.* New York: Praeger Publishers

DiLullo, Anthony J., 1981. "Service transactions in the U.S. international accounts, 1970–1980," *Survey of Current Business* (November): 29–46

Dinerman, Ina R., 1982. "Urban hierarchies and rural labor: shifting patterns of migration from two communities in Michoacan, Mexico," Unpublished paper, Wheaton College

Direction de la Documentation Française, 1986. "Politiques d'Immigration en Europe," *Problèmes Politiques et Sociaux* no. 530 (Feb. 21)

Directorate-General of Budget: [The Republic of China], 1979. *Monthly Bulletin of Statistics: The Republic of China*, Taipei: Directorate-General of Budget, Accounting, and Statistics

1982. *Monthly Bulletin of Statistics: The Republic of China*, Taipei: Directorate-General of Budget, Accounting, and Statistics

Dominguez, Virginia R., 1975. *From Neighbor to Stranger: The Dilemma of Caribbean Peoples in the U.S.* New Haven: Antilles Research Program, Yale University

Drake, St. Clair and Horace R. Clayton, 1962. *Black Metropolis*. New York: Harper and Row, Torchbook

Drennan, Matthew, 1983. "Local economy and local revenues," pp. 19–44 in M. Hornton and C. Brecher (eds.), *Setting Municipal Priorities 1984.* New York and London: New York University Press

ECLA [*Economic Commission on Latin America*], 1975. *Economic Survey of Latin America 1973.* Santiago: UN ECLA

1977. *Economic Survey of Latin America 1975.* Santiago: UN ECLA

1979. *Economic Survey of Latin America 1977.* Santiago: UN ECLA

1980. *Economic Survey of Latin America 1978.* Santiago: UN ECLA

1982. *Economic Survey of Latin America 1980.* Santiago: UN ECLA

Economic Consulting Services, Inc., 1981. *The International Operations of U.S. Service Industries; Current Data Collection and Analysis.* Washington, D.C.: Economic Consulting Services, Inc.

Edwards, Alba, 1943. *Sixteenth Census of the United States, 1940. Population. Comparative occupational statistics for the United States, 1870–1940.* Washington, D.C.: U.S. Government Printing Office

Edwards, Richard, 1979. *Contested Terrain: The Transformation of the Workplace in the Twentieth Century.* New York: Basic Books

Ehrenhalt, Samuel M., 1981. "Some perspectives on the outlook for the New York City labor market," *Challenges of the Changing Economy of New York City.* New York: The New York City Council on Economic Education

Emmanuel, Arrighi, 1972. *Unequal Exchange: A Study of the Imperialism of Trade.* New York: Monthly Review Press

ESCAP [*Economic and Social Commission for Asia and the Pacific*], 1977. *Economic and Social Survey of Asia and the Pacific, 1976.* Bangkok: ESCAP

1979. *Economic and Social Survey of Asia and the Pacific, 1978.* Bangkok: ESCAP

1981. *Economic and Social Survey of Asia and the Pacific, 1979.* Bangkok: ESCAP

Evans, Peter, 1979. "Shoes, OPIC, and the unquestioning persuasion: multinational corporations and U.S.–Brazilian relations," pp. 302–336 in Richard R. Fagen (ed.), *Capitalism and the State in U.S.–Latin American Relations.* Stanford: Stanford University Press

Fernandez Kelly, Maria Patricia, 1983. *For We Are Sold, I and My People: Women and Industry in Mexico's Frontier.* Albany: SUNY Press

Fishel, Leslie H. and Benjamin Quarles, 1970. *The Black American: A Documentary History.* William Morrow and Co.

Forman, Robert E., 1971. *Black Ghettos, White Ghettos and Slums*. Englewood Cliffs, N.J: Prentice Hall.

Freeman, Gary, 1979. "The political economy of immigration policy: labor supply and legitimacy." Paper presented at the Council for European Studies Conference for Europeanists, Washington, D.C., March 29–31

Fröbel, Folker, Jurgen Heinrichs and Otto Kreye, 1980. *The New International Division of Labor*. London: Cambridge University Press

Fuchs, Victor, 1968. *The Service Economy*. New York: National bureau of Economics Research and Columbia University Press

Furtado, Celso, 1963. *The Economic Growth of Brazil: A Survey from Modern to Colonial Times*. Berkeley: University of California Press

Galarza, Ernesto, 1964. *Merchants of Labor*. Santa Barbara: McNally and Loftin

George, Susan, 1977. *How the Other Half Dies: The Real Reasons for World Hunger*. Montclair, NJ: Allanheld, Osmun

Glazer, Nathan and Daniel P. Moynihan, 1963. *Beyond the Melting Pot: The Negros, Puerto Ricans, Jews, Italians and Irish of New York City*. Boston: MIT Press

Goldmark, Jr., Peter C., 1979. "Foreign business in the economy of the New York–New Jersey metropolitan region," *City Almanac* 14 (August): 1–14

Grasmuck, Sherri, 1981. "Enclave development and relative labor surplus: Haitian labor in the Dominican Republic." Unpublished Manuscript, Temple University

1982. "The impact of emigration on national development: three sending communities in the Dominican Republic." New York: Center for Latin American and Caribbean Studies, New York University, Occasional Papers, No. 34

Greenfield, H. I., 1966. *Manpower and the Growth of Producer Services*. New York: Columbia University Press

Grossman, Rachael, 1979. "Women's place in the integrated circuit," *Southeast Asia Chronicle 66–Pacific Research 9* (Joint Issue): 2–17

Grover, Wendy, 1983. "Industrial restructuring and state intervention: planning the development of Otay Mesa, California." School of Urban Planning, University of California, Los Angeles

Halliday, Fred, 1977. "Migration and the labor force in the oil producing states of the Middle East," *Development and Change* 8 (3; July): 263–292

Hansen, Marcus Lee, 1961. *The Atlantic Migration, 1607–1860*. New York: Harper Torchbooks

Hawkins, Freda, 1977. "Canadian immigration: a new law and a new approach to management," *International Migration Review* 11 (Spring): 77–94

Hechter, M., 1975. *Internal Colonialism: The Celtic Fringe in British National Development, 1536–1966*. London: Routledge and Kegan Paul, and Berkeley: University of California Press

Helleiner, G. K., 1973. "Manufactured exports from less-developed countries and multinational firms," *The Economic Journal* 83 (March): 21–47

Henry, Kragenau, 1979. *Internationale Direcktinvestitionen*. Hamburg: Institut für Wirtschaftsforschung

Herman, Edward, 1981. *Corporate Control, Corporate Power*. New York: Cambridge University Press

Herrick, B., 1971. "Urbanization and urban migration in Latin America: an economist's view," in *Latin American Urban Research*, vol. 1, ed. by F. Rabinowitz and F. Trueblood. Beverly Hills, CA: Sage Publications

Ho, Kwon Ping, 1980. "Bargaining on the free trade zones," *The New Internationalist* no. 5 (March)

Houstoun, Marion F., Roger G. Kramer, and Joan Mackin Barrett, 1984. "Female predominance of immigration to the United States since 1930: a first look," *International Migration Review* 28 (4): 908–963 (Winter)

Howenstine, Ned G. Gregory G. Fouch, 1982. "Foreign Direct Investment in the U.S. in 1981," *Survey of Current Business* 62 (8; August): 30–41

Hutchinson, Edward P., 1956. *Immigrants and Their Children*. London: John Wiley and Sons

*Immigration Commission* [The Dillingham Commission], 1911. *Abstract of Reports of the Immigration Commission*. U.S. Senate, 61st Congress. Washington, D.C.: U.S. Government Printing Office

ILO [International Labour Office] 1977a. *County Case Study: Sultanate of Oman (part one)*. Geneva: ILO, International Migration Project (Working paper)

1978a. *A Summary of Provisional Findings: Empirical Patterns, Past Trends and Future Developments*. Geneva: ILO

1978b. *Country Study: The State of Qatar*. Geneva: ILO

1978c. *Country Study: Arab Republic of Egypt*. Geneva: ILO

1978d. *Country Study: The State of Bahrain*. Geneva: ILO

1978e. *Country Study: The United Arab Emirates*. Geneva: ILO

1978f. *Country Study: Libyan Arab Jamahiriya*. Geneva: ILO

1981. *Employment Effects of Multinational Enterprises in Developing Countries*. Geneva: ILO

1982. *Yearbook of Labor Statistics, 1981*. Geneva: ILO.

1985. *Women Workers in Multinational Enterprises in Developing Countries*. Geneva: ILO

INS [Immigration and Naturalization Service], 1972. *Annual Report*. Washington, D.C.: U.S. Government Printing Office

1973. *Annual Report*. U.S. Gov. P.O.

1977. *Annual Report*. U.S. Gov. P.O.

1978. *Annual Report*. U.S. Gov. P.O.

1981a. *Annual Report*. U.S. Gov. P.O.

1981b. "Tabulation of immigrants admitted by country of birth, 1954–1979." Unpublished paper

1984. *Statistical Yearbook of the INS*. Washington, D.C.: U.S. Government Printing Office

1985a. *Annual Report*. U.S. Gov. P.O.

1985b. "Tabulation of immigrants admitted by country of birth, 1985." Unpublished paper

Institute of Social Studies, New Delhi, 1979. "A case study on the modernization of the traditional handloom industry in the Kashmir Valley: the integrated development project for the woollen handloom weaving industry in Jammu and Kashmir." Bangkok: Asian and Pacific Centre for Women and Development (May)

Jackson, J. A. 1963. *The Irish in Britain.* London: Routledge and Kegan Paul

Janvry, Alain de and Frank Kramer, 1979. "The limits of unequal exchange," *Review of Radical Political Economics* no. 11 (Winter): 3–15

Jasso, Guillermina and Mark R. Rosenzweig, 1982. "Estimating the emigration rates of legal immigrants using administrative and survey data: the 1971 cohort of immigrants to the United States," *Demography* 19 (3): 279

Jelin, E., 1979. "Women and the urban labor market." International Labor Office, World Employment Programme Research. Working Paper No. 77 of the Population and Labor Policies Programme (Sept.)

Jenkins Jr., Craig, 1978. "The demand for immigrant workers: labor scarcity or social control?", *International Migration Review* 12 (Winter): 514–535

JETRO [Japan External Trade Organization], 1981. "Japanese Manufacturing Operations in the United States." New York: JETRO

Jones, K. and A. Smith, 1970. *The Economic Impact of Commonwealth Immigration.* London: Cambridge University Press and National Institute of Economic and Social Research

Kaplan, David L. and M. Claire Casey, 1958. *Occupational Trends in the U.S.* Census Working Paper No. 5. Washington, D.C.: U.S. Government Printing Office

Kaufman, Franz-Xaver (ed.), 1975. *Bevölkerungsbewegung zwischen Quantität und Qualität: Beitrage zum Problem einer Bevölkerungspolitik in industriellen Gesellschaften.* Stuttgart: Ferdinand Enke Verlag

Keely, Charles B. 1979. *U.S. Immigration: A Policy Analysis.* New York: The Population Council

   1980. *Asian Worker Migration to the Middle East.* New York: The Population Council, Center for Policy Studies, Working Paper No. 52 (January)

Kelly, D. 1984. "Hard work, hard choices: a survey of women in St. Lucia's export-oriented electronics factories." Unpublished Research Report

Kindleberger, C. P., 1967. *Europe's Postwar Growth: The Role of Labor-Supply.* Cambridge: Harvard University Press

Klee, Ernst (ed.), 1975. *Gastarbeiter Analysen und Berichte.* Frankfurt: Suhrkamp Verlag

Krane, R. E. (ed.), 1975. *Manpower Mobility Across Cultural Boundaries – Social, Economic and Legal Aspects: The Case of West Germany and Turkey.* Leiden: E. J. Brill

Kritz, Mary M. with Douglas T. Gurak (eds.), 1979. "International migration in Latin America," *International Migration Review* 13 (Fall): Special Issue

   1985 "Work and household patterns among Colombian and Dominican women in New York City." Department of Sociology, Fordham University

Kuo Chia-Ling, 1981. "A study of the coping strategies of immigrant Chinese garment workers in New York's Chinatown." Department of Anthropology, City College, City University of New York

Lasserre-Bigorry, J., 1975. *General Survey of Main Present-Day International Migration for Employment.* Geneva: ILO. Department of Working Conditions and Environment

Lebon, A. and G. Falchi, 1980. "New developments in intra-European migration since 1974," *International Migration Review* 14 (Winter): 539–579

Lee, James, 1978. "Migration and expansion in Chinese history," pp. 20–47 in W. H. McNeill and R. S. Adams (eds.). *Human Migration: Patterns and Policies.* Bloomington: Indiana University Press

Legum, Colin, 1978, *Middle Eastern Contemporary Survey, 1976–1977.* Tel Aviv: The Shiloah Center for Middle Eastern and African Studies, Tel Aviv University.

Lenin, V. I., 1939. *Imperialism, the Highest Stage of Capitalism.* New York: International Publishers

Levitt, Theodore, 1976. "The industrialization of service," *Harvard Business Review*, 54 (September): 63–74

Light, Ivan, 1972. *Ethnic Enterprise in America.* Berkeley: University of California Press

Lim, L. Y. C., 1978. *Women in Export Processing Zones.* United Nations Industrial Development Organization, New York

　　1980. "Women workers in multinational corporations: the case of the electronics industry in Malaysia and Singapore," in Krishna Kumar, *Transnational Enterprises: Their Impact on Third World Societies and Cultures.* Boulder, CO: Westview Press

Little, Jane Sneddon (1983) "Foreign Investors' Locational Choices: An Update." *New England Economic Review* (January/February). Boston: Federal Reserve Bank of Boston.

MacDonagh, Oliver, 1961. *A Pattern of Government Growth, 1800–1860: The Passenger Acts and their Enforcement.* London: MacGibbon and Kee

McGee, T. G., 1978. "Rural–urban mobility in South and Southwest Asia: different formulations, different answers," pp. 199–224 in W. H. McNeill and R. S. Adams (eds), *Human Migration: Patterns and Policies.* Bloomington: Indiana University Press

Machlup, F., 1962. *The Production and Distribution of Knowledge in the United States.* Princeton, NJ: Princeton University Press

McWilliams, Carey, 1968. *North From Mexico.* Westport, CT: Greenwood Press

Marglin, Stephen, 1974. "What do bosses do? The origins and functions of hierarchy in capitalist production," *Review of Radical Political Economics* 6 (Summer): 33–61

Marshall, Adriana, 1983. "Immigration in a surplus-worker labor market: The case of New York." New York: Center for Latin American and Caribbean Studies, New York University. Occasional Papers, No. 39

Marx, Karl, 1970. *Capital*, vol. 1. New York: International Publishers

Melman, Seymour, 1965. *Our Depleted Society.* New York: Holt, Rinehart, and Winston

Myers, John, 1980. "GNP: Perspectives on services." New York: Conservation of Human Resources Project, Columbia University

Mines, R., 1978. " The workers of Las Animas: a case study of village migration to California." Department of Agriculture and Resource Economics, University of California, Berkeley

Mollenkopf, John, 1977. "The rise of the Southwest: problem and promise." Paper presented at the Roundtable Conference on the Rise of the Southwest, Phoenix, Arizona (April). Washington, D.C.: Urban Technical Assistance Office, Economic Development Administration

Montgomery, David, 1979. *Workers' Control in America.* Cambridge University Press

Morales, Rebecca, 1983. "Undocumented workers in a changing automobile industry: Case studies in wheels, headers and batteries." Paper presented at the Conference on Contemporary Production: Capital Mobility and Labor Migration. Center for U.S.–Mexican Studies, University of California, San Diego

Morokvasic, Mirjana (ed.), 1984. *Women in Migration. International Migration Review*, Special Issue, 18(4), Winter 1984

Multinational Monitor, 1982. *Focus: Women and Multinationals.* Washington, D.C. (Summer)

Myrdal, Gunnar, 1962. *An American Dilemma.* New York: Harper and Row

*NACLA* [*North American Congress on Latin America*], 1976. "Caribbean migration," *Report on the Americas* 11 (8)

1977. "Electronics: the global industry," Special issue, *Latin America and Empire Report* 11 (4)

1978. "Capital's Flight: The apparel industry moves south," *Latin America and Empire Report* 11: 3

1979. "Undocumented immigrant workers in New York City," Special issue, *Latin America and Empire Report* 12: 6

National Commission for Manpower Policy, 1978. *Manpower and Immigration Policies in the United States.* Special Report No. 20. Washington, D.C.: U.S. Government Printing Office

Nelson, Daniel, 1975. *Managers and Workers: Origins of the New Factory System in the United States, 1880–1920.* Madison: University of Wisconsin Press

Nelson, J., 1974. "Sojourners vs. new urbanites: Causes and consequences of temporary vs. permanent cityward migration in developing countries." Center for International Affairs, Harvard University

Netzer, Dick, 1974. "The cloudy prospects for the City's economy," *New York Affairs* 1 (4): 22–35

*New York State Department of Labor*, 1979. *Occupational Employment Statistics: Finance, Insurance and Real Estate, New York State, May–June 1978.* Albany: New York State Department of Labor

1980. *Occupational Employment Statistics: Services. New York State, April–June, 1978.* Albany: New York State Department of Labor

1982a. *Report to the Governor and the Legislature on the Garment Manufacturing Industry and Industrial Homework.* Albany: New York State Department of Labor

1982b. *Study of State-Federal Employment Standards for Industrial Homeworkers in New York City.* Albany: New York State Department of Labor, Division of Labor Standards

North, David S. and Marion F. Houstoun, 1976. *The Characteristics and Role of Illegal Aliens in the U.S. Labor Market: An Explanatory Study.* Washington D.C., New TransCentury Foundation: Linton

North, David S. and William G. Weissert, 1973. *Immigrants and the American Labor Market.* Washington, D.C.: Technical Information Service of the U.S. Department of Labor (April)

O'Connor, David C., 1983. "Changing patterns of international production in the semiconductor industry: The role of transnational corporations." United Nations, Center For Transnational Corporations [Mimeo]

*OECD* [*Organization for Economic Cooperation and Development*], 1974. "International migration and its relationship to industrial and agricultural adjustment policies." Paris: OECD [Mimeo]

1978a. *Labor Force Statistics.* Paris: OECD

1978b. *Investing in Developing Countries.* Paris: OECD

1980. *International Subcontracting: A New Form of Investment.* Paris: OECD

1981. *International Investment and Multinational Enterprises: Recent International Direct Investment Trends.* Paris: OECD

Omvedt, Gail, 1973. "Towards a theory of colonialism," *The Insurgent Sociologist* 3 (Spring): 1–24

Oppenheimer, Martin, 1974. "The sub-proletariat: dark skins and dirty work," *The Insurgent Sociologist* 4 (Winter): 6–20

Orlansky, D. and S. Dubrovsky, 1978. "The effects of rural–urban migration on women's role and status in Latin America." Paris: UNICEF, *Reports and Papers in the Social Sciences*, No. 41

Paglaban, Enrico, 1978. "Philippines: workers in the export industry," *Pacific Research* 9 (3–4)

Paine, Suzanne, 1974. *Exporting Workers: The Turkish Case.* Cambridge University Press

Papademetriou, Dimitrios, G. and Nicholas Di Marzio, 1986. *Undocumented Aliens in the New York Metropolitan Area.* New York: Center for Migration Studies

Parra Sandoval, R., 1975. "La desnacionalización de la industria y los cambios en la estructura ocupacional colombiana 1920–1970." Bogota: CIDE

Pessar, Patricia, 1982. *The Role of Households in International Migration.* Center for Latin American and Caribbean Studies, New York University: *Occasional Papers*, No. 34

Petras, Elizabeth McLean, 1980. "The role of national boundaries in a Cross-National labor market," *The International Journal of Urban and Regional Research* 4 (2): 157–195

Petritsch, M., 1981. "The impact of industrialization on women's traditional fields of economic activity in developing countries." New York: UNIDO

Pineda-Ofreneo, Rosalinda, 1982. "Philippine domestic outwork: subcontracting for export oriented industries," *Journal of Contemporary Asia* 12 (3): 281–293

Piore, Michael P., 1976. "Notes for a theory of labor market stratification," in D. Gordon *et al.* (eds.). *Labor Market Segmentation.* Washington D.C.: Heath
    1978. "The political and economic origins of dualistic structures in labor markets." M.I.T. Department of Economics
    1979. *Birds of Passage: Migrant Labor and Industrial Societies.* Cambridge University Press

Plender, Richard, 1972. *International Migration Law.* Leyden: A. W. Sythoff

Poinard, Michel and Michel Roux, 1977. "L'emigration contre le developpement: Les cas Portugais et Yougoslave," *Revue Tiers-Monde* 18 (Janvier–Mars): 21–53

Port Authority of New York and New Jersey, 1981. "Inventory of foreign-owned firms in manufacturing, by major industry in the New York–New Jersey metropolitan region," New York: The Port Authority of New York and New Jersey. Planning and Development Department, Regional Research Section
    1982. *Regional Perspectives: The Regional Economy.* 1981 Review; 1982 Outlook. Port Authority of N.Y. and N.J.

Portes, Alejandro, 1977. "Labor functions of illegal aliens," *Society* 14 (6): 31–37
    1978. "Illegal Mexican immigrants to the U.S.," *International Migration Review* 12 (Winter): Special Issue
    1979. "Illegal immigration and the international system: lessons from recent legal Mexican immigrants to the United States," *Social Problems* 26 (April)
    1983. "The informal sector: Definition, controversy, and relation to national development," *Review* 7 (Summer): 151–174

Portes, Alejandro and R. L. Bach, 1980. "Immigrant earnings: Cuban and Mexican immigrants in the United States," *International Migration Review* 14: 315–341

Portes, Alejandro and John Walton, 1981. *Labor, Class and the International System.* New York: Academic Press

Recchini de Lattes, Z. and C. H. Wainerman, 1979. "Data from household surveys for the analysis of female labor in Latin America and the Caribbean: appraisal of deficiencies and recommendations for dealing with them." Santiago: CEPAL

Reimers, David M., 1983. "An unintended reform: the 1965 Immigration Act and Third World Immigration to the U.S.," *Journal of American Ethnic History* 3 (Fall): 9–28

Reubens, E. P., 1981. "Interpreting migration: current models and a new integration." Paper presented at the New York Research Program in Inter-American Affairs at New York University on Hispanic Migration to New York City: Global Trends and Neighborhood Change (December)

Ricketts, Erol R., 1983. "Periphery to Core Migration: Specifying a Model." Unpublished Ph.D. dissertation, University of Chicago, Department of Sociology

Rist, Ray C., 1978. *Guestworkers in Germany.* New York: Praeger

Rossiter, William S., 1922. *Increase of Population in the United States.* Census Monograph, U.S. Government Printing Office

Safa, Helen I., 1981. "Runaway shops and female employment: the search for cheap labor," *Signs* 7 (2; Winter): 418–433

Salaff, Janet, 1981. *Working Daughters of Hong Kong.* New York: Cambridge University Press, ASA Rose Monograph Series

Salowsky, H. 1972. "Sozialpolitische Aspekte der Ausländerbeschäftigung," *Berichte des Deutschen Industrie Institut für Sozial Politik* 6:2

Samora, Julian with Jorge A. Bustamente and Gilberto Gardenas, 1971. *Los Mojados: The Wetback Story.* Notre Dame: University of Notre Dame Press

San Diego Chamber of Commerce, Greater, and The San Diego Economic Development Corporation, 1983. *1982 San Diego County Industrial Space and Land Guide.* San Diego: Greater San Diego Chamber of Commerce (Economic Research Bureau) and SDEDC

San Diego Economic Development Corporation, 1981. *Electronics Companies, San Diego County 1981.* San Diego: Economic Development Corporation

Sassen-Koob, Saskia, 1978. "The international circulation of resources and development: The case of migrant labor," *Development and Change* 9 (Fall): 509–545

1979. "Colombians and Dominicans in New York City," *International Migration Review* 13 (Summer): 314–331

1980. "Immigrant and minority workers in the organization of the labor process," *Journal of Ethnic Studies* 8 (Spring)

1981a. "The state in the oil-exporting countries." Unpublished paper

1981b. *Exporting capital and importing labor: New York City.* Center for Latin American and Caribbean Studies, New York University: *Occasional Papers,* No. 28

1984a. "The new labor demand in global cities," pp. 139–171 in M. Smith (ed.), *Cities in Transformation.* Beverly Hills, CA: Sage

1984b. "Growth and informalization at the core: the case of New York City." *The Urban Informal Sector: Recent Trends in Research and Theory.* Proceedings of the

Seminar on the Informal Sector in Center and Periphery. Baltimore: The Johns Hopkins University

1987. "The structuring of a new investment zone for the world market: Southern California." San Diego: Center for U.S.–Mexican Studies, University of California, San Diego

Sassen-Koob, Saskia and Catherine Benamou, 1985. "Hispanic women in the garment and electronics industries in the New York metropolitan area." Research Progress Report presented to the Revson Foundation, New York City

Savage, Dean, 1979. *Founders, Heirs and Managers: The French Industrial Elite in Transition.* Beverly Hills: Sage

Schapera, Isaac, 1947. *Migrant Labor and Tribal Life.* London: Oxford University Press

Scherer, F. M., 1980. *Industrial Market Structure and Economic Performance.* Chicago: Rand McNally

Schiller, Günter, 1974. "Auswirkungen der Arbeitskräftewanderungen in den Herkunftsländern," pp. 143–170 in Lohrmann and Manfrass (eds.), *Ausländerbeschäftigung und Internationale Politik: Zur Analyse Transnationaler Sozial Prozesse.* Munich: Oldenburg

Schmink, M., 1982. "La mujer en la economía en America Latina." Mexico: The Population Council, Latin America and Caribbean Region Office, Working Papers No. 11 (June)

Scott, Allen J., 1982. "Industrial organization and the logic of intra-metropolitan location II: a case study of the printed circuits industry in the greater Los Angeles region." Department of Geography, University of California, Los Angeles

Sha, N. M. and P. C. Smith, 1981. "Issues in the labor force participation of migrant women in five Asian countries." East–West Population Institute, East–West Center: Working Papers No. 19 (Sept.)

Shapira, Philip and Plant Closures Project, 1983. "Shutdowns and job losses in California: the need for new national priorities." Testimony Prepared for the Subcommittee on Labor Management Relations, Subcommittee on Employment Opportunities, U.S. House of Representatives, Hearing on HR 2847. Los Angeles, CA, July 8, 1983

Simon, G., 1973. "L'émigration tunisienne." *Hommes et Migrations – Documents* (April)

Singelmann, J., 1978. *From Agriculture to Services: The Transformation of Industrial Employment.* Beverly Hills and London: Sage

Snow, Robert, 1977. "Dependent development and the new industrial worker: the export processing zone in the Philippines." Unpublished Ph.D. dissertation, Department of Sociology, Harvard University

1980. "The new international division of labor and the U.S. workforce: the case of the electronics industry." Working Papers of the East–West Culture Learning Institute. Honolulu: East–West Center

Soja, E., R. Morales, and G. Wolff, 1983. "Urban restructuring: An analysis of social and spatial change in Los Angeles." *Economic Geography,* vol. 29 (April) no. 2

Solorzano Torres, R., 1983. "Female Mexican immigrants in San Diego County." Center for U.S.–Mexican Studies, University of California, San Diego. Research in Progress

*SOPEMI* [*Systeme d'observation permanente pour les migrations*], 1977. *Annual Report*. Paris: OECD, Directorate for Social Affairs, Manpower and Education [Mimeo]
  1979. *Annual Report*. Paris: OECD, Directorate for Social Affairs, Manpower and Education [Mimeo]
  1980. *Annual Report*. Paris: OECD, Directorate for Social Affairs, Manpower and Education [Mimeo]
Spero, Sterling D. and Abram L. Harris, 1968. *The Black Worker: The Negro and the Labor Movement*. New York: Atheneum
Stanback, Thomas M. Jr., 1979. *Understanding the Service Economy*. Baltimore: The Johns Hopkins University Press
Stanback, Thomas M. Jr. and Thierry J. Noyelle, 1982. *Cities in Transition: Changing Job Structures in Atlanta, Denver, Buffalo, Phoenix, Columbus (Ohio), Nashville, Charlotte*. New Jersey: Allenheld, Osmun
Stanback, Thomas M. Jr., Peter J. Bearse, Thierry J. Noyelle, Robert Karasek, 1981. *Services: The New Economy*. New Jersey: Allenheld, Osmun
Standing, G., 1975. "Aspiration wages, migration and female employment." ILO: World Employment Programme, Working Paper No. 23 of the Population and Employment Project (November)
Stigler, George, 1951. "The division of labor is limited by the extent of the market," *Journal of Political Economy* 59 (3): 185–193
Stone, Kathy, 1975. "The origins of job structures in the steel industry," in Edwards, Reich and Gordon (eds.), *Labor Market Segmentation*. Lexington, MA: D.C. Heath
Storper, Michael and David Walker, 1983. "The labor theory of location," *International Journal of Urban and Regional Research* 7 (1): 1–41
Survey of Current Business, International Investment Division, 1981a. "U.S. Business Enterprises Acquired or Established by Foreign Direct Investors in 1979," *Survey of Current Business* 61 (1; January): 28–39
  1981b. "1977 Benchmark Survey of U.S. Direct Investment Abroad," *Survey of Current Business* 61 (4; April): 29–37
Teitelbaum, Michael S., 1985. *Latin Migration North: The Problem for U.S. Foreign Policy*. New York: Council on Foreign Relations
Thomas, Brinley, 1973. *Migration and Economic Growth: A Study of Great Britain and the Atlantic Economy*, 2nd edn. Cambridge University Press
Tienda, M., L. Jensen, and R. L. Bach, 1984. "Immigration, gender and the process of occupational change in the United States, 1970–1980," pp. 1021–1044 in M. Morokvasic (ed.)
Tinker, I. and M. Bo Bramsen (eds.), 1976. *Women and World Development*. Washington, D.C.: Overseas Development Council
Tobier, Emanuel, 1979. "Gentrification: the Manhattan story," *New York Affairs* 5 (4): 13–25
Tomasi, S. M. and Charles B. Keely, 1975. *Whom Have We Welcomed? The Adequacy and Quality of U.S. Immigration Data for Policy Anlaysis and Evaluation*. New York: Center for Migration Studies
UNIDO [United Nations Industrial Development Organization], 1979. *World Industry Since 1960: Progress and Prospects* (ID/229). Vienna: UNIDO
  1980. *Export Processing Zones in Developing Countries*. Working Papers on Structural Change No. 19. New York: UNIDO

1982. *Changing Patterns of Trade in World Industry: An Empirical Study on Revealed Comparative Advantage* (ID/281). Vienna: UNIDO

United Electrical, Radio, and Machine Workers of America (UE), 1980. "Statement of the U.E. Electronics Organizing Committee made before the California Senate Industrial Relations Committee in support of S.B. 1494" (December 8)

United Nations, 1976. *Yearbook of Industrial Statistics 1976*. New York: United Nations

1977. *Statistical Yearbook 1977*. New York: United Nations

1978. *Transnational Corporations in World Development: A Re-examination*. New York: United Nations

1982. *Monthly Bulletin of Statistics, September 1982*. New York: United Nations

United Nations Centre on Transnational Corporations, 1979. *World Development: A Re-examination*. New York: UN Centre on Transnational Corporations

1981. *Transnational Banks: Operations, Strategies, and Their Effect in Developing Countries*. New York: UN Centre on Transnational Corporations

1985. *Trends and Issues in Foreign Direct Investment and Related Flows*. New York: United Nations

1986. *Foreign Direct Investment in Latin America: Recent Trends, Prospects and Policy Issues*. New York: United Nations

United Nations Economic Commission for Latin America, 1982. *Economic Survey of Latin America 1980*

United Nations Economic and Social Commission for Asia and the Pacific, 1982. *Statistical Yearbook for Asia and the Pacific 1980*

United Nations Economic and Social Council, 1986. *Recent Developments Related to Transnational Corporations and International Economic Relations*. Report to the Secretary-General. Commission on Transnational Corporations (6 February)

United States Department of Commerce, 1979. *A Report on the U.S. Semi-conductor Industry*. Washington D.C.: U.S. Government Printing Office

United States Department of Commerce, Bureau of the Census, 1957. *Census of Population, 1950*. Special Report, "Population mobility: farm and non-farm movers." Washington, D.C.: U.S. Government Printing Office

1960. *Historical Statistics of the U.S., Colonial Times to 1957*. Washington D.C.: Bureau of the Census

1953a. *Census of Population, 1950*. Special Report, "Nativity and Parentage". Washington D.C.: Bureau of the Census

1953b. *Census of Population, 1950*. Special Report, "Puerto Ricans in the Continental U.S." Washington D.C.: Bureau of the Census

1972. *Money Income of Households, Families and Persons in the United States, 1970*. Washington D.C.: U.S. Government Printing Office

1973. *1970 Census of Population*. Subject Report, "National Origin and Language." Washington D.C.: Bureau of the Census

1976a. *County Business Patterns, 1974*. Washington D.C.: U.S. Government Printing Office

1976b. *Statistical Abstract of the United States*. Washington D.C.: U.S. Government Printing Office

1976c. *Survey of Income and Education*. Washington D.C.: U.S. Government Printing Office

1978. *Microdata from the Survey of Income and Education*. Data Access Description No. 42. Washington D.C.: Bureau of the Census

1979. Current Population Survey, Supplement, (November). Unpublished data

1980. *Persons of Hispanic Origin in the U.S., March 1979.* Current Population Reports, Population Characteristics, Series P. 20, No. 354 (October). Washington D.C.: U.S. Government Printing Office

1981a. *County Business Patterns, 1979.* Washington D.C.: U.S. Government Printing Office

1981b. *1980 Census of Population, Supplementary Report.* Washington D.C.: U.S. Government Printing Office

1981c. *1980 Census of Population and Housing: Advance Report.* Washington D.C.: U.S. Government Printing Office

1981d. *Public Law File, 94–171.* Unpublished data

1982a. *Money Income of Households, Families and Persons in the United States, 1980.* Washington D.C.: U.S. Government Printing Office

1982b. *1980 Census of Population: General Population Characteristics, California.* Washington D.C.: U.S. Government Printing Office

1982c. *1980 Census of Population: General Population Characteristics, New York.* Washington D.C.: U.S. Government Printing Office

1982d. *1980 Census of Population and Housing Supplementary Report: Provisional Estimates of Social, Economic, and Housing Characteristics.* (March). Washington D.C.: U.S. Government Printing Office

1983. *Statistical Abstract of the United States.* Washington D.C.: U.S. Government Printing Office

1983b Current Population Survey, Supplement. (April). Unpublished data

United States Department of Commerce, International Trade Commission, 1970. *Economic Factors Affecting the Use of Items 807.00 and 806.30 of the Tariff Schedules of the U.S.* Washington D.C.: International Trade Commission

1980a. *Current Developments in U.S. International Service Industries.* Washington D.C.: International Trade Administration

1980b. *Import Trends in TSUS Items 806.30 and 807.00.* Washington D.C.: International Trade Commission

1980c. *Selected Data on U.S. Investment Abroad, 1966–1978.* Washington D.C.: International Trade Commission, Bureau of Economic Analysis

1982. *Foreign Economic Trends and Their Implications.* (Several Issues). Washington D.C.: International Trade Commission

1984. *International Direct Investment: Global Trends and the United States' Role.* Washington D.C.: International Trade Administration

United States Department of Labor, Bureau of Labor Statistics, 1979. *Employment and Earnings, for States and Areas, 1939–78.* Bulletin 1370–13. Washington D.C.: U.S. Government Printing Office

1980. *News.* New York: U.S. Department of Labor, Bureau of Labor Statistics, Middle Atlantic Region

1981a. *Geographic Profiles of Employment and Unemployment, 1980.* Bulletin 2111 Washington D.C.: U.S. Government Printing Office

1981b. *News.* New York: U.S. Department of Labor, Bureau of Labor Statistics, Middle Atlantic Region

1982a. *News.* New York: U.S. Department of Labor, Bureau of Labor Statistics, Middle Atlantic Region

1982b. "International Comparisons of Manufacturing Productivity and Labor Cost Trends, Preliminary Measures for 1981" (June)

1985. *Supplement to Employment, Hours, and Earnings, for states and areas, 1980–1984.* Bulletin 1370–19. Washington DC: U.S. Government Printing Office

United States Equal Employment Opportunity Commission, 1982. *EEOC 1980 Report: Job Patterns for Minorities and Women in Private Industry. 1980.* Vol. 2. Washington D.C.: U.S. Government Printing Office

United States Senate, Committee on Banking, Housing and Urban Affairs, 1982. *Foreign Barriers to U.S. Trade: Service Exports.* U.S. Senate 97th Congress, Hearing before the Subcommittee on International Finance and Monetary Policy of the Committee on Banking, Housing and Urban Affairs. Washington, D.C.: U.S. Government Printing Office

Urrea Giraldo, Fernando, 1982. "Life strategies and the labor market: Colombians in New York in the 1970s." New Research Program in Inter-American Affairs, New York University. Occasional Papers No. 34

USDA [United States Department of Agriculture], 1973. *Farm Population Estimates, 1910–1970.* Statistical Bulletin, No. 523

Van Den Bulcke, D., J.J. Boddewyn, B. Martens and P. Klemmer 1979. *Investment and Divestment Policies of Multinational Corporations in Europe.* Westmead, UK: Saxon House

Venezuela, Consejo Nacional de Recursos Humanos, 1977. *Informe Sobre la Situacion General y Perspectivas de los Recursos Humanos.* Caracas: Consejo Nacional de Recursos Humanos [Mimeo]

Vernon, Raymond (ed.), 1970. "The technology factor in international trade: A conference of the universities." National Bureau Committee for Economic Research. New York: National Bureau for Economic Research

Wachter, Michael, 1979. "Second thoughts about illegal immigration," *Fortune,* May 22: 80–87

Waldinger, Roger D., 1983. "Immigration and industrial change in the New York apparel industry," in G. Borjas and M. Tienda, *Hispanics in the U.S. Economy.* New York: Academic Press

Wallerstein, Immanuel, 1974. *The Modern World System, Capitalist Agriculture and the Origins of the European World Economy in the Sixteenth Century.* New York: Academic Press

Warren, R. and J.S. Passel, 1983. "Estimates of illegal aliens from Mexico counted in the 1980 U.S. census." Washington, D.C.: Bureau of the Census, Population Division

Weinstein, Jay, 1968. *The Corporate Ideal in the Liberal State: 1900–1918.* Boston: Beacon Press

Whichard, Obie G., 1981a. "Trends in the U.S. direct investment position abroad, 1950–79," in *Survey of Current Business* 61 (2; Feb.): 39–56

1981b. "U.S. direct investment position abroad in 1980," *Survey of Current Business* 61 (8; August): 20–39

Williams, Eric, 1970. *From Columbus to Castro: The History of the Caribbean. 1492–1969.* London: Deutsch

Williamson, Oliver, 1980. "Transaction costs economics: The governance of contractual relations," *Journal of Law and Economics* 22(2):233–261

Wilson, Francis, 1976. "International migration in Southern Africa," *International Migration Review* 10 (Winter): 451–488

Wilson, Kenneth L. and Alejandro Portes, 1980. "Immigrant enclaves: an analysis of the labor market experiences of Cubans in Miami," *American Journal of Sociology* 86: 295–319 (Sept.)

Wilson, William Julius, 1978. *The Declining Significance of Race. Blacks and Changing American Institutions*. The University of Chicago Press

Wolpe, Harold, 1975. "The theory of internal colonialism: The South African Case," pp. 208–228 in Oxaal, Barnett and Booth (eds.), *Beyond the Sociology of Development*. London: Routledge and Kegan Paul

Wong, A. K. 1980. *Economic Development and Women's Place: Women in Singapore. International Reports: Women and Society*. London: Change

Wool, Harold and Bruce Dana Phillips, 1976. *The Labor Supply for Lower-Level Occupations*. New York: Praeger

Work Relations Group (prepared by Jeremy Brecher), 1978. "Uncovering the hidden history of the American workplace," *Review of Radical Political Economics* 10 (Winter): 1–23

World Bank, 1980. *World Tables*. Baltimore: The Johns Hopkins University Press

World Bank Staff, 1975. "Internal migration in less developed countries." Washington, D.C.: International Bank for Reconstruction and Development, Bank Staff Working Paper No. 215. Prepared by L. Y. L. Yap (Sept.)

Youssef, N. H., 1974. "Women and work in developing societies." University of California, Berkeley, Institute of International Studies

Zolberg, Aristide R., 1978. "International migration policies in a changing world system," pp. 241–286 in W. H. McNeill and R. S. Adams (eds.), *Human Migration: Patterns and Policies*. Bloomington: Indiana University Press

# Index